G000135033

OWN YOURSELF

How to Form Your Conscience

WILLIAM J. O'MALLEY, SJ

Paulist Press
New York / Mahwah, NJ

The Scripture quotations contained herein are from the New Revised Standard Version: Catholic Edition, Copyright © 1989 and 1993, by the Division of Christian Education of the National Council of the Churches of Christ in the United States of America. Used by permission. All rights reserved.

"Tonight I'm Yours," Words and Music by Jim Cregan, Rod Stewart, and Kevin Savigar © WB Music Corp., Rod Stewart Pub Designee (NS) and Riva Music Ltd. (PRS). All rights reserved.

"Why Can't a Woman Be More Like a Man" (from *My Fair Lady*), Lyrics by Alan Jay Lerner, Music by Frederick Loewe © 1956 (Renewed) Alan Jay Lerner and Frederick Loewe. All rights administered by Chappell & Co., Inc. All rights reserved.

Excerpt from "The Hollow Men" from COLLECTED POEMS 1909–1962 by T.S. Eliot. Copyright 1936 by Houghton Mifflin Harcourt Publishing Company in the United States and Faber and Faber Ltd. in the United Kingdom. Copyright © renewed by Thomas Stearns Eliot. Reprinted by permission of Houghton Mifflin Harcourt Publishing Company and Faber and Faber Ltd. All rights reserved.

Cover image by Kundra/Shutterstock.com
Cover design by Joe Gallagher
Book design by Lynn Else

Copyright © 2016 by William J. O'Malley

All rights reserved. No part of this publication may be reproduced, stored in a retrieval system, or transmitted in any form or by any means, electronic, mechanical, photocopying, recording, scanning, or otherwise, except as permitted under Section 107 or 108 of the 1976 United States Copyright Act, without the prior written permission of the Publisher. Requests to the Publisher for permission should be addressed to the Permissions Department, Paulist Press, 997 Macarthur Boulevard, Mahwah, NJ 07430, (201) 825-7300, fax (201) 825-8345, or online at www.paulist press.com.

Library of Congress Cataloging-in-Publication Data

Names: O'Malley, William J.
Title: Own yourself : how to form your conscience / William J. O'Malley.
Description: New York : Paulist Press, 2016.
Identifiers: LCCN 2015030648 (print) | LCCN 2015042153 (ebook) | ISBN 9780809149773 (pbk. : alk. paper) | ISBN 9781587685903 (ebook) | ISBN 9781587685903 ()
    Subjects: LCSH: Conscience—Religious aspects—Catholic Church. | Christian Ethics—Catholic authors. | Conduct of life. | Catholic Church—Doctrines.
    Classification: LCC BJ1278.C66 O43 2016 (print) | LCC BJ1278.C66 (ebook) | DDC 170—dc23
    LC record available at http://lccn.loc.gov/2015030648

ISBN 978-0-8091-4977-3 (paperback)
ISBN 978-1-58768-590-3 (e-book)

Published by Paulist Press
997 Macarthur Boulevard
Mahwah, New Jersey 07430

www.paulistpress.com

Printed and bound in the
United States of America

OWN YOURSELF

For
Louis DiGiorno
Nil humanum alienum a se esse putat.

CONTENTS

PREFACE

Character is who you are when no one is looking.
                                                    —unknown

Any young man or woman leaving adolescence behind ought to
have at least a preliminary sketch of the person they will become
in "the real world," the genuine you—who you are when no one
is looking. What does character even entail? What does it cost?
Unlike puberty or personality, it doesn't just happen or build up
gradually by itself without effort. You surely know men and
women who have grown up but not become adults.

How do you make yourself an adult rather than just hope
it happens to you?

What steps must each individual take to be a self, not just
a pasteup of values imposed by parents, the media, schooling,
religion, and peers? What will any future employer have a right
to expect, not to mention your future wife or husband? It's too
late to prepare a parent when he or she receives a birth certificate.

If not now, when?

What gives you a right to feel good about yourself?

INTRODUCTION

BASIC ASSUMPTIONS

UNDERSTANDING VERSUS INFORMATION

Some purists insist your moral education is lacking if you've never read the classical thinkers. I'd beg to differ. Just as you can run a prosperous French restaurant without knowing French irregular verbs or run a conglomerate without knowing trigonometry, you can lead an admirable human life without having ploughed through John Locke. I don't regret reading page after page of Plato in Greek and Aquinas in Latin, but the experience has made me no superior to a farmer or assembly line worker who left formal learning in high school to be a caring husband and father and an honorable, dependable human.

The truths about being a decent human remain valid whether they were enunciated by Moses, Aristotle, Jesus, Mohammed, Gandhi, a church, or your Mom. Do they ring true? Does their advice lead to a richer, worthier human life?

It's more important that you value and feel a need for personal integrity than that you know what some of the greatest minds in history said about it.

It may be helpful to remind oneself of the friend whom the moral philosopher, Immanuel Kant, asked to comment on one of his manuscripts before publication. After a while, the friend wrote back that, as he hoped to preserve his sanity, he couldn't bring himself to read another line.

If you begin to despair of comprehending the classical moralists, Google or encyclopedias are always at hand to provide a rough, simple outline of the terrain before you begin to map in mountains and rivers, much less bushes and birds. Thus, if you're really (really!) stuck, you can click on the clever Three-Minute Philosophy segments on YouTube about almost any thinker. They are, indeed, only nanoseconds longer than three minutes, and give you the (very) barest, stick-figure ideas, even if they're as unsatisfying as one potato chip.

If you want to venture out into Plato's *The Republic* or Kant's *Critique of Pure Reason*, I bid you *bon voyage*. However, until you dare to sail those turbulent, monster-ridden high seas, let this text act as what primitive maps were to the first tentative explorers of this planet—rough approximations, to be sure, and inadequate, yet helpful on our long journey to pinpoint satellite images and GPS car locators.

One of the recommended resources is the Harvard ethics lectures of Professor Michael Sandel, a superb teacher—clear, clever, and down-to-earth.* Listening to Sandel, or any other college instructor, may be very different from the viewing you're used to. It's not entertainment, like a reality show, or even informational, like a mind-blowing *Nova* episode. You have to take notes.

Another excellent source of ethical societal dilemmas is the PBS series called *Ethics in America*, Socratic dialogues composed of panels of high-profile present-day thinkers—generals, a supreme court justice, news commentators, ethicists, military officers, physicians—discussing specific moral dilemmas in law, medicine, business, warfare, law courts, and news reporting.

A great deal of your previous schooling (ought to have) prepared you for this new, more grown-up college approach to learning. Many of your previous teachers hammered at the basic skills for both your reading and your writing. Now, your ability to grasp a central assertion and its complex supporting arguments must also become part of your listening skills: (1) What is the writer's/speaker's core insight—his or her topic sentence? (2) List all the arguments he/she puts forward to support that

---

*Michael Sandel, "Justice" (lecture series, Harvard University, Cambridge, MA), accessed August 9, 2015, http://www.justiceharvard.org/.

basic assertion. Without these, you're chained back in Plato's cave with the dull occupants, staring at shadows on a wall.

The point is to distill what's said into your own notes. You're not going to get by any longer with vague, unfocused feelings. And unless you're kidding yourself when you say, "I understand," you should be able to put your understanding into words. That's what *understanding* means—that you know the idea well enough to explain it to someone else, to teach it.

In this course, the medium is the message. The way you handle this challenge will be the evidence of whether you're developing a personal ethic or not, taking personal responsibility out of the hands of others and claiming autonomy.

MORAL DILEMMAS

One can guess that greybeard elders sat around cave fires when instructing younger tribal members not to make the same dumb, hurtful mistakes they themselves made. Quite likely, they were shared as stories, which kept being told and retold simply because they rang true. They were validated by the fact that the same dumb choices kept leading predictably to the same painful results.

These tales ultimately led to great collections like the Norse Eddur and the great Greek myth systems of the Olympian gods and their human protégés like Odysseus, Psyche, Theseus, Aeneas, and also to the life lessons of the Bible. That method of moral training persisted in a continuous unfolding of folktales that aimed to help young people to stand on their own, control their own basic urges, and become principled in order to join a spouse and form a stable enclosure for children: *Hansel and Gretel, Snow White, Pinocchio, Beauty and the Beast, Cinderella*—none of them actually happened, but all of them carry important human truths.

As prosperity, sophistication, and leisure led city dwellers away from the gods their forebears had so depended on, sustaining a cooperative society required the virtues the gods had (seemingly arbitrarily) demanded. Thinkers, like Pythagoras, maintained that "man is the measure of all things." There had to be reasons acceptable to both theists and nonbelievers, reasons more satisfying than "the gods say so." Men like Socrates, Plato, Aristotle, and later Cicero and Marcus Aurelius tried to train the young (almost exclusively male) to govern and teach their fellow citizens with laws that offered control to those unable to control themselves.

All along, a staple of moral education has been offering puzzling human quandaries that put the listener between the horns of a dilemma—two choices, each with its benefits and drawbacks. Plato, Jesus, and the Buddha each told parables to provoke puzzlement, pushing the listeners to stop waiting for some elder to dictate the choices and use their own wits to govern their own lives.

One of the oldest moral "chestnuts" is the overloaded lifeboat. The lifeboat is equipped to sustain six average-sized people. But in the classical dilemma, you have twelve clinging alongside, each of varying qualities: a Nobel Peace prize winner, a mentally impaired teenager, an Olympic swimmer, a ballerina, the ship's purser, and so on. You're the purser. Whom do you shove off? (When I've done that one, the very best students say, "I refuse. Let Fate decide.") The Internet provides hundreds more dilemmas.

From the time long before Plato's cave to last night's courtroom TV drama, moral dilemmas have been a staple of human communication and growth.

CONSCIENCE

As will become much clearer, a formed conscience is not innate. Other animals seem born with the instinct to choose foods that nourish and avoid the poisonous, but if humans knew from their first breath which specific actions degrade them to mere animals and which befitted their rational nature, there would have been no need for the wise elder cave men and women, nor the Greek philosophers or dramatists, nor, in fact, any schools.

Clearly, humans were not born ready to evaluate and accept the extent of pain that selfishness causes. They lack an inborn levelheadedness that would have refused war, robbery, rape, and every other kind of inhumanity. Every daily newspaper conclusively proves humans consistently refuse to act humanly, acting even against their own self-interests.

However, unlike other animals, humans are born with the *potential* for conscience. It needn't be actualized: simply witness fiends like Hitler and Stalin, soulless leeches like pimps and pushers, and garden-variety parasites who spit gum in public drinking fountains. Morality, which is formed by our conscience, has to be learned.

Rules and laws are made for people who are selfish, stubborn, or unable to think for themselves. There should be no need for laws forbidding parents to savage their own children or forbidding people to drive down city streets at 70 mph. However, since people (brainlessly) do that, women and men who know how to think try to form rules and sanctions that nonthinkers can understand. The philosopher, Bertrand Russell (1872–1970), said, "Most people would die sooner than think—in fact they do."*

This book is one more attempt to help keep people both living together and thinking.

CRITICAL THINKING (EVEN ABOUT THE EXPERTS)

Any prudent student should not be a vacuum, ready unquestionably to suck in anything from a textbook, any professor, or TV program. Being an adult thinker is cultivating the ability to smell rats, the sensitivity to soft spots in arguments, and a knowing eye to detect when even an expert is tap dancing around flaws or is, in fact, dead wrong.

Plato's own pupil, Aristotle, found fault with him because the strict unity his mentor wanted in the ideal republic had the potential flaw of smothering desirable contrary ideas and growth.

---

*Bertrand Russell, *The ABC of Relativity* (London: George Allen and Unwin, 1925), 166.

In turn, Aristotle's ideal of forming virtuous citizens (which Aquinas favored and furthered) has to be wary of desirable virtues run amok. For example, confidence unchecked by humility becomes arrogance, and chastity unbalanced by common sense devolves into smothering puritanism. Jesus, himself, can be (and is) misread by literalists as demanding self-mutilation rather than risk immoral activity (see Matt 18:9), and St. Paul's Letter to Philemon seems to take slavery as an unavoidable part of the human condition. Muhammed's assessment of Allah's demands can be (and is) misread to justify inhuman treatment of women. Bentham's Utilitarianism (the greatest pleasure for the greatest number) could lead to the judgment that the character Antigone and her motives are less valuable than the star of the "The Bachelorette." Immanuel Kant's inflexible moral demands would prevent an abolitionist from lying to a slave hunter at her door. Marxism overlooks human selfishness, and capitalism overlooks the rights of the talentless and impaired.

Keep in mind that moral principles very often conflict, on the one hand, with nobility and, on the other, with common sense. (Don't read more till you get at least a wobbly handle on that one. Think! It's a thrillingly dangerous way to spend your time!)

TRULY DUMB "PRINCIPLES"

The philosopher Immanuel Kant offers a good norm for judging the validity of a moral principle whereby *any* limit on human choices put forward should be capable of application everywhere humans exist and deal with one another. It should have universal applicability, grounded in the nature of rational beings.* In other words, "What would happen if everybody...?"

Why is each of the following "principles" (all of which I've heard voiced seriously in Ethics classes) dumb?

---

*See Immanuel Kant, *Groundwork for the Metaphysics of Morals* (1785), Rethinking the Western Tradition, edited and translated by Allen W. Wood (New Haven, CT: Yale University Press, 2002).

My opinion's as good as anyone else's.

>   Are you up for a debate on black holes with Stephen Hawking?

>   You never need to consult a doctor or plumber?

>   You know more about sex than your mother?

It's up to the individual!

>   Then you have no objection to my coming into your home and helping myself to your fridge, your bedroom, or your diary?

>   So, I'm free to treat Lysol the same way I treat Coke?

Morality (acting humanly) changes over time. What was immoral when you were young is not only not wrong today but recommended.

>   So what *human* means was different for Plato and Dante?

>   Rape is more tolerable for the victim today than five years ago?

>   Libraries are a terrible waste of money?

Society—the majority or the most powerful—just decides what to forbid, tells us, and expects us to conform.

>   So hiding Jews in Nazi Europe or runaway slaves before the Emancipation Proclamation was not only illegal but immoral, antihuman?

>   Sacrificing Inca virgins ceased to be objectively homicides because their society decreed it to be otherwise?

>   Until Magellan, the Flat Earth people were correct?

No one has a right to criticize anyone else's lifestyle.

>   World War II was an unjust intrusion on Adolf Hitler?

>   Ignore any criticism a teacher unjustly scribbles on your papers?

>   You dare not intrude on your children's freedom?

Here is an ironclad presupposition without which no learning can ever occur: you must admit that you need to learn and that there are problems you need help to grasp, to disentangle, to understand. Until you accept that, you've immobilized your mind.

MORALITY VERSUS RELIGION

Morality is not (repeat: not) identified with religion. The most inflexible atheists want their children to be moral, that is, responsible, dependable, honest, truthful, and so on. Although the spatial metaphor is inadequate, religion deals with a "vertical" personal relationship with a Creator, if one exists; morality is a "horizonatal" personal relationship with oneself and with all other occupants of the planet (including the planet itself), but especially with other human beings. Ethics/morality deals with obligations that exist whether there's a God or not.

Any reasonable human being should be able to see—embedded in the way each object is made—that there's an increasing inner worth as we move with the upward evolutionary progress. Clearly, apples are more valuable (in themselves) than snowballs, because apples can feed. Dogs demand more sensitivity from rational beings than apples do because they can feel pain. Humans deserve more cautionary treatment than dogs because each one possesses—again, by the evident way they're made—the same dignity each of us feels entitled to. Unlike any other species, we are aware that we are selves, and we have consciences that (unless they become corrupted) warn us that something is out of kilter.

Many equate morality and religion ("all those rules") simply because most of their moral training has come from religious sources. The original source of threats of punishment for human misbehavior was attributed to the gods, but even when the Greeks became more learned, sophisticated, and skeptical about divine influences, the most cynical realized that if we're going to live together for very long and with mutual profit, we have to acknowledge human value.

Furthermore, without being told, we see that some people are better at being human than others—more admirable, worthier of imitation. There is no need for a college degree to see that Abraham Lincoln was better at it than Saddam Hussein, but it does take a broadening of perspective to make a ghetto kid see the neighborhood pimp or drug pusher isn't as good at being human as the lady in the soup kitchen. First, humanity is a real, quantum leap from animal; second, humanity is a potential that (a) needn't be activated and (b) can keep intensifying—or not.

Ethics/morality means learning that no one can legitimately objectify a human being, even if the other person is willing—such as when men and women pose for skin magazines, when fathers in other cultures freely sell their children like animals, or when bureaucratic climbers use other people as stepping stones. It's wrong—plain and simple—not because the Bible says it is, or because society says it is, or because your parents say it is. The nature of the victim says it is.

This course is about discovering that humans-only potential, owning it, and setting it in motion toward its richest kind of fulfillment. You only go around once.

Part One

MORALITY IN GENERAL

1.

WHOSE TRUTH?

> The truth does not change according to our
> ability to stomach it.
> —*Flannery O'Connor*

The following statements are presented merely to set the pot
bubbling. Which of them do you believe are justified? Why do
you believe that? (Remember that without reasons, your assertion is words written on wind, baseless and beneath consideration—to avoid a coarser word, like *piffle*.)

1. Valid moral principles change from age to age and
   from culture to culture.
2. My opinion is as good as anyone else's.
3. What I feel about another person is more important
   than what he or she is.
4. True-for-me isn't necessarily the real truth.
5. Laws and commandments *make* an act moral or
   immoral.
6. Society decides what morality entails, then sees to it
   that the people act accordingly.
7. If there is no norm of morality independent of a particular society or individual, there is no such thing as
   morality, only current customs and lifestyle.
8. The question of the humanity of African slaves was
   settled by the Civil War.
9. We had merely a difference of opinion with the Nazis
   over the humanity of Jews.

10. The humanity of African Americans and Jews is debatable.

Who can dare tell me what I've got a right to believe or how I behave or what I can do with my own body? Parents? Anybody over 21? The law? My parents' religion? Teachers?

Only *one* authority has the right to limit what you can believe—only one.

The absolutely rock-bottom authority with a right to *command* your submission is the *objective facts*. You may not "allow" them to be true, but they're there, as unarguable as the toxicity of cyanide and the spherical shape of the earth. Ignore them at your peril. *Hear* that, yield to it, and accept it or you'll be wretched for the rest of your life.

Honestly confronting the *objective facts* is the only sure way to discover what's right and wrong, human (moral) or inhuman (immoral), justifiably permitted and justifiably prohibited. If anything said by parents, adults, the law, religion, or teachers *is* true, binding, or necessary, it's because what they recommend, demand, or threaten to punish is backed up by the *truth*—the natures of things, the way things are—flat-on, unprejudiced.

Everything comes to me. It tells me

—that it's there (*Existence*);
—what it is (*Nature*); and
—how I can legitimately use it (*Value*).

There couldn't be anything in education more fundamental than this.

If anyone sneers at that, insists to you that we can't access objective reality but can only interpret our unique responses to its stimuli, they're wrong. Park on their lawn and see if they respond negatively, and then suggest they go off and reassess their responses.

The steel objects pictured on the next page tell you all you need to know about them. And yet in college classes, with students who needed at least a 3.0 GPA just to apply, it takes me at least a half-hour to nudge even one student close to *how* he or she

| Image A | Image B | Image C |

knows what they're for. They say, "I've seen them before," "Somebody must have told me sometime," or "Everybody knows."

The objects tell the viewer what they are *by the way they're made*. If an aborigine in a jungle found those objects, she'd be befuddled. To intuit their purposes, she would need a *context*. It would be less difficult if she had found object A near an open lock; object B beside a little white ball; and object C covered in blood. Could you use object A to clean your ears, object B to swat flies, and object C to shave? It is possible, but it would be (A) painful, (B) ineffective, and (C) dangerous.

The first image (A) reveals its use by its shape. One end has a form coded to a single mechanism no other similar tool should compel to respond. The other end, simple and elegant (which shows it's not cheap stuff), gives the user a broader surface on which to exert needed pressure.

The second image (B) is at the end of a steel shaft and has the number 7 clearly incised on its foot. As the faces of irons gradually flatten out from a vertical-faced 1 to the almost horizontal 10, their uses become more for short-distance, high-loft shots. (The face is grooved so the ball will squish on impact and produce more backspin. Only the threat of death could have made me Google *why* you'd want that.)

Now our indigenous lady might have had a chance with image C. The sharp edge tells it all to anyone who's hacked vegetation. It also informs us by the way it's made that you can't expect to find one like this today at Target or Walmart.

How do we know the proper way to handle anything when there's no one more knowledgeable around to tell us? We simply go and look. Does it exist? How's it made? What's it for?

Does Santa exist? I'm not going to spoil that one. Have your parents charter a ski plane and fly around magnetic north till you run out of gas. Is the world flat? Beg Queen Isabella for three ships and sail west. If you don't fall off, come back and tell us. In *The Lord of the Flies*, the marooned boys were convinced there was an evil presence on the island, a tangible "Beast." Many had doubts, but they put them to rest in the absolutely dumbest way to establish truth: a vote. They crept up to the mountaintop, saw a wheezing "thing," and raced back down, resolutely convinced. Only Simon, the shy epileptic, had the wits and the courage to go up and *look*. He saw it was a corpse caught in a parachute.

Now, as you reach for a life out on your own, "in the jungle," you'll find questions get far more complicated, as well as more pressing for an answer...from you. Having sex used to be with someone you're committed to; then to someone you love; and now it's become just recreation. Is that true or not? Should I ask a cop friend to fix a speeding ticket? What's wrong with that? I don't do drugs, but a friend offered me good stuff, cheap, and I could resell it, easily. Is this abortion justified homicide or just the equivalent of an appendectomy? How can I be sure?

Which of the following statements do you believe are justified and why?

1. Your foot was over the line! You're out.
2. With a heavy heart, I concede the election.
3. Santa Claus is a delightful fiction with absolutely no literal basis in reality.
4. Never use bleach in a toilet bowl.
5. I'm sorry, but there's no pulse, no brain waves. The patient's dead.
6. You can't build a cabin there. This is my lawn!
7. Human sacrifice is premeditated homicide.
8. The rock that bloodied my knee isn't solid but packed with moving particles, and most of it is empty space.
9. There are undoubtedly other intelligent beings in the universe.
10. The results prove the Iraq War was necessary.

Those statements are *assertions* about the truth. But an assertion, all by itself, is simply that: no more than an opinion expressed with conviction, often with no support or attempt at proof. What could validate any one or all of those assertions above? Only the *objective facts* and unbiased *reasoning*.

1. The foot *was* either over the line or not. Each side stands to profit from the outcome. That's why we rely on sharp-eyed, honest umpires and judges.
2. You got 90 percent of the vote; I got 10 percent. Case closed.
3. That's magnetic North Pole down there. What do you see? (And psst! To pump up your joy, your parents gave credit for *their* hard work to a mythical old man.)
4. Ammonia in urine combined with bleach becomes chlorine gas, used to blind and kill British soldiers in World War I.
5. No one can function without a heartbeat or be self-aware without brain waves.
6. This legal deed testifies that I paid for all the land within these lines.
7. Any forensic physician can tell that the tissue from this body is human not sheep. The word *homicide* designates killing a human. Is this homicide *justified*?
8. If you blew up a hydrogen atom to the size of the Astrodome, the nucleus would be a grain of grit at midfield and the electron would be a speck on the roof, and the rest would be just...empty. Google "Atomic Bomb."
9. A statistical probability, no better. So far, no one knowledgeable and reliable has discovered unchallengeable evidence establishing that as an objective fact. It's still an open question.
10. What results justify a half-million deaths, four trillion dollars, plus uncountable maimed humans? Is it a different situation if they'd been used as food for the starving?

You're free to *do* absolutely anything you like, regardless of the truth. You're free to walk off the Sears Tower, drink cyanide, and tickle a tarantula—but *only* once. The huge plot of land now known as the Americas was *not* first discovered by a white European but by a whole lot of nameless Siberians. Furthermore, although you're completely unaware of it, you and everything else on earth are hurtling eastward at 750 mph, depending on how far you are from the equator. If it all weren't glued to the surface by mysterious gravity, we'd all go flying off into space. If the four unchallengeable physical constants (gravity, electromagnetism, strong and weak nuclear forces) were different in even the tiniest degree, life on earth would have been completely impossible. That's not religion. It's hard-nosed science.

It's also true that we all have a right to our own opinions. No argument. But that's not the same as assuring you the right to have that opinion accepted or respected. Nowhere is it established that you have a right not to have your uninformed opinions scorned and laughed at and you being judged (unkindly, but fairly) as dumb for voicing it. If someone rushes up and tells you, "Elvis Presley and Michael Jackson just went to the picnic at the house next door," it's prudent to go out into the yard and take a look for yourself.

The *only* way to have an opinion worth holding or expressing or being respected is the combination of objective (out-there) evidence and honest reasoning (without self-serving bias). I don't *want* it to be true that we all have to die, but unless I yield to the truth, I'll go mad trying to make the truth yield to me. And I'll never truly value what I have while I have it.

Objective evidence

Valid opinion   +

Honest reasoning

"I saw this show on TV once" isn't really as reliable a basis for an opinion as "They gave me a Nobel Prize in this field." Your opinion on physics is probably *not* as good as Stephen Hawking's. Your opinion on a performance is quite likely not as good as Meryl Streep's. When you come to a thorny question in class and your first-time opinion flashes up in fierce opposition to your teacher's (no matter how inexperienced), what are the odds you're right?

What follows might seem to be an unnecessary tangent into the way the mind works—or ought to. Actually, its intention is like the honest magician before he works his magic; this text has no aces up its sleeves or rabbits stuffed in concealed pockets. It wants to show *how* it arrives at its conclusions on fitting human behavior. Whatever moral precepts it offers are *not imposed*, like ready-made commandments carved in stone and inflicted from on high. Rather, before we set out to discover them, I want to show *how* they emerge from the evidence—from "the way things are"—not from the way any authority says they should be.

EPISTEMOLOGY: WHAT VALIDATES OPINIONS

Evidence

Evidence is the wherewithal you use to build an argument justifying a judgment, a valid conclusion. It's what banks demand for a loan, courts require for a conviction, scientists handle at the Federal Food and Drug Administration, the FAA, FHA, and a niagara of other guardian agencies that protect citizens in ways few can do for themselves.

Evidence—research, brainstorming—is like the huge pile of pitchblende Madame Curie had in her yard, which was ultimately refined down to a single vial of radium. Always, 95 percent of your research notes will end up wasted. But without that excess, your conclusions will be shaky, less trustworthy. Detectives solve crimes by eliminating wrong answers. It's the same with the SAT.

Evidence is of two basic types: *Real* knowledge is firsthand, experiential, and certain. *Notional* knowledge is secondhand, academic, and probable.

Real knowledge results from your own personal experience —either through actual contact with the object in question or common sense. I don't need anybody to tell me my parents existed or what they were like. And despite the fact I never met them, I know that *you* had two parents, also—one male, one female. That's called *a priori*: self-evident.

Notional knowledge results from research that *reasons* from certain evidence to probable conclusions: gather data, sift it, make an outline, conclude, and critique—from which you argue further. (If you don't know how to outline, you don't know how to think.) Most of what you accept as true—about almost anything—is notional knowledge: secondhand, the result of others' research and reasoning—testimony. You don't discover it yourself; you *accept* it. A great deal of its validity rests on the belief that most people tell the truth and have no occasion to deceive.

Argument

Argument—sequential logic, outlining, reasoning—begins with evidence that is reliable and argues to conclusions that are *probable*. Logical thinking rearranges the sifted evidence in an interlocked logical chain (outline) building to a conclusion. There are several major ways: *induction* (many parallel cases allow a general conclusion, such as water freezes at 32 degrees Farenheit); *deduction* (tested general principles applied to a particular case, such as it's below zero, therefore, this water will freeze); *analogy* (explaining something by comparing it to something similar, such as the statement "Alfie is a pig"); or overwhelming *convergence* (arrows pointing to one outcome: "Because we've been through hell together so many times, we've stayed married for fifty years."

That process—making trustworthy decisions—has been the fundamental goal of the last twelve-plus years of your learning life. *Did it work?* It's what you ought to be prepared to do before you choose a career, get married, buy a house, or have sex. Are you rightfully confident that you not only know *how* to think logically and confidently, but that you can actually *do* it?

PERSONAL REFLECTION

For too many years, you've spent class and homework time scribbling down what *other people* think. These reflections are a chance to begin to discover what *you* think, and more importantly, why.

1. Describe a time when you took an instant dislike to a person but then changed your reaction completely and became good friends. What triggered the instant dislike? Then, what occurred that began the change to a totally different response? Was it quick or gradual?

2. Why did I ask this question? (Be sure to ask that of *all* the proposed reflections.)

2.

ACCUMULATING EVIDENCE

> Everyone's entitled to their own opinion. Not to their own facts.
>
> —*Daniel Patrick Moynihan*

Do you agree or disagree with the following statements?

1. Personal experience—"street smarts"—is more useful in life than a lot of book knowledge.
2. A college degree is necessary to become very successful financially.
3. Without personally felt curiosity, education is impossible.
4. The true purpose of college is learning how to handle sex and alcohol responsibly.
5. An educated person has begun to form a continually evolving perspective on reality.
6. Experience is not the best teacher; only experience that is *reflected on*.
7. The majority of the time, eyewitness testimony is highly unreliable.
8. When a famous athlete recommends a brand of cereal, that's a reliable norm.
9. Most of the celebrities on late-night talk shows are worth listening to.

10. Most of what we claim to "know," we're taking on someone else's word.

Owning yourself means assuming responsibility for who you are and the choices you make. To accomplish that, you have to know (like the key, seven iron, and axe) how *you* are made, which opens other questions like, for example, What does it take to be a *worthwhile* human? Those questions that we all share are the subject of this book. Answering them is easier if we consider our own answers next to the experiences of others. (That's what libraries are for—biographies, novels, history, psychology, and the sciences.) Just as scientists can tell you what foods are safe, diagnose diseases, and offer treatment, everyone who's lived on earth for a while can give you invaluable hints on what will make you happy or sad, upbeat or downcast, proud or ashamed. There is no need to start from scratch. You can profit from their painful experience without having their painful scars. (Google "vicariously.")

Regarding statement 2 above: Abraham Lincoln, Henry Ford, Thomas Edison, and Mark Twain never even finished *grade* school, and yet each became not only well paid and influential but also impressively articulate. You might say, "Well, those were simpler days." (Correct! No books or computers.) Walt Disney, Frank Sinatra, Robert DeNiro, Lucille Ball, Simon Cowell, and Jim Carrey never finished high school. Nine United States' presidents never graduated from any college, nor did Sergey Brin, Winston Churchill, or Tom Carvel. Frank Lloyd Wright, J. D. Salinger, Steve Jobs, Mark Zuckerberg, Russell Simmons, Ted Turner, Oprah Winfrey, F. Scott Fitzgerald, John Glenn, Ralph Lauren, Steven Spielberg, Woody Allen, Tom Hanks, Clint Eastwood, and Michael Dell never finished college. Eugene O'Neill, William Faulkner, John Steinbeck, and Ernest Hemingway managed to win the Nobel Prize for Literature without A.B.'s. Bill Gates never finished college! (That's called argument from examples.)

Is there no end to the ways we continue to kid ourselves? There must be some *other* reason your parents are spending $120,000 (minimum) to postpone your need to support yourself.

Beyond basic literacy and computational skills, all you need to be financially successful are the four D's: discipline, drive, and determination—and a dream, which motivates the other three. I don't know any graduate school that teaches those. Certainly, few, if any, high schools do. Most reward much less noble qualities: cheating, minimalism, and indifference. And if you plan to spend your college years learning to socialize and fine-tune those unemployable skills, you have no need of other enemies than yourself.

Before you set out to discover for yourself what morality (humanity) means and entails, this text can give you confidence in the *process* by examining how you discover what *anything* means, what *anything* is for, how *anything* can be legitimately used. I have a hunch no one's done that with you yet. If so, your moral (human) life is enslaved to people who *do* think.

PERCEIVE

The first essential step is *to perceive what's there. See* the facts, *hear* what's said, *examine* the object or action in question, and *discover* how it reveals itself.

That's not easy—not as easy as most people bombarded by stimuli every moment might at first believe. Centuries ago, when people had fewer distractions, they were forced to be more attentive, quicker on the uptake, and better at sizing-up. For evidence of that, merely skim the extraordinary long verse choruses of Greek dramas, which held audiences transfixed for hours, or Shakespeare's comedies, whose classical references and sharp wit came leaping like popcorn off the stage, but which most moderns have to approach as if translating Mandarin Chinese, with as many footnotes on every page as there is text.

Would you make a reliable witness even of the data of your daily life? How many names do you know of those who sit near you every class? Do you know the color of your English professor's eyes? Does he or she wear a watch? Do you know the name of the person who clears your breakfast table? Mops your bathroom? Are they as real as your pets, your clothes, your hair, or your CD's? Those facts aren't really important, but they suggest how observant you are.

If you're drunk and think a store mannequin winked at you, your opinion is stupid. And of course if *you* look stupid enough, people will repeat the story. If you answer a professor's question without having read the book, don't blame the professor for the scowl. If you haven't looked at the speedometer in a while, don't growl at the state trooper as you roll down the window. Surely you're not dumb enough to believe that you can concentrate on a text better with music blasting in your headphones. Can you follow an argument when everybody talks at once? Does construction noise help you to listen to a class lecture? The one person you should *never* deceive is yourself.

Most people make very poor eyewitnesses. You, yourself, must admit that you'll write any drivel to fill space on a quiz. Three-quarters of cases overturned by DNA testing were caused by misinformed but confident eyewitnesses. When you say, without thinking, "We've *heard* all this before," does that mean you're ready for a quiz on it?

CATEGORIZE

One of the prime functions of the human mind is to simplify the bewildering clutter of stimuli by clustering things with those like them under "umbrella terms" like *mineral, vegetable, animal, human,* and further specifying them as *iron, gold, plutonium; orchid, carrot, lima bean; oryx, panda, hairy-nosed wombat;* and *male, female, Caucasian, Asian.*

Just as people are lazy in perceiving, they're also predictably slovenly here—and often much more positive about their opinions than they have evidence for. You see a woman lurching along the street, hair and clothes disheveled, and with empty eyes. You might jump to the conclusion that she is drunk. This is quite possible, of course. Also possible is that she might be suffering from a diabetic attack, epileptic fit, or rape. Or if you see a young man "walking funny" and categorize him as "gay," you've taken an enormous leap, based on almost no evidence, to make a life-judgment on a stranger. Perhaps you've never done that or at least never had to apologize to your victim.

EVALUATE

This is a step beyond pigeonholing. You're passing further judgment on how you can legitimately *use* this item, given the nature you've discovered by analyzing it. Could you use facial tissue to type a term paper? Again, it is possible, but... Are you free to swim across Niagara Falls? Sure! But only once. Can you treat gin like ginger ale? Yes, for awhile.

Consider this trivial example: while walking along a college corridor, I saw a guy cramming *Of Mice and Men*. "Good book," I said. "It stinks," says he. I said, "Well, he did win the Nobel Prize." He snorted, "It still stinks." Noticing his index finger in the text, I asked, "How much have you read?" "Twenty pages," says he.

He was saying nothing about that novel, John Steinbeck, or the Nobel Prize Committee. He was evaluating *himself*. What he really had a right to say was, "What I've read doesn't appeal to me at all." Instead, he said—equivalently—"I'm an idiot, and I don't mind proving it." Attempting to mask his inability to appreciate it, he blamed the book and looked stupid.

Before you dump the moral dos and don'ts of your parents, teachers, religion, and the like, it's wise to give them an *unbiased* appraisal. It could be like unloading an antique table from your dad's spinster aunt for beer money, then finding out it was a big-ticket heirloom.

Juries sometimes arrive at an opinion that will send the defendant to death. Such a decision would be beyond obscene if, for instance, the evidence establishes that the prisoner was out of the country at the time of the murder or physically incapable of handling the lethal weapon. It would be even worse if the jury arrived at the death verdict mainly because the defendant was of a different race, badly dressed, or ill-mannered. (It's wise to recall that fact when you're tempted to snap out a negative term when you see someone "odd.")

This is the stage where baseless prejudices can mess up the whole operation. Evaluation takes an honest, impartial mind. We should be able to hope for it from one another as we do from civil judges. But it's wise not to *expect* it: "Everybody's got an angle!"

We'll see a bit later that those special "angles" are sometimes not only justified but valuable. Conservatives need the balance of liberals and vice versa. Theology and science need one another. What's poisonous at this stage of assessment is *unfounded* prejudices—racial, sexual, ethnic, as well as blind rejection of liberals by conservatives or theologians by scientists. The absolute requirement for discovering is honesty and open-mindedness. Even one's most iron certitudes ought to be open at least to fine tuning.

EXPRESS

"I understand it. I just can't put it into words." That is self-delusion. *Understand* means you *can* put it into words. You can explain it to someone else. The first step toward wisdom is calling a thing by its *correct* name.

That was the real—and completely lost—purpose in all that vocabulary for the SAT: Do you have a treasury of words you can recognize and use to grasp what others say and express your own thoughts in a way others can grasp without misunderstanding you? Using words in structures is the reason to study Latin. Theoretically, if both parties really understand one another, there'll be fewer reasons for war, drive-by shootings, and date rape.

However, if you don't make the effort to say exactly what you mean, don't blame me. "Well, you know what I *meant*," you might say. No. I can't know anything except what you say or write. If I send you a note saying that I will send you five hundred dollars, and you write back, "I except your gift," don't expect to get it. You've written the exact *opposite* of what you meant. *Except* means "leave out, omit." If you meant *accept*, you should have written that.

Using the wrong word incautiously harms not only the one labeled but also the speaker. A male, for instance, calling another male "gay" clearly is too dull to realize there's only *one* way his accusation could possibly be certain, beyond doubt.

CRITIQUE

It is always prudent to check out your opinion—moral or otherwise—with someone you think wise and trustworthy. That's why teachers write comments on papers, and why so many students don't profit from them but look only at the grade.

People were burned at the stake for claiming everything revolved around the sun, barred from lifetime jobs for having attended a few communist meetings in college, imprisoned for protesting the Vietnam War. On the other hand, millions have lost their lives or limbs without having any reason other than, "Or else...!" or "Your country needs you." *Why* is this worth my one life—my children's parent?

The media constantly tell us that money, fame, sex, and power are the yellow-brick road to "success, happiness, and ful-fillment." It's a nearly universal conviction. But if that *were* true, how do you explain Elvis Presley, Marilyn Monroe, Janis Joplin, Jimi Hendrix, Jim Morrison, Kurt Cobain, River Phoenix, Michael Jackson, and Robin Williams—money, fame, sex, and power to the max! Did they anaesthetize themselves with drugs for years (from life) because they were so happy? Did most of them finally kill themselves because they were so fulfilled they couldn't take it anymore?

Opinions are definitely not *self*-justifying, automatically true simply because I choose to like them. They're true—valid, worth trusting—*only* if they're substantiated by objective facts.

Subjective opinions are those in my head; what
   I assert.
Objective evidence is the facts; what's out there as it
   exposes itself *to* me.

Whatever your personal, subjective opinion—on *any* conceivable subject—it's only valid as the objective ("out-there") evidence and honest reasoning ("in here") backing it up.

When a lawyer enters a plea in court:
Where's your **evidence**?
When you give your opinion of a poem:
Where's your **evidence**?
When you argue with your parents:
Where's your **evidence**?
When a test prompt says, "Explain":
Where's your **evidence**?
When you contemplate an abortion:
Where's your **evidence**?

PERSONAL REFLECTION

The subject for this reflection is one you know better than anyone else who ever lived: you. What keeps most of us going—more or less on course, confident—is that most people are decent, good humans. That, then, includes you. What is the evidence and argument that substantiate that highly probable opinion?

Remember: Evidence means concrete, specific actions—not windy, unsubstantiated assertions like, "I'm nice to people...I love my family." What evidence would hold up in court? Who would testify on your behalf? What would they offer to convince a jury? How would you testify on your own behalf?

Many students shy foolishly from such questions. How can you give yourself away in marriage if you have only the vaguest notion of who you really are? The whole purpose of this time of your life is not merely to make a living but to find out what human living is for. It's the only "you" that you'll ever have. How can you trust it to take you anywhere if you're too pseudo-humble to check it out?

(Always remember: writing is not the same as typing.)

3.

POINTING EVIDENCE TO A CONCLUSION

> Most people would die sooner than think—in fact they do.
>
> —*Bertrand Russell*

Consider the following statements. Do you agree or disagree?

1. If you don't know how to outline, you don't know how to think.
2. Charm and personality will get you in the door. It won't keep you there long.
3. Fail to learn how to think for yourself, others will inevitably do your thinking for you.
4. Specialists usually get jobs quickly, but those who succeed are those skilled in coping with questions no one has answers for beforehand.
5. One of the greatest pitfalls in theorizing is reductionism—leaving out pertinent evidence that might threaten the thesis.
6. Any professor who gives even a D for an essay that's a mess of disorganized, surface, ill-considered fluff should be dismissed.
7. As with scientific realities and theories, the *subjects* of moral theories remain the same but our *insights* into them should be constantly better focused.

8. People without doubts or hesitations are the most boring people on earth.
9. No one—absolutely no one—writes a read-worthy first draft.
10. Lack of proofreading is like static on the radio. It takes little time before you get turned off.

The combination of objective evidence and honest reasoning is just a less complicated way of expressing the scientific method, and it should be applied as rigorously to moral questions as it is to the atomic theory. It consists approximately of the following six steps:

1. Be genuinely puzzled. Without curiosity, learning can't happen.
2. Gather all pertinent objective information about the point at issue.
3. Put evidence into a logical sequence (an outline) so you can...
4. Make an educated guess—a "hypothesis"—about the best possible answer to your question.
5. Design an experiment (research) to test your hypothesis.
6. Evaluate the results: Does your hypothesis, in fact, work?

For instance, during the Crimean War (1853–56) between Russia and the major European powers, a very determined young woman named Florence Nightingale volunteered, along with a handful of other trained nurses, to serve the British wounded in Turkey. Until that time, care of the sick and injured had been a contemptible job unfit for proper ladies. When Florence arrived, she discovered wounded British soldiers were dying in far higher percentages than any others. War wounds accounted for only one death in six. Typhus, cholera, and dysentery killed by far the majority. The in-hospital death rate was 42 percent. Why (*puzzle*)? So she listed all the reasons: men were kept in rooms without blankets or decent food, unwashed, still wearing gore-soaked battle uniforms. There was no soap, towels,

21

clean clothes, or waste disposal (*evidence*). She presented her solution (*hypothesis*) to the learned doctors and officers: lack of hygiene and nutrition, untreated pustulant wounds, and chaotic surroundings. They scorned her: "Meddling old maid!" (*unfair bias*). So she wrote to *The London Times*, which triggered, almost immediately, an order from the War Office for proper cleaning, constant care, and kindness (*testing*). The doctors grudgingly yielded, and the death rate dropped to 2 percent. Since then, Florence Nightingale's methods have become standard operating procedure for hospitals all over the world (*results*).

HOW LOGIC WORKS

What separates human beings from other animals—even the smartest (like the dolphin) and the most affectionate (like the Labrador Retriever)—is that, while other animals can know facts (thunder, danger, bitter weather), we have the potential to understand. While animals can even give up their lives for their own babies, we can give up our lives for people we don't even like or for an abstract idea or value, like our country or religion.

> Thinking does *not* mean just having thoughts but *skillfully* directing evidence to legitimate conclusions.

Here, we concentrate on understanding, since the course promises to give reasons that validate claims about fitting moral behavior specific to humans. The goal of schooling, since human beings lived in caves, has been trying to fine tune our human wits so we can be less afraid. The first task is to train children to use the right names for things, and then to associate the words *Ah, good!* and *No-no-no!* with each one. Without a vocabulary that remains consistent, communication is impossible. Then, the child learns to express relationships among objects and people. Nobody has to teach a little girl her doll is hers and no one else's! But she's going to need sentences to complain to her mom when her nasty brother is holding it hostage.

That first stage is called induction, like the game *Password* where one team member calls out specific examples that lead to a single unifying idea—"potato chips, ocean water, tears, anchovies = salty." That skill is the basis of thinking: seeing logical relationships. It is the basic skill of the sciences: whenever I put water out and the temperature goes below 32 degrees, it turns to ice; everything drops at 32 feet per second. It's also the basis of moral judgments: over the course of the last fifty centuries, every time the powerful dehumanize the masses, the masses will somehow get their revenge; dogs have feelings; wasting food is bad; human sex is hugely different from simple animal coitus.

Those generalizations become useful in solving new questions. That logical skill is called *deduction*. No human ever saw a live dinosaur, but the evidence for their existence is all those bones. So, knowing how muscle and bone interact in creatures living today, we can make legitimate, educated guesses how dinosaurs were fleshed. Likewise, arguing backward from the evidence of the Hubble Telescope, we can deduce that the universe is expanding. The same is true of moral judgments. What dehumanizes people has always harmed both victim and perpetrator.

STRATEGIES FOR ORGANIZING EVIDENCE

Many students are sure they've outwitted their English teachers (who are mostly kind by nature) by guilting them into at least a C for a paper unworthy to wrap fish—no brainstorming or research, no recognizable organization, and quite often not even a stab at the spell-checker.

They are their own victims and will pay for their momentary relief for the rest of their lives. Managers don't pay salaries for people who generate waste paper. Second-rate minds are always trotting behind, wondering what the smart guys are jabbering about.

Here are just a few ways of manipulating your accumulated evidence so that it will begin to make sense, cease to be a jumble of mismatched beads, and instead become strung together like a chain of DNA that clarifies into a conviction about human life and its business.

Induction works from the bottom up, from the concrete and specific to abstract, universal conclusions. Induction accumulates particular examples or similar recurring patterns into a reliable generalization. On a simpler level, we begin using umbrella words to categorize similar objects and people, such as *animal, vegetable, mineral.* Induction is also a way we can study *behaviors* and draw conclusions from invariant results, such as without fail, ice melts above 32 degrees; fire burns; rape is brutal and terrifying.

Once we've validated persistent—almost invariant—patterns of causes and their effects, we can establish a code of dos and don'ts, which in the vast majority of cases, will have good or bad results. The more examples of human beings we can gather—not just from people right at hand, but from recorded understandings going back to the burial practices of prehistorical humans—the more confident we can be predicting good or bad outcomes. Evidence from all over the globe substantiates our trust in what almost all humans have believed is fitting.

It will never be 100 percent sure. You will always find a society here or there that differs, such as headhunters, suicide bombers, or cannibals. Nor should we ground our assertions solely on the preponderance of people who hold a moral conviction, for example, voting on whether there are evil spirits or if tomatoes are poisonous.

Lawmakers and rulers, since the first societies arose, have discerned that certain activities invariably cause suffering. So they draw up laws—inductive conclusions—trying to help those too slow, selfish, or pigheaded to figure that out for themselves. Sometimes the law seems doubtful when applied to a particular situation. For example, I should repay honest debts on time. But my house burned down last night. Therefore, give me more time. That's why we need judges.

Deduction works from the top down. It begins with trust-worthy generalizations produced by induction and concludes that these new but identical circumstances will produce the same results as have occurred in the past. For example, one may reason, "Water freezes at 32 degrees Fahrenheit; it's now 32 degrees Fahrenheit; this water will freeze if I put it out there." When parents say, "You're gonna get in trouble doing that young lady/man," they have no crystal ball. They've been around the track more often, and every time they've seen these actions, they've invariably turned out painfully.

The point of this present digression into epistemology is to establish that this course is *not* deductive—legislating from on high, which is what most students have become used to in their upbringing: "This is the law...this is the commandment...society says we must...." This course is *inductive*: assisting you in your own *personal* search for the evidence and arguments that will validate your *personal* ethical generalizations, your own ethical self.

Analogy tries to give insight into something less known by comparison to something better known. For example, someone might say, "You never met Alfie. Well, he's an outright pig." Some things you can say about pigs give you a better insight into this unknown guy; some you can't—no pointy ears, cloven feet, curly tail. But even without carefully dissecting the metaphor, you know more:

ALFIE = PIG

Overweight

Slovenly

Smelly

Unshaven

"My love is like a red, red rose"—except for the thorns.
"War is hell!"
"It's a jungle out there."

"Airplane seats are torture chambers."

Analogy can give insight into far more complex situations—tangled moral dilemmas, like abortion. The pivotal question is not whether the *method* is brutal or humane, but *what* are you killing? Is it a clot of formless cells or a human being? Is this a human as worthy as Abraham Lincoln, or a tumorous object like an appendix? *It* tells a forensic scientist that it's a product of two human cells. If you leave it alone, you won't get just a banana or a chimp (*fact*). Its DNA is 50 percent different from its host mother (*fact*). *However*, half of fertilized ova never implant in the uterus; therefore, if they were persons from fertilization, half of humanity died before it was born (*fact*). Well? Which is it? Almost everyone has an opinion—often fierce. But is the opinion valid?

Take an analogy. An abortionist is out hunting. He hasn't seen anybody in two days. He sees the bushes move. Is he free to shoot? Most people would say no, not until he's sure what he's killing, that it's demonstrably *not* a human being. Can you terminate a fetus if you don't know what it *is*?

That doesn't settle the abortion debate. But it does show the question is a *lot* more complex than most ill-informed "experts" on either side believe.

Convergence of probabilities operates on the conviction that when *almost* all the arrows seem to whip around and point to the same obvious conclusion, the answer has a reliable degree of probability. That's the method of understanding that allows a jury to conclude that a defendant is not only guilty but should be executed—"beyond a *reasonable* doubt." Be careful, though: their vote (in fact, any vote) doesn't establish the *truth*, only the action representatives of this community believe from the evidence is *fair*. A more representative case of convergence would be asking a couple at their fiftieth wedding anniversary why they stayed together so long. They'd look at you like you're dull-witted: "Why? Well...everything."

Eliminating Unsatisfactory Answers. Google "Twenty Questions." Avoid the sites that ask for a name and address, and find one that will let you play the game against the machine, or even better, play it on a long car trip. Get an object or person in mind, then type in "animal" or "vegetable" or "mineral." The machine—or the other player—will ask you umbrella questions, answerable with "Yes," "No," "Maybe," or "Doesn't matter," to eliminate large *clumps* of possible answers.

Think back (or forward) to your choosing of a college. Picture a map of the whole United States. Then, ask an umbrella question, like Do I want to come home for Thanksgiving and Christmas? For most, answering yes cuts off more than three-quarters of the possible choices. Then, an equally excluding umbrella question for most would be, What colleges are likely to accept my SAT scores?

Watch detective and courtroom TV shows. They are not at all academic, but good practice.

Either/Or: When you can narrow the possible answers to only two—as in, Is this the person to marry or not?...Guilty or not?...Raise the bet or fold?—simply draw a line down the center of a sheet of paper, with a plus above one side and a minus above the other. At random, simply list the pluses and minuses of each alternative. When you're exhausted, you won't have the answer, but you'll be less confused. Then, go through the two lists and weight each entry with plus-and-minus numbers given according to each reason's importance. At the end, you still won't have the answer, but you'll have more information on which to take a *calculated risk*. And in nearly every decision you ever make, that's the best you're ever going to get.

LOGICAL FALLACIES

You don't have to memorize the following specific types of faulty assertions/conclusions. They're listed here merely to sensitize you to smell rats in unethical statements. Not everything said, printed, or broadcasted deserves credence.

- *Ad hominem* arguments are the tools of scoundrels and idiots, therefore invalid.
- If you had any consideration for my feelings, you wouldn't argue from **appeal to pity**.

- What would your mom say if you argued from **appeal to sentiment**?
- I can't understand how anyone could argue from **appeal to incredulity**.
- If you argue from **appeal to force**, I'll bash your face in.
- You're surely far too intelligent to accept an **appeal to vanity**.
- **Circular reasoning** (begging the question) means assuming what you intend to prove. This form of argument is invalid because it's circular. (You use this ruse when you merely restate the quiz question as a positive assertion.)
- As Aristotle said, most arguments from **appeal to authority** are invalid.
- *Post hoc ergo propter hoc* (**After this, therefore because of this**) arguments precede false conclusions. Hence, this type of argument is unacceptable.
- *Argumentum ad consequentiam* (**Arguing from unpleasant but irrelevant consequences**) often leads to bruised feelings, therefore, avoid it.
- *Argumentum ad nauseam* (**wearying repetition**) is invalid, is invalid, is invalid. If three repetitions haven't convinced you, I'll just have to say it again: *argumentum ad nauseam* is ineffective because it doesn't work. (This is also taxing when the test taker resorts to writing down the side of the page.)
- Ancient wisdom teaches that **argument from antiquity** is unjustified. Therefore, refrain from citing the Flat Earth Society.
- If we accept **slippery-slope** arguments, sooner or later we'll find ourselves having to accept other hare-brained arguments, and sooner or later, we can't argue at all.
- No decent logician would accept the "**No True Scotsman**" fallacy. If anyone makes loyalty the determinant of truth, he or she has no right to claim to be logical.

Practice your sniffing skills on one evening's commercials or one slick magazine's ads. Loads of them are unmasked on the Internet. Google "logical fallacies in commercials examples." Some are a real hoot! It may also be revealing if you applied your rat-smelling skills to the "explain" prompts on your last few quizzes and tests.

SOME LOGICAL PRACTICE

There is no need to apply the correct label, but what invalidates each of the following?

1. Most people who show up for church are just as bad as anybody else during the week.
2. I'll add twenty bucks a week to your allowance, if all your grades are at least C+.
3. Oh, Mom! *Everybody* does it.
4. Why? Because I told you to!
5. If you start drinking beer, there's no telling what you'll get into next.
6. The whiter the bread, the sooner you're dead.
7. My country, right or wrong. (Compare with Nero, Torquemada, Pio Nono, Adolf Hitler, Ku Klux Klan, Sen. Joe McCarthy, Dick Nixon, Dick Cheney, ISIS.)
8. If you loved me, you'd have sex with me.
9. The Nazis had nationalized health care.
10. How could someone eat a dog? It's a living being!
11. Saddam must have had weapons of mass destruction; the president wouldn't have lied to us.
12. It depends on how you define sex.
13. You don't support the Israeli occupation of Palestine? You must be an anti-Semite.
14. Because of global warming, piracy has decreased in the Caribbean.
15. If we legalize gay marriage, people will then want to legalize polygamy.

PERSONAL REFLECTION

Describe a time when you were in an argument—perhaps with your parents—when, all of a sudden, a light flashed in your brain and you silently muttered, "Oh, my God. They're right!" But you kept arguing. In all honesty, what was going on then?

4.

ASSESSING VALUE

> I conceive that the great part of the miseries of mankind are brought upon them by false estimates they have made of the value of things.
> —*Benjamin Franklin*

Consider the following ten statements and whether you agree or disagree.

1. Willy Loman was right. A smile and a shoeshine are the key to success.
2. Like table manners, moral guilt becomes part of a child's personally validated psyche by repetition and consistent rewards and punishments.
3. It is unlikely that a man like Abraham Lincoln could be elected president today.
4. Those who specialize their career choice early will continue to get higher salaries than those who generalize in courses like humanities.
5. A lie detector doesn't detect lies but only offers evidence on which to base an educated guess about the subject's truthfulness at the moment.
6. *Scientific proof* means not certainty but, at best, a high degree of probability.
7. Survival of the fittest is the most deeply rooted *human* impulse.
8. People who avoid complex human problems live more serene lives.

9. The silver medalist is simply the first of the losers.
10. For any writer, the content is more important than engaging the reader.

SUBVERTING HUMANITY

Morality is an objective fact; conscience is a subjective opinion.

One day, nearly by accident, Dr. Justin McBrayer, a philosophy professor at Fort Lewis College in Colorado, discovered that his second-grade son's potential to become a fully moral human being was being destroyed at the very root by his kindly teachers and their supervisors.

His child and little companions were being inculcated, like the children in *1984* and *Brave New World*, with the conviction that the difference between human babies and baby seals was merely a matter of subjective opinion. Of course, the teachers never would have thought of their instruction that way, which, of course, is the problem. But their bumper sticker assertions about values—as opposed to facts—make the principles of moral (human) behavior more or less arbitrary—temporary social customs, morality as lifestyle choices, a matter of taste—like a Fiat compared with a Ford, chocolate rather than vanilla.

Crammed into a student's desk at a PTA meeting, Dr. McBrayer began to realize why "the overwhelming majority of college freshmen...view moral claims as mere opinions that are not true or are true only relative to a culture."*

On the neatly arranged second-grade classroom wall were two innocently ignorant slogans, just like the barn motto in *Animal Farm*: "Four legs good, two legs bad." The two slogans, which were viewed daily—unavoidably and uncritically—by the children, read thus:

Fact: Something that is true about the subject and can be tested or proven.

---

*Justin P. McBrayer, "Why Our Children Don't Think There Are Moral Facts," *The New York Times*, March 2, 2015, http://opinionator.blogs.nytimes.com/2015/03/02/why-our-children-dont-think-there-are-moral-facts/.

Opinion: What someone thinks, feels, or believes.

Later, McBrayer sat with his six-year-old son and tried to determine just how badly well-meaning teachers and the school system, which our Founding Fathers insisted on in order to form decent citizens, had perverted his most precious treasure.

> McBrayer: *I believe George Washington was the first president. Is that fact or opinion?*
>
> Son: *Fact.*
>
> McBrayer: *But I believe it. And you said what someone believes is an opinion.*
>
> Son: *Yeah, but it's true.*
>
> McBrayer: *So it's both true and an opinion.*
>
> Son: *[Blank face. No response.]*

Then the father found worksheets that asked kids to identify which was fact and which was opinion, such as:

> –Copying homework is wrong.
> –All men are created equal.
> –Some freedoms must be limited to protect us from terrorism.
> –No one under age 21 should be allowed to drink alcoholic beverages.
> –Students should not bring deadly weapons to school.

When I read Dr. McBrayer's article in the *New York Times*, I yearned to grab the principal of that school (and of how many others?) by the ears, and demand a few addenda:

> –The difference between Coca-Cola and Lysol is a matter of personal taste.
> –Because of societally accepted moral norms, the humanity of Jews and Slavs was less than the humanity of white Aryans wherever Nazi Germany

held power. Any difference of opinion was settled
by World War II.
–The rape of conquered females was once a legitimate
prize of war.
–Concentration camp workers were exonerated because
they were only following orders.
–Guilt trips are bad for you.

The first day of every course, I say, "This is the most important statement I'll make while we're together. I won't say it till
everybody is ready to write it down....Okay. Here it is: 'The tree
comes *to* me. That's the whole megillah."

There are blank looks—like McBrayer's little boy—but
these are college upperclassmen. "If you remember nothing else
of what I say, remember that! The tree comes *to* me. IT tells ME:

1. That it's there.
2. What it is.
3. How I can legitimately use it."

The same is true for Coca-Cola and Lysol, a live person and
a corpse, an embryo and a tumor. The tree itself is *not* an opinion! The tree is the *evidence* for any opinion, which is valid (that
is, not stupid) depending *entirely* on the evidence the tree offers
and the honest reasoning that processes that evidence. As noted
earlier, your opinion on black holes isn't as good as Stephen
Hawking's and your opinion on a performance is probably not
as good as Meryl Streep's. However, your opinion on a band is
surely better than mine, because on that subject, I don't know
what I'm talking about and therefore have no right to an opinion worth hearing.

Why is it that, despite fifty years of hearing people say, "My
opinion's as good as anybody else's," I'm still stunned that
twenty-year-olds (exactly like McBrayer's six-year-old) haven't
the slightest notion that truth is out there, waiting to be discovered and processed. After ten weeks, there are still some who
claim that objective fact is a valid opinion and a subjective opinion is questionable.

Year after year, I hold up my keys and jangle them. "What are these for?" That question takes very little time to answer: "To open things."

Now for the killer question: "How do you know that?"

The question never fails to produce blank looks.

"Uh...er...like...I mean...people have told me."

"How do they know? What right do they have to impose on your freedom?"

This is obviously getting heavier than they're used to or more likely completely stupid.

"Uh...you, like, try them in a lock."

"How did that occur to you?"

I kid you not. These students had to have sufficient SAT scores to get into college (and I've done this in four of them). But it takes at least a half-hour—and a few heavy hints—before one of these genuinely bright young people finally says, "You know what they're for by the way that they're made!"

The same is true, unvaryingly, about hula hoops, mouse-traps, gerbils, coal, diamonds, DVDs, IEDs, BVDs, GREs—not to forget the universe, old horses, rivers next to chemical plants, welfare recipients, impaired children, sex, alcohol and alcoholics, tobacco, the ozone layer, homosexuals, Mexican immigrants. Yet people continue to say, "Don't bother me with facts, my mind's made up."

Violate the inner natures of things and sooner or later those natures will rise up and take their rightful revenge. You can count on that—whether you acknowledge it or not, like it or not, or refuse to accept it as true.

That's an opinion, to be sure. But it's an opinion backed up by (roughly) fifty centuries of recorded human history. The reason we have libraries—and ethics classes—is so you don't make the same stupid, hurtful mistakes humans have always made.

Justified moral principles are not arbitrary or whimsical like fashions—"acceptable" skirt lengths, tie widths, or the decency of bathing suits. They depend on the evidence, that is, the *inner worth* of objects as they present themselves to honest minds. At least in your imagination, line up four objects on a table: a rock, an apple, a puppy, and a baby. No one has to tell you, do they, that there's a big difference from one to another?

There are stark differences in uses of the word *value*. But for the moment, be warned that the judgment infusing that word *value* shifts—sometimes only marginally, often fiercely. For example, there's a difference between the value of a single soldier to a general back at headquarters during a major battle and to his mother back at home. Consider the value of a human body to a couple on their honeymoon, as opposed to in a hospital or an anatomy class. Consider the value of a fifty-dollar bill to a vagrant and to a billionaire. Consider the value of an atomic bomb to Harry Truman and to the citizens of Hiroshima, Japan on August 6, 1945.

What scientific mechanism or process can establish and evaluate the very real difference between *soldier* and *son*? Do the words *priceless* and *invaluable* have substantive meaning? Is there any truth whatsoever to the statement, "Some things you just can't put a price tag on"? The following come to mind: human life, friendship, family, your body, your integrity, and your reputation.

Martin Luther King Jr. said, "If a man has not discovered something that he will die for, he isn't fit to live."* How do you react to that? Are there things you'd die for? If so, what, specifically?

It is often most difficult to discern the differences in value between the insights and skills of empirical sciences—physics, chemistry, biology, computer sciences—which deal with material realities that can be quantified, and in contrast, the insights and skills of the humanities—philosophy, theology, ethics—which are just as real but incapable of being captured in numbers. A million dollars in gold and a schoolyard full of kids both have real value.

- Scientific equipment, correctly programed, can determine which object is poisonous or healthful, diamond or glass, human tissue or platypus tissue. However, it

*Rev. Dr. Martin Luther King Jr. speaking at Syracuse University in July of 1965, http://www.syracuse.com/kirst/index.ssf/2015/02/newly_found_tape_of_dr_martin_luther_king_jr_in_syracuse_there_are_some_things_w.html.

can't determine a witness's truthfulness or a defendant's guilt. A lie detector doesn't recognize truth but measures a person's heartbeats and sweat: nervousness. You'd probably get a more reliable judgment from the person's mother. Why?

- Science doesn't have the reasoning expertise to tell— even vaguely—the moment a human embryo possesses the qualities that make it a person and not an "it." Or even isolate restrictively what those human-vs-"it" qualities *are*. Why?
- There is no Geiger counter that can give an engaged couple evidence convincing enough to dispel all doubts about whether this is the right person to marry. Why?
- It would be quite reckless to program into a computer all the pros and cons of entering a preemptive war, and let the machines decide. They just don't have the "equipment" to make that kind of value judgment. Why?
- How trustworthy are the value judgments simply assumed by advertisers? Why? Have you ever tried to analyze their assumptions about human beings? Why not?

BILATERAL BRAINS

A crucial element is lost in so-called "value-free education." It's caused by the absurd confusion of morality (relation to humanity) with religion (relation to a God). The same confusion supports the claim that "church is church; business is business," as if, once you exit the church door, you can join all the savages. Such a judgment is literally half-witted.

Neurologists believe there are two different but related functions of the human brain, located in the left and right lobes. (That specialization is by no means that simple, but it allows for discussion of the two very real but different functions.) The left lobe is associated with the rational, and the right lobe with the intuitive.

LOGIC VERSUS INTUITION

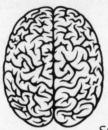

Analysis	Synthesis
(Take apart)	(Put together)
Science and Math	Art and Insight
Quantities	Qualities
SAT	Art
Isolating causes	Judging in context
Linear	Holistic
Abstractions	Analogies
Definitions	Hunches
Clarity	Ambiguity

Those of us trained in the western world have been, without realizing it, more influenced by the manner of thinking preferred by the Greeks and Romans who dominated life, warfare, business, and philosophy in Europe for centuries. We believe subjective and personal hunches and feelings should be exiled from any attempt at clear understanding; they just clutter up what should be totally objective. At its strictest, this manner of thinking results in dangerous *dualism*—either/or—which is handy in showing contrasts, but is often too simplistic, as in the statement, "Four legs good, two legs bad."

Furthermore, this was a matter not of *exclusivity* of one way of thinking over the other, but rather a *preference* for clarity, decisiveness, and practicality over "the big picture," exceptions, and differences. But it has had a much stronger influence on practical decisions about values. For example, in a budget pinch, which would a school cut first: math, physics, or art? Football or school plays?

In contrast, thought systems from Asia and the New World emphasize and value more strongly the input of the intuitive mind; they are more comfortable with *paradox*—more/less, both/and: "So the darkness shall be the light, and the stillness the dancing." American Indians gave a perfect example when they called the Europeans' whiskey "fire-water." The Hebrew Scriptures use the word *know* not in the clinical, abstract sense of the Greeks but in the manner in which a couple knows each other in sexual intercourse, not by abstraction but by involvement.

Without your early teachers drawing attention to it, modern science, which has long been restricted in ordinary understanding to icy, impersonal, left-brain clarity is now far more opened up to ambiguity by quantum physics. The electron, for instance, is no longer considered *just* a pellet like a seed but also a wave like an aerosol puff. Rather than abstracting themselves from the submicroscopic dance, the observers must insert themselves into it!

Therefore, those who seek "scientific proof" to undergird their moral precepts are looking for a rigidity with which most genuine scientists are no longer comfortable.

Psychologists like Carl Jung made the same more/less (*not* either/or) distinction between predominant "masculine" and "feminine" methods of approaching understanding. Not the brute distinction between "Me Tarzan; You Jane," but a difference between being psychologically more judgmental or more relational. We will take this up later in differences of sex and gender.

You likely have heard of the *Tao*, the Confucian belief that means "The Way." Its symbol is a circle divided by a wavy line, one half white and one half black—but each with a small circle of the other color. This symbolizes a balance, within each individual, of the aggressive, decisive, rational so-called masculine and the embracing, intuitive, creative so-called feminine. It's a basis for all human activity, for morality, for establishing a sense

of personal worth. In the ideal, it's a perfect, fluid harmony within each human, among humans, and within nature—everyone and everything doing what their inner constitution reveals that they're intended to do, in balance. It is the world as it ought to be: a *synthesis* of rest and movement. Its flexible complementarity is the diametric opposite of Western dualism: either/or. The *Yang* is hot, clear and dry, rambunctious, masculine, and *Yin* is cool, moist, receptive, dark, restful, watery, earthy, feminine: a total balance.

The fully realized female ought to be as decisive and confident as any male, and the fully realized male should be as empathic and vulnerable as any female. Many strict empirically trained graduates of high school science can't handle those kinds of shadings. It has to be black or white, not both at once. Genuine post-Newtonian scientists are much more comfortable with a more flexible assessment than such dogmatic certitude.

CONTEXT

There are external standards by which we can measure *quantitative* differences: weight, height, density, DNA. But how do we differentiate between *unquantifiable* values, like honesty, love, dignity, worthiness of admiration and imitation? Numbers —the speciality of the sciences—have no effectiveness in such questions. Love gives off no measurable force, yet it's not only real but essential to human life. How can a human keep going in god-awful circumstances like a concentration camp without a sense of purpose and meaning? This sense of purpose is immeasurable but essential.

Confederate money is relatively valueless now because it's lost its context: the Confederate States of America. In Nazi Germany, Jews and Slavs were *Untermenchen*—"less-than-human"—not because of their inner, objective lesser worth, but because of Hitler's arbitrary designation, backed by the deadly Secret State Police, the Gestapo.

Picture a little girl with a fifty-dollar bill in one fist and her teddy bear in the other. There are three very distinct values in that picture: the money, the doll, and the girl. The money has economic power, a real value. The teddy bear has little or no value to coldly objective, rational observers, but a real, if intangible, value to the little girl (and to any observer with greater sensitivity than a tax assessor). And within the little girl herself resides a truly real, if unquantifiable, value (no matter what Hitler asserted or how much power he had to enforce it).

Honest scientists must be humble enough to realize and accept that *any* of our verbal and formulaic traps cripple the elusive truth they try to encompass. All scientists must submit to the truth rather than try to dominate it.

The quantum principle of complementarity tolerates ambiguity, approximation, probability, paradox, bipolar magnets and brains, the different sexes—not antagonisms, but fertile togetherness; not indifferent potentiality, but *eagerness* to be fruitful and multiply. Why pretend we understand what defies comprehension? Despite former inflexible certitudes, matter is not basically solid. $E = mc^2$ *means* energy (E) *is* the *same* as mass (m) times the speed of light squared. Mass is solidified energy!

PERSONAL REFLECTION

Give your personal response to this assertion made by a Nazi propagandist and give your reasons for that response:

> The human body contains sufficient fat to make seven cakes of soap, enough iron to make a medium-sized nail, a sufficient amount of phosphorus to equip two thousand match heads, enough sulphur to rid oneself of one's fleas.

In effect, this reflection is asking you to take hold of your own reasons for morality: your answer to this chapter's claim that left-brain empirical science simply cannot decide when someone's lying, how a *person* differs from an *it*, how to take the risk out of a wedding, how to declare war, how to discern the relative difference between 80 pounds of dirt and 80 pounds of child.

5.

How Do Humans Differ?

The world is very different now. For man holds in his mortal hands the power to abolish all forms of human poverty—and all forms of human life.

—*John F. Kennedy*

Consider whether you agree or disagree with the following ten statements.

1. Humans are just higher-level animals.
2. Thinking can be reduced to the interactive powers of chemicals and electricity.
3. Loving can be reduced to the interactive powers of chemicals and electricity.
4. All nonhuman species—animal, vegetable, and mineral —are programmed to perform only within strict limits.
5. No lion can refuse to be leonine, but humans can refuse to act human.
6. What constituted acceptable human behavior has constantly changed.
7. As far as we can tell, tigers and sharks suffer no pangs of conscience.
8. No one has yet determined how inert matter developed the skill to reproduce.
9. No effect can be greater than the sum of its causes.

10. All the preceding questions are strictly a matter of personal opinion.

In his novel *Cat's Cradle*, Kurt Vonnegut, the genial pessimist, inserts his own little story of creation:

> In the beginning, God created the earth, and he looked upon it in his cosmic loneliness. And God said, "Let Us make living creatures out of mud, so the mud can see what We have done." And God created every living creature that now moveth, and one was man.
> Mud as man alone could speak. God leaned close to mud as man who sat, looked around, and spoke. "What is the purpose of all this?" he asked politely.
> "Everything must have a purpose?" asked God.
> "Certainly," said man.
> "Then I leave it to you to think of one for all this," said God.
> And He went away.

Note that, at least for Vonnegut—and for the author of Genesis, as well—the man doesn't *give* things their inner purposes. He himself *discovers* even his *own* purpose in the task of examining everything he comes across and discerning its purpose, hard-wired inside of it, and then naming it. No matter your personal position on the God questions, whether there's a God or not, we still find the need—unlike other species—to *look* for the natures of everything and how we can use them without danger of being ambushed. All the other species at least seem to go about the business of daily living with all that information already packed into their programming. Only Mud-as-Man has to figure out which are safe, which are unsafe, and which are risky.

Even if it's a definite intrusion on your freedom of discovery, it's reassuring if we have parents and tribal teachers who've already done the tedious work of picking up all that stuff, analyzing its workings, discerning its assets and liabilities, and cataloging all that information in their heads. In most cases, even they haven't done *all* that scut work themselves but have relied on previous analysts also. That's why there are libraries—and Google!

So, long after Mud-as-Man, we have considerable help resolving nitty-gritty decisions about trustworthy foods and even thornier choices—like ways of behaving—that almost always end up painfully, no matter how innocent your motives. It's unwise to take a bone from a dog, or take your neighbor's chicken, or have impetuous sex with the King's daughter—who in many stories was already promised to a richer king before she was born.

You may think that personal experience is the best and only teacher, but I suggest that you don't need to have your fingernails pulled out to decide, short of actual experience, that you'd prefer not. Also, just as no sane person needs a rule that says, "Don't run wildly with scissors," it doesn't take a doctorate in anything to conclude that roadkill is unappetizing. In the same way, when Hansel and Gretel leave the nest, they'd better have a pretty firm grasp on those self-protective suggestions imposed on them up to now: what Freudians call the superego. There are ogres and witches out there, even if they're artfully disguised as managers and time-study people.

But you need not merely bow like a slave to the inflexible decrees of your parents, nor of your society, teachers, religion, or peers! This is the time in your life when your new ability to think clearly and your natural urge to become more independent *demand* that you investigate and evaluate all those rules— uncritically swallowed, up to now—and decide, as an adult, which ones *you* want to stow into your backpack as you set out, and which you want to leave behind with the Barbie dolls and the Matchbox cars.

The way to do that is just the way Mud-as-Man had to do it. If you don't want to be a victim of your parents' rules and society's dictates, it's going to take effort. Gather the facts; categorize them; evaluate their nature, worth, and uses; give them a name; and see if others agree that you're not a fool. At least in your imagination, line up those four objects on a table again: a rock, an apple, a puppy, and a baby. No one has to tell you there's a *big* difference from one to another. The objects do that for you—but you've got to examine them.

It takes no advanced theoretical degrees in any field to discern a progression in the objects. You should see indisputable evidence for increased complexity and sophistication in their different internal qualities that force clear distinctions of value as you move from mineral to vegetable to animal to human. Evolution progressed in the same way.

The rock informs you by just the way it's made. It has mass, weight, some kind of electrical charge, and it just sits there. If you kick it, there are no complaints. Don't expect it to start growing or gestating new pebbles.

The apple has all the qualities of the rock, but it's a quantum leap more potent. It can take in nourishment, grow, and reproduce, which no rock can do. You know without doing it that you can bite the apple, not the rock. You can plant its seeds and get even more apples. Not so with rocks!

The puppy has all the qualities of both the rock and apple, but it can feel pain, exhibit affection and pleasure, see and hear, sense danger, and move itself, which no rock or apple can possibly do. Its makeup dictates the wrongness of roasting it alive as you can do with the apple.

Ah, but the baby! Humans have potentials far in excess of any other creatures we know so far. He or she isn't limited to biological and instinctual constraints. Although nature didn't endow humans with the ability to fly, to swim endlessly, we have the *wits* to make machines that can. If there's another ice age, humans needn't struggle as far as we're able, like other animals, and then just die. We can take their pelts, make fire, and survive. If we're wounded, poisoned, or attacked by disease, we're able to counteract those, too. Humans have the potential beyond all the other species to ask *why*—to seek to understand. Other animals can know facts. A hunted stag, for example, can know *that* danger is "back there." But as far as we can tell, he doesn't ask, "What'd I do to that guy?

Why's he after me?" Other animals feel loss and grieve; some even give their lives for their own babies. But there's no evidence so far that they can give up their lives for animals they don't even know, don't even like, or even hate. We can even die for something inaccessible to other animals: for a *principle*.

No other species we know needs a book like this. Why? **Because no other species can do wrong!**

There is no such thing as a bad dog, cabbage, or rock. They have no choice. If a dog wets the rug, it's just doing what comes naturally. If a cabbage begins to decay, it's merely following the laws of chemistry. If a rock falls on your head, you can rest assured that it was merely yielding to the force of gravity. On the contrary, humans have, in a very profound and significant degree, the ability to control those forces or to give in to them.

Domesticated animals can be trained to fear punishment, to cringe, but as far as we can tell, no other animals but humans feel *cheapened* by actions even when no one else is around. Conscience isn't just a discriminant between humans and animals but between humans who live up to the challenge of their nature and those who refuse to act any better than lesser animals. Every newspaper and magazine testifies that a great many humans reject the challenge to act better than other animals. They can vegetate. They use other humans as stepping-stones.

What's wrong with that?

Does any rational being need convincing that it's degrading for human beings to raise other humans for food—as we do with sheep and broccoli—or that there's something unarguably wrong setting a live cat on fire, the way we easily do with a Christmas pudding? Does any rational human need convincing that it's simply unfitting to treat cupcakes as insensitively as we do snowballs—that it's as inappropriate as using a nine iron to play softball, using flamingo heads for croquet mallets (like the Queen of Hearts in *Alice*), or using your little brother for third base (not to *play* third base, to *be* third base). That's just not the way humans are made.

There are elements—powers, skills, needs—within the human species that we at least can't find in any other species. At least as far as we can discern, no other creature shows regret—

fear of punishment, maybe, but not the need to make amends. No other creature makes judgments. No mountain stream has to decide which side of a rock it will pass on; no carrot uproots itself because the soil looks better on the other side of the fence; and no animal commits suicide from despair over a meaningless existence. (Lemmings don't commit mass suicide as once thought.)

But the most persnickety, irritating, inescapable, and exclusively human *compulsion* is asking *why*. When attacked, other animals (and inadequately evolved humans) either fight or flee. This is universal. But no one has recorded a time any animal has said, "Okay. Let's just hold on a minute. We can settle this." Asking *why* distinguishes us. Little kids are relentlessly asking unanswerable questions like, "Why is the sky blue?" and "Why does Mrs. Mergatroyd have a moustache?" Teenagers whine, "Why do I have to...?" And more painfully, "Why can't I make him/her love me as much as I love them?" When a child dies: "*Why?*" The bereaved parents don't want *causes*—scientific analysis. They want a *reason*—something to make this awful moment make *sense*, justify it, and help them to accommodate it. It's not a left-brain question but a right-brain groping.

Science can give causes, not reasons. A cause is an agent that precipitates an effect. A reason is what *motivates* precipitating the effect. If you find a turtle on top of a fence post, something other than the turtle must have caused that. The reason, the motive, may have been to drive the one who discovered it nuts. If in backing the car out of the driveway, you smash into the house, the cause could have been a thousand inseparable accidents with no reason/motive at all, or it could have been caused by an intentional swerve and motivated by anger at your dad.

And there is the ultimate humans-only need: a reason to keep going, a purpose in living, when the quicksand is up to your eyes. The agnostic, Camus, put it perfectly: "There is but one truly serious philosophical problem, and that is suicide. Judging whether life is or is not worth living amounts to answering the fundamental question of philosophy."* Why keep going?

*Albert Camus, *The Myth of Sisyphus: And Other Essays* (New York: Alfred A. Knopf, 1983), 3.

All is well and good for the first twenty years or so, when you're subsidized, protected, spoiled, given the best your parents can afford, and bailed out. But "welfare" is fast running out. These last twenty years have been the ever-so-slow preparation to *leave* that behind, like the first stage of a rocket, and set out on your own. It's time to find your *own* validation.

Nietzsche put it well: "[Whoever] has a *why* to live for can bear almost any *how*."* This is one of the last times in your life you'll have the leisure to find your *why*.

One way to solve, or at least avoid, that gut-human question of a purpose is to deny that it is either real or meaningful. Richard Dawkins "solves" the question simply by asserting that it's an un-question. Forget grunting around for a reason because there is none. He writes remorselessly,

> This is one of the hardest lessons for humans to learn. We cannot admit things might be neither good nor evil, neither cruel nor kind, but simply callous— indifferent to all suffering, lacking all purpose....
>
> We humans have purpose on the brain. We find it hard to look at anything without wondering what it is "for," what the motive for it is, or the purpose behind it. When the obsession with purpose becomes pathological it is called paranoia—reading malevolent purpose into what is actually random bad luck. But this is just an exaggerated form of a nearly universal delusion.†

Again, all well and good—provided you can live with being purposeless or negligible, except perhaps for the meaningless games you invent or discover to kill the time and before time kills you. Then, Pffft!

Furthermore, you've been born into a society whose principal task is to provide distractions—always remembering too that, for Victorians, *distracted* was a synonym for "insane."

*See Friedrich Nietzsche, *The Twilight of the Idols and the Anti-Christ: or How to Philosophize with a Hammer* (New York, NY: Penguin Classics, 1990), 33.

†Richard Dawkins, *River Out Of Eden: A Darwinian View Of Life* (New York, NY: Basic Books, 1996), 112.

The umbrella term most societies use for that humans-only factor in us is *soul*. Unfortunately, it has become so enmeshed in the idea of religion that many wrongly identify the soul and *spirituality* with *religion*, whereas the former is about human relationship and the latter is about divine relationship. But even if you personally find the idea of a Creator unacceptable, you're still left with our commonly shared humanity. You remain human. So the study of your inescapable humanity will be eased if you allow the word *soul* to stand—at least for the sake of discussion—for all the unquantifiable aspects of humanity that we find in no other entities, such as hope, humor, and honor. Altruism seems incomprehensible to other animals—and to humans who have yet to realize their inborn differences from other animals. In fact, lack of altruism suggests such human beings haven't evolved from the animal in them.

The question isn't whether you lose your soul in hell, but whether you ever own it.

In order to make Freud more acceptable in the pragmatic New World, his followers purposely *mis*translated key Freudian terms, effectively turning an introspective psychology into a behavioral one, making the person an object ruled by "mechanisms." ("Don't blame me; it's my synapses, my DNA, my socialization.") Each occurrence of "soul" in Freud's works is rendered as *mind*. They make us believe Freud is talking about our intellect, turning what its discoverer intended to be a science of humanity into just one more mechanistic natural science.*

Freud uses "soul" as the overarching entity that encapsulates all the other functions, conscious, and unconscious: ego, id, superego (which he wrote as "me," "it," and "over-me"). This is not merely intellect, but the whole *self*—what holds "the whole thing" together, paradoxes and all.

The crucial insight is that I don't *have* a soul. I *am* a soul. I have a body, which is surely a constitutive part of myself and influences me all the time. It is that part of me that I hope and trust I'll outlive—simply because the inner core of me is immaterial, not subject to the second law of thermodynamics, which insists even

---

*Bruno Bettelheim, "Reflections: Freud and the Soul," *The New Yorker*, March 1, 1983, 52–93.

granite is in the process of decaying. There is no annihilation, only transformation. Anyone who was ever privileged to witness the instant of a person's death knows that whatever served as the source of integrating aliveness before is incontestably gone.

"Soul" reflects the core of one's personal existence: the whole living being of an individual. But there are aspects of that reality that are often used as synonyms, yet can be considered and better understood as separate facets of the one reality: spirit (*unifying vitality*), character (*conscience*), and personality (*ingrained habits of adapting*). As Victor Frankl put it, spirituality is our human search for meaning. We are the only species whose choices are not branded into our fibers. We must *choose* to be who we are. But before we can do that, we have to discern what human beings are *for*, what will make us happy. Therefore, ethics—a personal morality—is a set of guidelines to help an individual act like a human being and not just like an animal, a vegetable, or a rock.

Three aspects of humans stand out as crucially different: knowing (understanding), loving (selflessly), and becoming more intensely human. No rock becomes harder, no cabbage becomes more vegetative, and no pig becomes more porcine. However, it's clear from our ordinary experience that some people are more intensely saturated with the qualities that differentiate us from beasts: love, joy, peace, patience, kindness, large-mindedness, generosity, faithfulness, and self-control. Anyone knows, almost without reflection, that Mother Teresa was a finer human being than Adolf Hitler. In fact, we can see that humanity is a spectrum, ranging from pimps and drug pushers at one end (just over the line from beasts), through most of us, all the way to exemplary humans like Martin Luther King Jr. and Bill and Melinda Gates.

This book invites you along that spectrum.

THE HUMAN SPECTRUM

Thinkers who restrict their informational intake to only what can submit to left-brain, value-free assessment find the whole concept of the human soul inadmissible to meaningful human study or discussion. Since that *ipso facto* excludes any contribution to understanding human nature and praiseworthy human behavior from the less constricted right brain, such exclusion seems unjustifiably reductionist. Properties that for millennia have been understood as beyond the powers of bodies and brains we share with other animals are ignored—simply because they refuse analysis by the dissecting brain—even though they delight the equally evident and powerful right brain. In fact, delight is a reality utterly inaccessible to minds restricted to GPAs, GDPs, and SATs.

What follow here are quotations to ponder from writers of exceptional intelligence who might not outright deny the human soul if put on the spot but who at least seem to restrict the soul's influence and the extent of its powers. Read them with others and bounce them around like a volleyball match for the mind.

> Prisoners in European Nazi camps were rented for ten to twelve hours a day to war industries, such as Krupp, IG Farben, BMW, and Bayer, as slaves and lab specimens for experimental drugs. Their rental was six Reich marks per day (about US $15.00 in 1940).

Daily rental of prisoner	-RM 6.00
Deduction for food	-RM 0.60
Deduction for use of clothes	-RM 0.10
Value of prisoner per day	-RM 5.30
Multiplied by the usual lifespan (270 days)	-RM 1,431.00
Rational disposal of corpse: (fillings, clothes, bones)	-RM 200.00
Cost of cremation	-RM 2.00
Total value of prisoner	-RM 1,629.00
	(US $2,400.00 in 1940)

> Multiplied by 15,000,000 prisoners equals US $36,000,000,000,000.00*

*Rev. John M. Lenz, *Christ in Dachau* (Ft. Collins, CO: Roman Catholic Books, 1960).

Mr. Gradgrind, a model of Utilitarianism, speaks to the school he supports as an adjunct to his factory. Its function is to determine which children can become managers and which will be "the hands," the workers.

> Now, what I want is Facts. Teach these boys and girls nothing but Facts. Facts alone are wanted in life.... This is the principle on which I bring up my own children, and this is the principle on which I bring up these children.*

> I don't really want to challenge you
> Marry you or remember you.
> I just wanna make love to you....†
> —Rod Stewart, "Tonight I'm Yours"

> I have a goddess of a wife who sweats ambition and empathy and a daughter who reminds me too much of what I used to be, full of love and joy, kissing every person she meets because everyone is good and will do her no harm. And that terrifies me to the point to where I can barely function. I can't stand the thought of Frances becoming the miserable, self-destructive, death rocker that I've become. (Kurt Cobain, Suicide Note).

> [He] had everything necessary to the Modern Man,
> A phonograph, a radio, a car and a frigidaire.
> Our researchers into Public Opinion are content
> That he held the proper opinions for the time of year;
> When there was peace, he was for peace: when there
>   was war, he went.
> He was married and added five children to the
>   population,

*(Charles Dickens, *Hard Times: For These Times* (London: Bradbury & Evans, 1854), 3.

†Jim Cregan, Rod Stewart, Kevin Savigar, "Tonight I'm Yours (Don't Hurt Me)," from *Tonight I'm Yours*, WB Music Corp. and Riva Music Ltd.,1981, compact disc.

Which our Eugenist says was the right number for a
 parent of his generation.
And our teachers report he never interfered with their
 education.
Was he free? Was he happy? The question is absurd:
Had anything been wrong, we should certainly have
 heard.
—W. H. Auden, "The Unknown Citizen," lines 20–29

I have a dream that one day on the red hills of
Georgia, the sons of former slaves and the sons of former slave owners will be able to sit down together at
the table of brotherhood. I have a dream that one day
even the state of Mississippi, a state sweltering with
the heat of injustice, sweltering with the heat of
oppression, will be transformed into an oasis of freedom and justice. I have a dream that my four little
children will one day live in a nation where they will
not be judged by the color of their skin but by the
content of their character. (Dr. Martin Luther King Jr.,
"I Have a Dream" speech, 1963)

In a Newsweek interview, [Gen.] Eisenhower again
recalled the meeting with Stimson [Secretary of War]:
"...the Japanese were ready to surrender and it wasn't
necessary to hit them with that awful thing."*

Admiral William Leahy, Chief of Staff to Presidents
Franklin Roosevelt and Harry Truman, wrote,

The lethal possibilities of atomic warfare in the future
are frightening. My own feeling was that in being the
first to use it, we had adopted an ethical standard
common to the barbarians of the Dark Ages. I was not
taught to make war in that fashion, and wars cannot
be won by destroying women and children.†

---

*"Ike on Ike" interview, Newsweek, November 11, 1963.
†William Leahy, I Was There (New York, NY: McGraw Hill, 1950), 441.

When I asked General MacArthur about the decision to drop the bomb, I was surprised to learn he had not even been consulted. What, I asked, would his advice have been? He replied that he saw no military justification for the dropping of the bomb. The war might have ended weeks earlier, he said, if the United States had agreed, as it later did anyway, to the retention of the institution of the emperor.*

Once you introduce exclusively rational, quantitative values into the human equation, once you limit "human" to no more than "reasoning animals," anything—absolutely anything—becomes not only conceivable but, eventually, tolerable.

PERSONAL REFLECTION

Beyond the bedrock skills to survive in the marketplace—literacy, computation—what are the personal skills you will need to make habitual before you graduate in order to be a fully functional adult employee, spouse, parent—none of which are taught in schools? Most are presumed by all three of your future major roles, such as reliability, punctuality, spunk, honesty, and so on. Merely list them in columns and in no particular order.

If those are not already functioning habits in your life, how will you take concrete, specific steps to make them habitual? If not now, when? The day you get your first contract, or your marriage license, or your first child's birth certificate will really be too late!

---

*Norman Cousins, *The Pathology of Power* (New York, NY: W W Norton & Co., 1987), 65, 70–71.

6.

WHAT DO I DESERVE?

> Nobody owes anybody a living, but everybody is entitled to a chance.
>
> —*Jack Dempsey*

Consider the following statements. Do you agree or disagree?

1. Consistent hard work and good intentions will sooner or later result in success.
2. The Declaration of Independence guarantees Americans the right to happiness.
3. After childhood, the purpose of parents, teachers, and bosses is to give young people flinty places against which to sharpen their adulthood.
4. A game where neither side can possibly lose is not worth playing.
5. A story without conflict (like ogres, demons, mutant bees, murderous aliens, serial killers, other people's agendas, meter maids) is usually not very interesting.
6. True happiness means feeling good, well fed, and secure most of the time, and exempt from most serious intrusions on one's freedom.
7. Any understanding of *happiness* that doesn't factor acceptance of suffering into the definition is a fatally flawed assessment of the truth.
8. Parents who attempt to shield their children from any kind of suffering also shield them from adulthood.

9. People who pursue happiness as an end in itself usually end up frustrated because happiness is always the *by-product* of a greater quest.
10. The most important fact of life parents keep from children is that life is not fair.

ENTITLEMENT

In 1993, McDonald's was unsuccessfully sued over a car accident in New Jersey. While driving, a man who had placed a milkshake between his legs, leaned over to reach into his bag of food and squeezed the milkshake container in the process. When the lid popped off and spilled half the drink in his lap, this driver became distracted and ran into another man's car. That man in turn tried to sue McDonald's for causing the accident, saying the restaurant should have cautioned the man who had hit him against eating while driving.

In 1933, Billy Rose and Eddie Heyman wrote a song that became a hit only twenty years later with the fabled Andrews Sisters. But the lyric still gives voice to a feeling that echoes just as surely in the hearts of emergent adults today, and was probably just as true for adolescents in Shakespeare's London or Socrates's Athens:

> I'm in no mood to resist,
> And I insist the world owes me a loving.*

It may well be true that you're not only willing but eager to stop resisting temptation, but it's a manifest and cruel perversion of the truth to suggest, much less believe, that the world owes you a loving. There are some entitlements you do have, simply because you're a human being and not a dog or a cabbage

---

*"I Wanna Be Loved" is a popular song with music by Johnny Green and lyrics by Edward Heyman and Billy Rose, published in 1933.

or a rock. However, being loved, or even being happy, is not among them.

Everybody wants to be happy; nobody (except crazies) wants to suffer without a reason. That desire is as universal as the pull of gravity or the humiliation of rape, and therefore, there *ought* to be a law entitling each of us to be happy all the time (or most of it) and free of setbacks, intrusions on our freedom, and pain. The only time we should feel any inconvenience is when we're waiting (momentarily) for the next thrill. Even *instant* gratification shouldn't take that long. That's why travel agencies spend so much on ads that show miles of palm-shaded white beaches where your every whim is gratified. That's why the most formative story in Western history starts in a Garden where everything was once free and easy. Face it! We all yearn to get back there, but we can't. In fact, accepting that fact is a big clue to life!

Although we have that undeniable yearning, there *isn't* a law that says we have a right to its fulfillment, nor can there be—at least not *here*. You might as well spend your one life yearning in vain for movie star looks, the body of a Greek statue, the mind of Einstein, unlimited funds, *and* the assurance you can make anyone and everyone love you. (You do *really* wish for all those things, don't you?) If your idea of happiness is "having it all," feeling good and being free of suffering, you really ought to find transport to a different galaxy, agree to settle for a life of endless frustration, *or* change your idea of what success/fulfillment/happiness means.

Believe it or not, life can be even more difficult for young men and women who actually *do* start off their adolescence with the killer smiles of Tom Cruise and Julia Roberts—the enviable bodies, the irresistible charm. They're usually teachers' pets, quarterbacks, and prom queens, and engender fierce envy (not to mention homicidal thoughts) in the hearts of their peers. Such early-gifted young people have even more grounds on which to base the fraudulent hope they might just make it as a world-class model or film star. Sadly, even if they do have some *substantial* talent, the odds of even such initially gifted people sitting on the couch next to the host of "The Tonight Show" are as slim as their chances of winning the state lottery, quarterbacking the Jets, or monopolizing the covers of *People*. The fact is that "things" will *not* adapt to your wishes. They will *not* go away.

In the daily newspaper, alongside all those ads that promise thousands of keys to the perfect world, there are stories of the nearly infinite ways in which human beings can make one another (and themselves) utterly miserable—how they sabotage the Garden of Eden not just for others but for themselves. That's another intriguing fact: in a world whose inhabitants universally crave perfection, nearly all of us undermine our own chances for it. Why?

For the sake of their own sanity and happiness, American Dreamers should be forced to meet Willy Loman, the "hero" of Arthur Miller's *Death of a Salesman*. He never really existed, any more than Adam and Eve did, but his story, like theirs, tells a heavily important human truth. Willy believed, all his life and with all his heart, in that corrosive American Dream: "Personality always wins the day" (act. 1, pt. 8, p. 48). Willy convinced his sons that success—happiness—came to "the man who creates personal interest....Be liked and you will never want" (act. 1, pt. 3, p. 21). The fact was that Willy himself was wretchedly unhappy. One son was "wasting" his life herding cattle, and the other was a well-heeled cad who seduced his best friends' fiancées the night before their weddings. They kept lying—to themselves—that they were victims of temporary bad luck. At the end, Willy crashed his car and killed himself so his wife and sons could have his insurance. In stark reality, he was worth more dead than alive. The reason for all three men's unhappiness was the fact they'd built their lives and their sense of self-worth on something completely false. It can't work, no more than lead can change into gold.

Elvis Presley, Marilyn Monroe, Janis Joplin, Jimi Hendrix, Jim Morrison, Kurt Cobain, Heath Ledger, Philip Seymour Hoffman, and Robin Williams actually had *achieved* everything Willy and his sons (and probably most Americans) believe guarantee happiness: money, fame, sex, and power beyond most imaginations. And yet, just like the failure, Willy Loman, they also killed themselves. Many of them died on silk sheets.

That's not to say that you can't have money, fame, sex, and power and be happy. What it does say is that, if you have them and you're happy, *they* aren't the reason for your happiness.

As noted earlier, you have only three ways to face life as it really is: migrate to a more accommodating galaxy, redefine your idea of happiness to accommodate suffering, or agree to spend your life in frustration. There is, to be truthful, that fourth option that Willy and all those fabulously "successful" people chose—suicide. In fact, since statistics for suicide among well-to-do teenagers exceed suicides among poor teenagers, one is left with the ironic possibility that affluent suicides may have been led to believe—like Willy and the others—that life *should* deliver more than life *can* possibly deliver.

SUFFERING IS ONE OF THE GIVENS

> We hold these truths to be self-evident, that all men are created equal, that they are endowed by their Creator with certain unalienable Rights, that among these are Life, Liberty and the pursuit of Happiness.
> —*The Declaration of Independence*

Note several elements in that foundation statement which even many of those familiar with it overlook. First, the truths it professes are "self-evident," that is, they needn't be established by rational proof nor *can* they be. They are as self-validating as the truth that it's either raining or it isn't. Second, it says "all men" (i.e., *homines*, humans) have these manifest rights, not because they're Americans but from the simple fact that they're human and not of a lesser species. They are *moral* (human) rights, not *legal* (conferred by some society's laws). Third, the newly founded United States does not *bestow* these rights; it merely *acknowledges* them. They originated long before there was any thought of a United States. Fourth, they are inalienable, that is, they cannot be *legitimately* surrendered or taken away. Fifth, the framers of the document were very careful about the wording: *happiness* is not a right, only the liberty to *seek* it.

Finally, note the words "among these." The three rights mentioned are not the only rights due to all human beings (remember: not just American citizens). If an individual has the right to life, then he or she, *ipso facto*, has the inborn right to those factors without which life is impossible: food, clothing, and shelter. In turn, those absolute necessities are impossible without the funds to grow or lease or purchase them, which, further, leads inevitably to the right to *work*, which is the only way (short of crime or of sheer luck, such as inheritance or the lottery) to come by money. So, also embedded in those rights, is the right to private property, education to learn a trade, basic respect due to an equal—no matter how deprived or depraved. Therefore:

Life ⟶ Food (etc.) ⟶ Money ⟶ Work

But what of those who, by any honest judgment, simply *cannot* work? In the United States, such people are restricted to *only* four groups: children, old people, the disabled, and the blind, who, because of situations over which they simply have no control, are unable to work. Therefore, they have no direct control of the money they need for food and shelter, and thus no access to that most basic human right: to live. These are the people who most societies determine have the *right* to expect community support simply because they are human. Thus, we provide welfare and public assistance.

Curiously, we find, here, a sticking point for many of the readers of this particular book: young people who, for most of their lives, have been members of that first group (children) and who, by their very helplessness, *deserved* to have their physical needs taken care of by someone else. From the instant you passed physical puberty, that situation became no longer true. This is one of the most wrenching challenges of adolescence: shifting one's basic attitude from being one provided for to one who provides. This is a radical conversion.

In order to rise to that challenge, you must, before all else, accept that it is, in fact, true. By the very nature of the human body and psyche, you've begun to resent being "treated like a

kid." This is perfectly natural. However, it entails the very difficult decision to stop *acting* like a kid—not just in refusing to act
silly, to gripe and moan about requests, to pout when you don't
get your own way, but beginning positively to take the small,
concrete, specific steps to learn the *habits* of adult responsibility that you used to take for granted in others. *You* are now one
of *them.*

Before, you were expected to do what you were told; now
you have to develop the alertness to see what needs doing and
take the steps to do it yourself: "Mom, I'm out of clean
blouses....Dad, can you pick me up after practice?...Mom, Joey
keeps getting into my stuff! ...It's raining, and I don't have anything to do!" It's what your spouse and kids will expect of you,
and you won't learn it overnight. Bad habits are very, very
painful to break. Ask anyone who smokes, who drinks too much,
who treats sex like a conquest, and who's always had somebody
to pick up after them. Certainly, you will not easily overcome fif-
teen-plus-years' habits of being cared for and replace them with
the demanding habits of being the care provider. It will not happen automatically and without real effort. And here we
encounter again the inescapable life-truth of suffering. You have
to learn to look at challenges not as hateful intrusions but as
invitations to a larger life.

In its very broadest sense, suffering means giving up something comfortable, taken-for-granted, and accepted. Suffering is
anything that intrudes on your freedom, anything that reminds
you, even in a trivial way, that we are a long way from the
Garden of Eden. In that sense, even getting out of bed in the
morning is "suffering," leaving the warm womb of the covers in
the hope of a more interesting (i.e., challenging) day. Birth itself
is a seeming setback: ejected from a place where every possible
need was taken care of into the cold and noise, complete with a
slap to make you breathe. And that is just the first in a consistent
pattern of intrusion on your comfort: weaning, potty training,
having to leave Mommy to play with other kids, school, adolescence, each of them presenting a crisis/challenge and inviting
you into a broader circle of being alive.

Why do you think all those centuries-old folktales start with the hero/heroine being called out of comfort into challenge: Odysseus, Psyche, Abraham, the Buddha, Osiris, Aeneas, Jesus, Arthur, Robin Hood, Siegfried, Dorothy, Eliza Doolittle, Snow White, Frodo, Luke Skywalker, Harry Potter, and Spider-Man? The list is, literally, endless, because that *is* what life is all about: dealing bravely and skillfully with the unexpected.

That dream for uninterrupted leisure and freedom is precisely that: a dream. If you want to live—to eat, be clothed and housed—then you have to suffer. Like it or not, your freedom will be intruded on by *the natures of things*. You're free, of course, to do anything you want, like leave the wheel of your Winnebago to make a cup of coffee, ease into the swampy ooze of passivity, gorge on junk food, use sex as a carefree recreation. But you *will*, like it or not, pay the price. If you want an attractive body, you'll accept a lot of effort and self-denial. If you want to be a CEO, you'll have to learn how and make a lot of sacrifices you may not really want to make. If you want to live a comfortable life, you have to forego treating gin like ginger ale. If you want to escape the domination of your parents, you have to learn the skills that will enable you to live without them.

What is true of your body is true of your soul: what Don Richard Riso calls "the law of psychic retribution." We needn't fear immediate or later punishment at the hands of a vengeful God for our wrongdoing, he says. "On the contrary, because of the nature of the psyche we bring some kind of punishment on ourselves because we inevitably pay a price for every choice we make."* Concretely, if you act like a swine, you will *become* a swine, and everybody will be whispering about it behind your back and hating you. And your misery will be self-induced. If you defy the natures of things, the natures of things will sooner or later rise up and take their revenge. Count on it!

Your freedom will also face the obstacle of *other people* with legitimate expectations of you, as well as contrary values and agendas. You're free to ignore your mortgage and credit cards, leave junk all over your front lawn, drive at seventy miles

---

*Don Richard Riso and Russ Hudson, *Personality Types: Using the Enneagram for Self-Discovery* (Boston: Houghton-Mifflin Co., 1996).

per hour on a city street, deny your own parents an honest day's work for an honest day's pay—free, that is, for a while. Furthermore, other people who want exactly the goal you want will come to the contest with more talent, more influence, more money, more charm. Read the papers: other people will work out their frustrations by shooting up school cafeterias, raping strangers, robbing people poorer than they because they believe they deserve Nikes and iPods. Why have I been forced to give up my job, my house, and my kids' dreams because fat-cat financiers all over the world played fast and loose with the money entrusted to them?

Even beyond the limits you can expect from the way things are made and from other people's contrary desires, there are also—always and everywhere—the *un*predictable intrusions: drought, tornadoes, cancer. Why did Hurricane Katrina flood mostly the homes of African-American poor people and not the hilltop homes of the wealthy people who could more easily rebound from it? What did the parents of Down syndrome children do to "deserve" their fate? Surely, their children couldn't have merited such a "challenge." Why did my grandmother disappear into the living-death of Alzheimer's? Why are human beings, by the mere fact of being born (over which we have no responsibility), condemned, without a fair trial, to death? "That's just not *fair!*" you say. You're right! But it just happens to be the inescapable truth.

However, there's a flip side to the unfairness of being condemned to suffer and die. Realize, too, that you did nothing to deserve being *born,* either. Think of all the people you rejoice to know and love, all the things and activities that give you joy. How could you possibly list them all? And yet, in truth, you might never have known them.

It might come as a setback to comprehend that your parents didn't *have* to have you. They could have saved the quarter-million bucks they committed themselves to and bought a nice piece of land in Florida. Like so many elements in our lives, we take even our lives themselves for granted, as if we'd done something to *merit* living. So, whenever someone says, "How ya doin'?" I usually answer, "Probably better than I deserve." They very often object. "Oh! What a terrible thing to say! Of course you deserve...." What? I didn't exist. How could I possibly have *deserved* anything? That's worth thinking about, too.

PERSONAL REFLECTION

The Founding Fathers presumed that all human beings are created equal, which is clearly true about the basic rights of life, liberty, and the pursuit of happiness. But it's equally clear that all human beings are *not* created equal. Some begin life in Hollywood mansions, others in Appalachian cabins. Some are guaranteed Harvard or Yale (regardless of their qualifications), others need to drop out to support a single-parent family. Some luck into looks, charm, personality, while others seem colorless, dull, and charmless. How does your developing, ethical self react to that foundational fact?

7.

GROWING UPWARD
(ERIKSON)

> It is only after a reasonable sense of identity
> has been established that real intimacy with
> others can be possible. The youth who is not
> sure of his or her identity shies away from
> interpersonal intimacy, and can become, as
> an adult, isolated or lacking in spontaneity,
> warmth or the real exchange of fellowship in
> relationship to others; but the surer the per-
> son becomes of their self, the more intimacy
> is sought in the form of friendship, leader-
> ship, love and inspiration.
>
> —*Erik H. Erikson*

Consider whether you agree or disagree with the following ten
statements.

1. Beyond argument, life is not fair.
2. As their bodies mature, humans have gone through
   the same unwelcome but predictable life crises since
   the caves.
3. People who have never seriously suffered are the
   most boring people alive.
4. True happiness means feeling good and having no
   serious problems.

5. Wisdom means humbling your mind before reality, the unchangeable.
6. The first step toward growing up is to shed the "if only I..." delusions.
7. Every suffering is an invitation to become a profounder person than you had been.
8. Sooner or later, science will have disposed of most human unhappiness.
9. All the centuries-old folktales show that every society knew that the road from childhood to parenthood consists almost solely of obstructions.
10. Becoming an adult is merely a matter of time and more experiences.

THE WIZARD OF OZ

When Dorothy lands in Munchkinland and the Wicked Witch of the West shows up to collect her sister's ruby slippers, Glinda the Good magically transfers them to Dorothy's feet. As those who have seen the end know, the slippers will be Dorothy's mode of travel back to Kansas. Dumb question: Why doesn't Glinda say, right there and then, "Just tap your heels together three times, and think to yourself, 'There's no place like home'"?

Well, for one thing, it would dead-end not only the movie but the whole *point* of the story. Why?

When Dorothy is whipped from black-and-white Kansas into her Technicolor dream, she's been just a kid on the edge of adolescence. In her eyes, she's pretty much useless or just in the way, longing to cross "over the rainbow" into a place where she's *somebody*. (Sound familiar?) The three farmhand friends who show up in her dream embody what she feels she lacks: courage (the lion), love (the tin man), and intelligence (the scarecrow). Like any other adolescent, male or female, Dorothy has to face and rise above challenges (snarling trees, deadly poppies, winged monkeys, and the powerless wizard) in order to find her true self, her identity.

Why did she have to go through all that? Where was the power of magic? The trials that the foursome (and Toto) endured brought out their *potential* courage, love, and wits, which were inside them all the time! The obstacles made her grasp the truth: that the magic in the shoes is *Dorothy*.

So it's been for every human being—from kings and queens to ploughmen and scullery maids—it's only step-by-step that you discover and own your true self, your soul.

Sigmund Freud discovered that every individual, every group, every society is motivated at the core by either one of two powers: *eros*, the life wish, or *thanatos*, the death wish. *Eros* craves challenge—exploring beyond the baby blanket, risking loss for a better life, and setting off beyond the horizon. *Thanatos* craves being unbothered—the warm, pampered security of the womb, the South Sea Island, the Garden of Eden. *Eros* impels you to try out for a play or a team, to take on a service project, or sit at lunch with someone different. *Thanatos* is senioritis, griping rather than changing, holding lethal grudges. Right there, you have your most basic choice. And what counts is not what you say, but what you do. Are you truly alive or the walking dead?

Other psychologists have studied the seemingly invariant challenges of life and distilled from them which ones further evolutionary powers, bringing them to the surface as our bodies mature. Erik Erikson calls them "crises of disequilibrium," challenges that throw us off-center and demand that we rethink our *selves*. If we rise to the "call" within the crisis, we reach higher as responsible members of families and societies and, at the same time, send down deeper roots within ourselves. We *become* confident by *acting* confidently. If we evade the crisis, we become stranded in a labyrinth of games, self-delusions, and pitiful imitations of life. Psychologist Carl Jung says all neuroses are rooted in the refusal to accept and meet legitimate life challenges.

What follows is a skeletal outline of your life, and mine, along with every other human's.

Birth. The first painful crisis or shock is birth itself. For nine months, you lived as a fetus in bliss in the womb—warm, fed, floating, without a care in the world because you couldn't think. Then suddenly, through no fault of your own, you're ejected out into the cold and noise. You have to learn to adapt. But without that traumatic experience, you'd have died.

Infancy. For the next year and a half or so, your parents supplied everything you needed. If you threw up or cried out at night, they were there. But then, being human, they started to get tired of slavery, and more importantly, through no fault of your own, you began to develop muscle control and teeth! So you were weaned onto an impersonal bottle—unnerving. You became able to manage your toilet habits, but you could also pull down lamps on your head. So you began to hear two words you'd never heard: *good* and *bad*. You are thrust into a complex set of rules that Freudians call the superego. If mothers can't face their infant's angry resentment of such unwelcome (and incomprehensible) intrusions and yield to it, the children never gain independence and remain demanding all their lives, like Hitler who some believe wasn't fully weaned till he was five.

Play years. For your own good, when you wanted to stay warm inside, your mom probably shoved you out to play in the cold with other kids. Without that nudge, you'd never learn to solve your differences without an adult. And you had to learn to compete without rancor and discover ways to occupy yourself.

Schooling. Then there was the awful betrayal at the kindergarten door, when the Fairy Godmother became the Wicked Stepmother, stranding you with all those strangers. Students have told me they thought they were being left for adoption! But you have to learn the skills of the tribe so sooner or later you can subsist on your own. You needed to learn competency and industry.

Adolescence. By late grade school, everything had settled into complacent equilibrium. Then, through no fault of your own, your own body betrayed you. Secret distilleries send out magic potions into your blood, and your limbs go gangly. The change isn't just physical but psychological. You have to reassess what "everybody says," all that parents and media have taped on your superego. You have to test them against the objective truth or remain a victim.

Young adulthood. The natural purpose of that impulse to separate from dependence on your parents and to find personal identity is so that you can offer that self to someone else in a union of intimacy and partnership, which is not easy. It means giving up a separate story and weaving a new one, giving up a room of your own, compromising—working out which equal partner holds the remote.

Parenthood. Usually, once that new union begins to take shape, the couple, incredibly, jeopardizes it by inviting into it a stranger for whom they dedicate themselves to raise a quarter million dollars even though they won't even see or approve him or her for nine months, and whose schedule will totally disrupt the dual equilibrium they've fought so long to achieve. But without it, the couple is less alive, less creative.

Aging. Then, after all the sacrifices of time, emotion, forgiveness, and work, the couple rejoices when the child comes and says, "I've found someone I love more than you. Bye!" And you have to start all over as a couple again, without the focus that gave meaning to your lives for twenty years. What is worse, you have to face slowing down, retiring, and clinging to a reason to keep going!

As Burger, the psychiatrist in the movie *Ordinary People*, tells Conrad: "If you can't feel pain...you won't feel anything else either." No pain, no gain.

PERSONAL REFLECTION

Guatama Siddhartha (c. 563–483 BCE), who later became the Buddha, had been brought up by his kingly father, who resolved to outfox a prophecy that said the boy would be a great king *or* a great world-defying mystic. The king wanted to make sure his heir would find no attraction in anything other than a life of being pampered, revered, and obeyed. So the boy was kept secure in the palace compound and never had contact with anything upsetting.

However, Siddhartha was curious, and four nights running, he bribed the charioteer to take him out into the city. What came from those adventures has become known as the Four Distressing Sights. The boy was amazed to encounter facts of life his father had forbidden from the palace: a sick man, an old man, a dead man, and finally a begging monk who'd forsworn the world to find the wisdom that could make sense of suffering: why we get sick, why we grow old, and why we die.

Most parents, like Siddhartha's father, feel two duties: to give their children the best they can afford and shield their children from suffering. In what ways has your upbringing been shielded as Siddhartha's was? Has the solicitude in any ways limited your ability to cope with life as it surely will be delivered to you? Has it hampered your realistic growing-up?

8.

GROWING OUTWARD (KOHLBERG)

> The most exciting breakthroughs of the 21st century won't occur because of technology but because of an expanding concept of what it means to be human.
>
> —*John Naisbitt*

Consider the following ten statements. Do you agree or disagree?

1. Like any instinct, human conscience is innate, that is, hardwired and ready for use without the need for further learning.
2. If my brother were dealing drugs, I'd protect him rather than his victims.
3. Sex, hunger, survival, aggression, and escape are human drives, but unlike animal instincts, they can be overridden by their host.
4. In an exclusively capitalist economy, greed is a good and necessary virtue that benefits both the individual and the common welfare.
5. No one on a public bus has the right to tell someone else to turn a radio down.
6. At a children's race at a summer camp, a disabled person deserves a head start.

7. People in third world poverty have the same hopes as people in wealthy countries.
8. Those whose parents have worked hard have a right to more of this world's goods than children whose parents have not.
9. In the United States, only those explicitly declared "persons" by the law have legal rights.
10. Every human has a right to a reasonable chance, even if the rules have to change.

CONSCIENCES CAN GROW

Ed and Dorothy Ryan from San Jose, California, have worked hard, raised a family, and are ready to retire to a cottage in the Salinas Valley on their savings and whatever they can get for their house. The problem is that the only families who inquired about the house are African American. The neighborhood is all white—assimilated Irish, Poles, and Italians. Dorothy is a tangle of nerves. If they sell to black people, the neighbors will hate them; if they don't, the blacks could get violent. Ed is completely calm: "We paid our dues, Dot. And they're so eager to get outta wherever they are, they'll probably even pay more than white folks, right?"

Mike and Judy Falco and their three children live in a fashionable suburb in Denver, Colorado. Mike runs a collision shop, and Judy is a full-time mom. Driving home from a party one New Year's Eve, their oldest daughter, Kim, a college senior, completely sober, struck a drunken derelict who had stumbled onto the street. She stopped and ran back, but he was dead. In a panic, she sped home and blurted out the story to her parents. Her mother took her upstairs, gave her a sleeping pill and put her to bed. As she came back down, Mike was on the phone. "We have to tell the police," he said. Judy yelled, "Mike, no! No one will know he's even dead. She's never hurt anyone. It's bad enough she has to know. Not all of Denver." Mike sighed, "Judy, what would happen if everybody decided when they're beyond the law?"

George and Maggie Ackroyd teach in a local high school in Shreveport, Louisiana. Their children are grown, and they've rented a room to Cynthia Thomas, a single woman who teaches French at their school. Late one evening, Cynthia came home in tears from a school board meeting where she'd been fired because she was homosexual. She'd fought it all her life, but during the previous summer vacation, there had been an episode with a woman her own age. The woman tried to blackmail Cynthia. When Cynthia refused her demands, the woman told the board. There had been no review or hearing—simply a dismissal. George exploded. He went to the phone to see how many members of the faculty he could get to challenge "that bunch of damn fascists!" Maggie was calmer. As she held her weeping friend, she said, "Cynthia, if it means our jobs, so be it. We couldn't live with ourselves if we just let this go."

If you read sensitively, you can see a definite shift in the motivations of these six people, each one's motivation spreading out to a broader number of people, each one becoming less *self-centered* than the previous. How does each one *justify* his or her moral behavior?

Lawrence Kohlberg has sketched out a useful pattern to help understand this difference. He divides motivations into three distinct *levels*, paralleling roughly the spectrum of humanity we saw earlier, stretching from the "Pre-Conventional" (just over the line from beasts: for example, graffiti artists, hoods), through the "Conventional" (traditional, common: most of us), to the "Post-Conventional" (beyond the usual: Lincoln, Rosa Parks). The most basic level is completely self-centered (the Ryans), the middle level spreads out wider to others, but limited (the Falcos), the third level is selfless, governed by reason rather than emotion or lockstep conformity, recognizing a "law beyond the law": human dignity.

The first Pre-Conventional Level is governed by what Freudians call the primitive id, the presocialized animal from which humanity invites us to evolve. This is the *Child*, whom all societies have seen must be taken in hand and led (*e-ducere*, "to lead out") slowly first to self-control, then self-motivation. No matter their age, they're not concerned with the action in itself or with others but solely with themselves. Morality is external. This shouldn't imply that all adults stranded at this level are grunting and uncouth. They do what they must to be accepted, but it's purely utilitarian, not done from conviction—being good means being un-bad or at least not getting caught.

The middle, Conventional Level is a big leap up and out from the confines of the self to a larger, though limited, group of those closest to them and then to the wider community, which we all depend on for services we can't provide for ourselves, no matter how wealthy. This is at least the outskirts of The Golden Rule, which is found in every moral code: "Do unto others as you would have them do unto you." That has nothing to do with God, only with living together. Like the bottom level, these midlevel people aren't concerned with the *act*. Unlike them, they are principally concerned with the cost to those they value. It's by no means altruistic, but not as cravenly utilitarian as Level One. They differ from the higher level by the fact that, for the most part, their motivation is accepted *uncritically*. They're governed by what Freudians call the superego, the complex of dos and don'ts taped on their psyches by parents, peers, media, teachers, religion: their *Inner Parent*.

The highest, Post-Conventional Level is self-reasoned and self-defined. It doesn't disdain laws but no longer needs them. If all the police in the world went on strike, they would still be self-governed, autonomous selves. Unlike the previous levels, they are concerned with the *act*, no matter the cost to themselves or to others. They govern themselves by principles they themselves ground logically: gather, sift, outline, conclude, critique. Not many ordinary folks have the time, or inclination, to do that. These Level Threes are what Freudians call the healthy ego. They are personally validated *Adults*.

Kohlberg and his colleagues subdivide/ refine each of these three levels of motivations into two "stages" or "groups." The very bottom, lowest human motivation is *fear* (Dorothy Ryan). For her, conscience comes down simply to "What's it going to cost me?" Although she's probably a "nice" woman, her moral scope is just a little broader than that of a circus lioness: the whip. Equality of human beings is as remote from her concerns as spherical geometry. She'll go with whichever option will cost her the least.

She's the kind of uncomplicated person hell "was invented to scare." It's relatively easy to get lockstep good behavior when the slightest misstep could land you in the eternal bonfire. It's even more effective if those in charge can build the bonfire right there in the town square for the entertainment and education of all.

Even before infants are capable of reasoning—of seeing cause and effect—they intuitively fear their parents' scowls, because the parents are, after all, the source of food and assurance: "I'll conform! I'll scarf down the lousy spinach; I hate detention more than I like goofing off; I hate summer school more than I hate studying; I'll wear a hateful tie to work because I don't want to lose my job; God help me if I ever get pregnant or catch a sexually transmitted disease." Very often, people can do the right thing, even if not for the best of reasons.

The second stage of the bottom level is *hope of reward* (Ed Ryan). For him, conscience means simply asking, Is it worth the risk? Where's the payoff? Although he's a cautious man, he's a step up the moral scale from his wife, but he's in exactly the same "game" as the three-card monte crook or the sidewalk watch salesmen in Manhattan: "There's a sucker born every minute." They have a nose for loopholes: "It depends on how you *define* sex."

This perspective is likely to reason in the following ways: "I'll study just enough for a C because (a) my parents will get off my back, (b) I'll be eligible to play sports, or (c) in the long run (so they tell me), I'll get a better-paying job. I'll worship on weekends because it's insurance for heaven and also the boss favors people who are "religious." I'll give blood when they give that sticker to put on your lapel, and everybody can see I've got the guts to face the needle." The United States gave arms to the Taliban as long as they would fight the Russians in Afghanistan. Tobacco companies brush up their image by offering free advice to those who try to quit. Donating an organ for ten thousand dollars is quite different from donating it out of sheer kindness and concern for someone dying (cost/benefit analysis).

The first stage of the second level (stage three) is motivated by loyalty to the small group—family, gang, team, and platoon (Judy Falco). Judy Falco's motive is not self-centered. She believes the heartfelt but ill-considered dictum, "Blood is thicker than water"—or, for that matter, than the truth. She's a genteel woman but no more or less moral than one of the feuding Hatfields and McCoys.

Some examples of this are the following: "I'll study because my parents have a right to expect it of me. I'll worship because it strengthens the family cohesion (at least when the kids are younger). The platoon needs me to stay alert." But one could also do the wrong thing for what only seems to be a powerfully right reason: "The gang will think I'm disloyal if I don't get into this turf war. Those kids vandalized our school; we've got to get revenge. I have to brag about sex or they'll think I'm a wuss."

However, what happens to a young psyche when the local hero is a pimp or pusher? To a less dangerous degree, often, the ill-considered opinions of the supportive group limit an individual's freedom in a corrosive way. I'm not *really* free to like different music, dissimilar styles, and people the group considers unacceptable. In such cases, the person may seem to be motivated by group loyalty but is actually lower on the scale of genuine values, acting really out of fear of rejection or hope of continued acceptance.

The next stage in this level (stage four) goes beyond the small group to a *collectivity*—city, nation, church—and their published rules (Mike Falco). For Mike, conscience is the law. He hasn't reasoned it out any more than Judy has reasoned out her motherly protectiveness, but law and order makes him comfortable, like a tangible lifeline. Society's been good to him; it deserves cooperation in return. World War I soldiers used to say, "Leave the thinking to the officers and to the horses. They have bigger heads."

A genuine advance in this frame of mind is a willingness to sacrifice for the greater good, the efficient and mutually profitable beehive. Here is the perennially tragic flaw in the totalitarian society, like Nazi Germany, the Soviet Union, the utopias of *1984* and *Brave New World*: human beings are more than mere "rational animals."

Even in otherwise admirable societies, leaders can send young people to death in battle for causes that, arguably, do not justify such an expenditure of precious lives. To accept blindly "my country," even when it's wrong, isn't the act of a truly good citizen. A truly devoted member would stand up and challenge a misguided leadership. But that is a much higher stage.

The third and upper level is more difficult to grasp. Both stages in this level are beyond the law; both rely on personally considered principles; the *whole human family* rather than any special segment. However, the best way to discern between the two stages in this level (stages five and six) is that the former group (George Ackroyd) tends to be more abrasive than the more serene final stage (Maggie Ackroyd). During the Vietnam War, the actress Jane Fonda risked a lucrative film career, which depended heavily on popularity, in order to protest the inhuman and unjustified savage attack on a sovereign nation that had done nothing to us. She certainly seemed sincere, but she did many stupid things to express her indignation. In fact, there are some Americans who still shrivel in disgust if she's even mentioned.

Often stage five people bring on more antagonism than enlightenment. They can step back from their own particular society and judge it honestly: Does it make its people more honorable, freer, and more fulfilled? Such people don't deny the need for law, but they go *beyond* the law to the reasons for it. They still revere such normative sources as the Bible and the Constitution, but they want also to grasp why those sources are interpreted in such-and-such a way in this case. They're also courageous enough to challenge whether even those revered sources could be misapplied, such as the original Constitution of the United States allowed continued "importation of persons" at least until 1808 (art. 1, sec. 9); in censuses, slaves were to count as "three-fifths of a person" (art. 1, sec. 2); anyone "held in service" should, by law, be delivered back to the proper owner if they managed to run away (art. 4). Few sane people would argue that was just, though it was legal.

Stage five people will overcome their reluctance and join a protest line over unfair cafeteria prices, even if some of their professors say it's too disruptive. They won't back down from a dorm debate, but unlike other convinced believers, they *will* honestly admit it if they're out-argued by valid points. The more mature of them find the truth more important than dominating.

Very few manage to arrive at stage six. For these people, conscience means their inviolable soul. They say, "I will die rather than do that..." or "Even if you kill me, I won't...." Not many have the courage to die or endure long imprisonment for something as intangible as a principle—Socrates, Jesus, Hypatia, Joan of Arc, Galileo, Thomas More, Gandhi, Bonhoeffer, Trotsky, Solzhenitsyn, Mandela, and Martin Luther King Jr. might have died of old age if they'd kept quiet.

Such people work not merely on principles but on empathy. They put themselves "into the skins" of all the persons and issues involved in a dilemma, such as the sanctity of human life, the humanity of the fetus, and also the anguish of the pregnant woman. Good Samaritans, outcasts themselves, reached out to the Nazi camp prisoners living on no more than a small roll a day to share bits with their weaker fellows.

Genuine "altruism" means completely unselfish concern for the welfare of others, without any kickback to the giver and without even any hope for basic compensation (e.g., any good parent). No other animal is as altruistic as humans. No other animal goes out of its way, sacrifices its own welfare, not just for its own offspring or species, but for others it can't stand! Such selflessness in some animals is carelessly called *biological altruism*, a doubly contradictory phrase. In the first place, altruism is a matter of intention, of personal *choice*, and no other animal and no biological element, factor, or agent has the intelligence to see options and choose, not even Mother Nature *itself*. Secondly, by its very nature, altruism operates to the complete exclusion of any possible repayment.

There is no evolutionary basis for that "humans-only" trait. True altruism—as opposed to its misuse in cases of mutual profit—does not make its host more reproductively potent.

People who give their lives for others clearly cannot pass on their noble natures to their offspring.

There are several cautions to the Kohlberg scheme. First, his colleagues' research bears out that the stages are invariant. You can't jump a step and go immediately to a broader area of human concern. Second, the steps aren't conditioned by age or IQ. Many youngsters and illiterates are quite genuinely and freely moral, while some grown-up and highly schooled people are merely childish. Third, the experts have established that no one can even *comprehend* the motivation of anyone two steps above him or her. For instance, Ed Ryan would think Mike Falco was stupid and Maggie Ackroyd a featherhead liberal idiot.

Perhaps the most significant caution comes from Kohlberg's protégé, Carol Gilligan, in her book, *In a Different Voice*. She argues, rightly, that Kohlberg's research was too tilted toward the left-brain "masculine" bias: western, urban, intellectual preferences. They are, after all, for both the subject and the psychologist, left-brain analytical judgments of what was, in the actual choosing, an essentially right-brain, intuitive decision. One concrete example demonstrates this point: a young boy in the study said, "Moral dilemmas are just like math problems, but with people." Such a mind-set opens the door to such questionable utilitarian judgments as treating young men in battle as merely personnel or assets that have no more inner worth than a grenade or tank. As we saw, such reductionist judgments are half-witted, no matter how self-justifying.

Kohlberg is sharply correct about justice. What he ignores is caring and kindness.

For those in all four of the early moral stages, morality is *external* to them. Society, parents, God, or some power governing them make the rules—too many, and probably arbitrarily—and impose(s) them on us. We conform or get rejected, denied, imprisoned, or exiled. How do those in charge—parents, teachers, legislators—help newcomers to adult society *internalize* moral principles, rather than dumbly *obeying* out of fear, cunning, loyalty, or duty? How do you do it for *yourself*? At first, we obey with motives no better than trained circus animals or chimps who connect words on flash cards to a physical response

that brings food—the superego. Gradually, a youngster inte-
grates attitudes, values, standards, and the opinions of others
into one's own identity or sense of self. But how do we facilitate
that to become a *free personal choice*, so that the individual rec-
ognizes and accepts that this behavior is not only expected or
demanded but also worthy and desirable *in itself*?

One state of mind that is indispensable, but which I've seen
few suggestions for developing, is *reciprocity*, that is, the real-
ization that the other person is also a *me*. How do we help a
child—or a childish adult—feel empathy for those who are *not-
me*: when I hit her on the head, she feels exactly what I feel when
she hits me; people with different color skin or funny accents
want the same things—to be found, to love, and to be loved;
impoverished peasants in third world countries dream of the
same things for their children?

Shylock rightfully asked his Venetian fellow citizens:

> Hath not a Jew eyes? hath not a Jew hands, organs,
> dimensions, senses, affections, passions? fed with the
> same food, hurt with the same weapons, subject to the
> same diseases, healed by the same means, warmed and
> cooled by the same winter and summer, as a Christian is?
> If you prick us, do we not bleed?*

Internalization is at least analogous to religious conversion—a complete turnabout when the individual's eyes are
shocked open by an epiphany, a sudden intrusive insight that
blasts their horizons. Some who seem stuck at lesser motivations encounter some person or an experience that makes them
see life in a new way. For instance, if a small child from the black
family interested in purchasing the property got up on Ed Ryan's
lap and fell asleep, he might see that this child's pigmentation
doesn't make her different from his own kids. The Falcos might
differ so strongly about informing the police that they seek
some insight from a professional who makes them consider why

---

*William Shakespeare, *The Merchant of Venice*, Act 3, Scene 1, vv. 60–65
(Oxford: Oxford University Press, 1979), 47.

laws are formulated in the first place and submit their unexamined convictions to rational examination.

It's worth noting that this awareness, radiating outward from the self to the group, from the group to the nation, and from the nation to the whole human family should also expand the beginning moralist to a more adult understanding of *love*— a label as slippery in meaning as *value*. People at stage one remind me of the plaintive voices of so many "in-love" songs. Stage two brags to friends on Monday about "scoring." Stage three can make going steady more exclusive than marriage. Stage four can end up holding the friend or lover "for downs," cataloguing faults and cherishing grudges. At the top levels, the individual is far more understanding and forgiving.

One might draw a powerful lesson from these researchers. If we want to lessen the likelihood of crime, war, drive-by shootings, date rape, and suicides, we might spend every effort to teach as many people as possible to *think* clearly and honestly and to shatter horizons!

SUMMARY

A. Pre-Conventional: ID - CHILD—SELF (Conscience equals Self-Interest)
    1. Fear: Cost; punishment; "whip"; hell
    2. Reward: Risk; benefit; "treat"; heaven
B. Conventional: SUPEREGO—PARENT—OTHERS (Conscience equals Uncritical Loyalty)
    3. Group Loyalty: Deep relationship; "gut connection"; blood
    4. Law and Order: Intuitive "contract"; mutual dependence; justice
C. Post-Conventional: EGO—ADULT—TRUTH (Conscience equals Reasoned Self-limits)
    5. Principle: natures of the conflicting elements; validity of a law
    6. Integrity: the demands of human dignity; impartiality

PERSONAL REFLECTION

The course is about owning yourself, looking yourself over more sensitively than you would a new car or house—the only "you" you'll ever have. As honestly as you can, try to put into words where your conscience "fits" in the Kohlberg scheme in the ordinary moral choices of your life: work, money, sex, honesty, and so forth.

If you need a specific case to deal with, consider the story of the Good Samaritan. You're driving along a relatively untraveled, heavily wooded road and see a car pulled onto the shoulder. The trunk is up and the back off-road wheel is up on the jack. But a man is lying face down next to the jacked-up axle. He might have had a heart attack. He also might be a ruse, with accomplices hidden in the trees. You have no cell phone.

Be honest with yourself, even if you don't get it down on paper. The one person it's unforgivable to deceive is yourself.

Part Two

GETTING DOWN TO SPECIFICS

So far, we've been considering morality in general. What issues do we each have to confront in order to live up to the human challenge? Now we shift focus more closely on the task of your own self-apprehension. This involves two fundamental questions: First, who am I, or rather, How do I embody humanity as a unique individual? And second, How do I personally fit into the web of human relationships that is society?

First, let's consider the unique personality you bring to the formation of a worthwhile character. Achieving that means much more than merely being un-bad, not just avoiding evil but doing good—respecting yourself and others, helping to expand your soul and theirs. So we will study virtues, the worthwhile habits needed for any human working toward integrity. Then, we will branch out, as the Kohlberg scheme suggests, into wider and wider relationships: work, romance, marriage, family, society, and humanity.

Second, we will consider specific moral questions that seem to generate more friction and could be a constant test of your own moral convictions when applied to a particularly complex human dilemma.

9.

PERSONALITY

> Staying on the surface all the time is like going to the circus and staring at the outside of the tent.
>
> —*Dave Barry*

Consider the following ten statements. Do you agree or disagree?

1. Today, nothing succeeds like the appearance of success.
2. Personality is who you are to others. Character is who you are.
3. Personality is a set of habits formed uncritically by a child before age three.
4. People wouldn't feel so helpless if they took charge of their own lives.
5. In today's threatening world, it's wise to keep your guard up all the time.
6. Admitting your mistakes to others is a sign of weakness.
7. Today, schooling is pretty shallow; it is about making a living, not what living is for.
8. Whether you're preoccupied with your assets or with your liabilities, you're pretty much paralyzed from growing up emotionally.
9. Most people in *People* magazine are really more important than most people you know.
10. You're nobody till somebody loves you.

YOUR FIRST "SELF"

What follows in this chapter are only two of many valid—and equally short-of-perfect—paths to understanding your unique personality better. Where are you coming from?

On the one hand, studying personality profiles that have been formulated over thousands of years, and more recently given substance by the studies of Jungian psychologists, is not as superficial as a fortune teller's assessment or as surefire as a DNA test. They are helpful only in giving you a better focused and less sketchy idea of the individual you're dealing with when you set out to own your unique self. The Internet has short versions of Myers-Briggs and Enneagram tests that could help in clarifying what each personality type entails and could help narrow down your grasp on what traits operate most significantly in your daily attitudes and choices. They're hardly definitive. They're more like dwarfs and foxes that heroines and heroes in folktales meet on their journeys, pointing the ways to find themselves.

These personality types sketch out different temperaments or styles. No type is better or worse than another, nor are they linked to intelligence or indicative of mental health. They are not blameworthy, since they're a complex of habits developed gradually and uncritically before you were about three, and were developed in response to your genetic makeup (nature) and socialization (nurture). Like your eye color or your writing hand, or the fact you had these specific parents, or that you were born into this specific economic spot—they're just there. At this point in your life, the only worthwhile question is What will I make from them?

To understand the power of these uncountable factors on your everyday practices, write your name as you have become habituated to do it. Then sign it with the other hand. The first signature was personally natural to you; the result wasn't planned. You could always use the other hand in a pinch, but it would be "unnatural," and the result probably wouldn't pass a bank teller. It's not "you," even if it's your hand that drew it. Many people put on fake selves, masks, persons they'd rather be than the persons they started out with. It takes little time—even for people less critical than Holden Caulfield—to see through the masks and look elsewhere for friends.

Just as with our signatures, we have the same kinds of habits in our preferred ways to perceive, judge, learn, understand, and respond to others. As our habits intensify, some aspects prove themselves assets to exploit, while others are real liabilities to control or even uproot. At the very least, all our habits deserve our attention.

Genetic physical and mental capabilities impact not only how you perceive yourself, but how others react to the way you then deal with them. In turn, you react to their reactions. And remember, this is a little kid reacting to people whom he or she sees as six-foot giants. If you, through no fault of your own, have poor hand-eye coordination and can't hit a softball, or if, because of poor nutrition, you can't concentrate at school, you may be made to feel inadequate or even incurable. That becomes a self-fulfilling prophecy as you keep assuming you're inferior. Also, your health and appearance, especially in this jungle of commercials, influence your personality development. You may be fragile or overweight, or have a learning disability that you are not responsible for having. Hereditary factors can make you generally optimistic or pessimistic, naturally confident or fearful, but they're *not* like genetic diseases! They can be changed, with resolve and effort. Ponder Stephen Hawking, Beethoven, and Helen Keller.

Socialization—your unique experiences of childhood—clearly affects your personal acquisition of values, beliefs, and expectations. But an individual's reactions to almost all the same early influences can be exactly the opposite of someone else's. Children from intensely religious parents can adopt their values and become dedicated missionaries, or they can react angrily and become dedicated atheists. The first child of understandably nervous parents can intuitively sense the apprehension and, without the reasoning power to make distinctions, become tense, fearing they might alienate the sources of food and warmth, and instinctively try to "hold back." This is what Freud called "anal retentive." Through nobody's fault, the child could begin, and continue to be, cautious and introverted. On the contrary, a second child comes under the influence of the same parents but a different environment because of the older sibling. He or she could intuit the other child's tension and resolve not to be that way, becoming willful and extroverted. Of course, it's never that simple, but you get the idea.

In all societies, males and females are socialized differently, getting wordless messages from their parents, the media, and their peers about what's "appropriate" for them. Is anything objectively, by nature, wrong with a boy loving dolls or a girl loving trucks? Even in advanced societies, girls are expected to point themselves toward household tasks and boys, whose parents hope they'll be surgeons and lawyers, are set to build up their muscles and compete. Despite the evident success of the women's movement, the most sophisticated parents get a twinge of unease if a son wants ballet lessons and a girl comes home with a tattoo. Despite our stereotypes, like virile musketeers in curly wigs, baseless certitudes can distort the growth of a young psyche for life, and unjustly cramp their expectations of what's possible for them—and they're completely independent of the individual's sexual orientation.

Just as genetic factors in personality formation are not immutable, so are socializing factors. Extraverts can become thoughtful, and introverts can become confident. Each person comes into adolescence like Dorothy after the tornado, with new opportunities: "Now what do I build from this rubble?"

MYERS-BRIGGS

The Myers-Briggs Type Indicator, the most widely used test in the world, is a questionnaire elaborated from Carl Jung's typological theories by psychologists Katharine Cook Briggs and her daughter, Isabel Briggs Myers, to study psychological preferences in individual's perception of the world and decision making. Many students have taken the test before college, but often the results are of more interest to their teachers as indicators of different learning styles. (However, over fifty years in countless schools, I've never heard a teacher refer to a problem student by his or her Myers-Briggs type.) Nonetheless, of the Fortune 100 companies, eighty-nine find it useful for understanding applicants for employment and finding the best uses for their talents.

Remember that the results are *not* restrictive or certain, like a blood type or DNA. Their estimates are indicative, and useful, but only approximations, like a skilled teacher's grade on an essay or all scientific judgments: educated guesses that are not definitive.

Some students who have taken the questionnaire spout off the four-letter major type-indicators—INTJ, ESFP, and so on— and haven't the slightest notion of what they connote or any idea in what way they may indicate any "victim's" assets and liabilities, or what parts of their personalities need cultivation and which need pruning. This chapter may help clarify the specifics of each type.

The same warning applies for what comes after the explanation of the Myers-Briggs in the more down-to-earth Enneagram types. Furthermore, it's hardly ethical to use these types as a kind of parlor game to pigeonhole others.

Jung identified different basic aspects of any personality: (1) attitudes: extrovert/introvert; (2) ways of perceiving: sensing/intuitive; (3) ways of deciding: thinking/feeling, and (4) ways of lifestyle: judging/perceptive.

Attitudes: usually people prefer to be upfront (E = extrovert) or reserved (I = introvert). Extroverts are talkers, "people persons," have broad interests; they challenge: Napoleon, Pope Francis, and John F. Kennedy. Introverts are more comfortable listening, waiting, seeing, and processing: Einstein, Lincoln, and Tolkien. Extroverts recharge their energy interacting with people; introverts recharge spending time alone, reading, taking walks.

Ways of perceiving: Some people approach new challenges in a hands-on, commonsensical way, and they may miss the big picture (S = sensing): Dr. Phil, Mother Teresa, and Princess Diana. Others approach novelty theoretically, associating it with other known factors, and may over-simplify (N = intuitive): DaVinci, Steven Colbert, and Celine Dion. Sensing people distrust hunches and go for facts; intuitive people are interested more in the wider context than just immediate solutions.

Ways of deciding: Some are more concerned with truth than with subjective feelings; they see the world as it ought to be. They use the left brain and are more detached (T = thinking): Heisenberg, Barak Obama, and Madame Curie. Others are more subjectively involved in any judgment; value-oriented, Eastern, the gut, getting inside things (F = feeling): Mark Twain, Anne Frank, and Kurt Vonnegut.

Ways of lifestyle: There are those who want their lives orderly and clear, structured, purposeful, and seeking closure (J = judging): Margaret Thatcher, Bill Gates, and Madeleine Albright. Others are more spontaneous, empathetic, keeping options open, flexible, adaptable (P = perceptive): Jane Austen, Tina Fey, and C. S. Lewis.

Any of those specific examples are, of course, merely educated guesses about individuals, a judgment based solely on observation of their way of handling things and what interests them.

THE ENNEAGRAM

Another similar approach to the Jungian types is the Enneagram (*ennea* = "nine"), which is a set of nine personality types that is less academic but nonetheless has been widely used in both business and spiritual retreats. Unlike extensive either/or choices of other methods, the Enneagram asks the participant to choose which of nine sets of choices most *feels* right.

The *-gram* part of the title refers to a circle with nine points, lines crisscrossing to connect types, indicating, with surprising accuracy, which other personalities exhibit qualities someone of that particular type could profit by imitating and which suggest bad habits of other types to avoid or uproot. Like the Myers-Briggs, the Enneagram is a sketch, not a photograph.

Which of the following sets feels right for you, personally? There will be statements in each that apply to you; you're *not* a specimen. However, which type, overall, are you drawn to most strongly? First, ask yourself if, in most of your dealings, you're

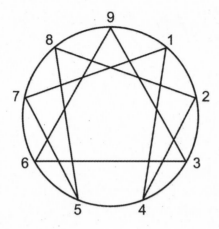

Extrovert (Ext) or Introvert (Int). That will cut the possible answers in half. Put a check next to the statements you feel strongly about.

ONE—REFORMER (Ext)

1. I'm often bothered because things aren't the way they should be.
2. I hate to waste time.
3. Often the least flaw can ruin the whole thing for me or, at least, "take the top off."
4. There's frequently a critical voice chattering in my head, about others and me.
5. I feel compelled to be honest.
6. Being right (not correct, but honest) is important to me.
7. If something isn't fair, it really bothers me.
8. I've often felt that, in order to be loved or even just respected, I have to succeed.
9. Quite often the truth is more important to me than kindness to someone obviously and courageously wrong.
10. I strongly admire crusaders against evil.

TWO—HELPER (Ext)

1. Many people depend on my assistance and unselfishness.
2. I take pride in my ability to help.
3. I like people to need me and depend on me.
4. I regularly compliment people, with no pretense.
5. I feel a duty to help people, even when at the moment I'd rather not.
6. At times, I feel weighed down by people needing me.
7. I admit that, at times, I feel underappreciated.
8. I like to feel "close" to people.
9. At times, I'm irritated by the suspicion I'm a patsy, being used.
10. Despite it all, I feel an obligation to help.

THREE—ACHIEVER (Ext)

1. I like to be on the go.
2. Success means a lot to me.
3. I like grades, prizes, and tokens of progress.
4. Image is very important to me.
5. You sometimes have to compromise your principles.
6. I have a strong memory of my past mistakes and why they occurred.
7. I have a very hard time forgiving betrayal.
8. I believe appearances are essential.
9. I'm better at spinning out possible solutions than the nitty-gritty of implementation.
10. First impressions count a lot.

FOUR—ARTIST (Int)

1. Most people don't appreciate how beautiful life can be.
2. I try to look casual and natural.
3. Symbols mean a lot to me.
4. I suspect most people don't feel as deeply as I do.

5. Often, other people seem careless about how I feel.
6. I don't want to think of myself as ordinary.
7. I can get caught up in sad ideas like suffering, loss, and death.
8. I seem to absorb the feelings of a group pretty easily.
9. I've sometimes been accused of being "hard to reach."
10. I can easily absorb myself in the arts.

FIVE—THINKER (Int)

1. I don't share my feelings easily.
2. I dislike chitchat, gossip, and small talk.
3. I like to take things apart, see where everything fits.
4. I don't need a lot of people around, and I like private space.
5. At parties, I'd rather observe than mix in.
6. I can easily get lost in thought. I enjoy that.
7. I'd rather puzzle out a question myself than get into a discussion.
8. I strongly resent being considered ill-informed or naïve.
9. If I hesitate to speak out or publish, the reason is that I hate uninformed criticism.
10. When I'm angry, I use the words *stupid* and *idiot* a lot, even about myself.

SIX—TEAM PLAYER (Int)

1. I'm basically a middle-of-the-road person. I hate over-the-top folks.
2. Loyalty to a tested group is very important to me.
3. I take a long time to assess all the options.
4. I often suffer doubts about others and myself.
5. I like those in charge to provide clear guidelines for work.
6. I seem more aware than others of possible danger.

7. When I go on a car trip, I always have the MapQuest map and step-by-step directions.
8. People compliment me on being levelheaded, steady, and dependable.
9. I dislike shifty people, blowhards, and cowards.
10. As a kid, my peers used to call me "The Boy/Girl Scout."

SEVEN—SAMPLER (Ext)

1. I'm less wary of people than others are.
2. I'm almost always optimistic. Things will always work out.
3. I wish people were less uptight and more upbeat. Life's too short.
4. I like to have adventures so I have good stories to tell.
5. My theory is: if something's good, more's better.
6. I like to savor life; you only go round once!
7. I don't like getting into heavy issues, and I'm often bored by those who do.
8. I tend to jump from one thing to another rather than go into anything in much depth.
9. When I'm bored, I'm really bored.
10. I remember my childhood as happy.

EIGHT—BOSS (Ext)

1. I stand up and fight for what I want.
2. I sense others' weak points better than most.
3. When I'm dissatisfied, I say so.
4. I have an inner sense of who really calls the shots in any group.
5. I don't like showing my tender, "feminine" side.
6. You've got to keep both feet firmly on the ground.
7. Generally, I don't go in much for self-analysis or "airy" stuff.
8. I don't like to be either cornered or subordinate.

9. I have trouble just letting things be when they're screwed-up.
10. When I take on a job, it's definitely going to get done.

NINE—PEACEMAKER (Int)

1. Most people get too worked up about things.
2. I like time just to do nothing.
3. People seem to see me as easygoing, mellow, and laidback.
4. I can't remember the last time I had trouble sleeping.
5. Generally, I don't get either too enthusiastic or too upset about things.
6. I often put things off, especially unpleasant things. I usually need to be pushed.
7. I have no trouble seeing both sides of questions or even other sides entirely.
8. I generally take the line of least resistance.
9. I don't think of myself as all that important.
10. Why walk when you can ride; why stand when you can sit?

The numbers of the types are value-neutral.

Reformers (One) are conscientious and confident, not so much in themselves but in the truth and whatever specific aspect of truth engages them most: race, sexism, poverty, or whales. Their greatest asset is objectivity, and when they're at their best, they make fine umpires, judges, or crusaders, but usually they are less successful diplomats and mediators because they have hawks' eyes for flaws. Their biggest obstacle is that the world simply won't line up and act rationally. As a result, when they're "in a bad stretch" or psychologically unhealthy, they lose hold of their main asset—objectivity—and sink into a swamp. They become resentful, melancholy, self-righteous, and angry. They need to avoid the broody bad habits of the unhealthy Four, the Artist, and take lessons from the carefree Seven, the Sampler, in order to stop brooding and take a vacation. Examples of this type are John McCain, Vanessa Redgrave, and Mr. Spock.

Helpers (Two) are caring, selfless, and openhearted. The best will pick you up at 2 a.m. when you're stuck on the highway—and never expect thanks. They make excellent caregivers and teachers, but would suffer greatly at solitary work. However, the world is saturated with selfish, ungrateful users. As a result, when Twos lose their main asset—self-forgetfulness—they fall into the possessive, demanding bad habits of the unhealthy Eight, the Boss. They begin to demand gratitude ("After all I've done for you....") and inflict guilt ("Oh, go ahead and enjoy your life. Forget me!") They use love as a weapon. They need to look at the kind of carefree dreaminess a healthy Four, the Artist, has. They need to go on a retreat and find out the world can, indeed, get along without them. Examples of this type are Pope Francis, Mr. Rogers, and Jerry Lewis.

Achievers (Three) are self-confident, charming, and ambitious. They excel at sales, politics, advertising, and think tanks, but would be unhappy at scientific research or any job that has rare payoffs. At best, they're authentic and inner-directed. At worst, they can become depressed, envious, deceitful, withdrawn, and defeatist. When they lose their main asset—confidence—they need to emulate healthy, trusting Sixes, team players, who don't take themselves too seriously. Examples of this type are Oprah Winfrey, Bill Clinton, Lance Armstrong.

Artists (Four) are reflective, reserved, creative, and transformative. They can take the ugliest aspects of humanity and make them accessible to anyone, but they'd be miserable at repetitive assembly line work or being in charge. When they lose their main asset, empathy, they wallow in the unhealthy, clingy habits of the unhealthy Two, the Helpers. They need lessons from the healthy One, the Reformer: "Will you just cut the crap?" Examples of this type are Paul Simon, J. D. Salinger, and Kurt Cobain.

Thinkers (Five) are clear-headed and objective, like Ones, but they're less involved in nitty-gritty problems and more abstract observers. They are best at painstaking academic work, but are less drawn to engaging the public. Their biggest temptation is withdrawal, using the objective world only as a source for theorizing and, losing their objectivity, imposing theories on reality. They begin to resent honest criticism and, irrationally, take on the devil-may-care enthusiasm of the unhealthy Seven (the Sampler), overindulging in alcohol and drugs. What they need is the confidence of the healthy Eight, the Boss. Examples of this type are Isaac Asimov, Bill Gates, and Dr. Frankenstein.

Team-Players (Six) are warm-hearted, like the hero of the film *Rudy*, eager to be helpful, dedicated, and responsible. They succeed naturally in the military, police, and clergy. They have a keen sense of trouble and react to it like antibodies. They are healthiest when they keep hold of the serenity of the healthy Nine (the Peacemaker), but when their main asset—trust—is threatened, they can regress to the self-centeredness of Threes (the Achievers), who have lost confidence. They react in either of two ways, yielding to fear (Woody Allen characters) or defying fear (Jack Nicholson in *A Few Good Men*). Examples of this type are Ellen DeGeneres, Mel Gibson, and Charles Manson.

Samplers (Seven) are spontaneous, effervescent, always "up," nervy, and on the prowl for new experiences. They are very gifted at think tanks, popping out imaginative ideas, but they can become flighty, frivolous, childishly demanding, and drugged out. What they need most is control and a schedule, which are the virtues of the healthiest Ones (the Reformers). What's worst for them is to regress to the aspects of the unhealthy Fives, which are single-minded, shrewdly hiding their drugs and bottles. Examples of this type are Bette Midler, Robin Williams, and John Belushi.

Bosses (Eight) are confident, sure of themselves, though not in their principles (like Ones). In fact, Eights are more shrewd than thoughtful. They have little time for self-examination or rumination other than concocting operational plans. They're aggressive because very often, as children, they dominated their mothers, as Hitler did. They're not good at yielding or taking orders. What they need is the vulnerability of healthy Twos (the Helpers), to spend some time helping out in a facility for impaired children. What they need least is to lose confidence in themselves and regress to the single-minded cunning of a

Five (the Thinker), as Hitler did. Examples of this type are Russell Crowe, Lucille Ball, and Don Vito Corleone.

Peacemakers (Nine) are accepting, open, placid, sometimes unhealthily putting their serenity even before weighty problems. But they're remarkably able to see all sides of questions and make excellent diplomats and counselors but poor judges and decision makers. They need to emulate the confident energy of the healthy Three (the Achiever). As they become less healthy, they degenerate to the self-surrender of an unhealthy Six (the Team Player), and become listless, slothful, and disengaged. Examples of this type are Clint Eastwood, Elizabeth II, and Neville Chamberlain.

The ideal result of becoming familiar with the Enneagram is not just to find out more about your own assets and liabilities, but also to provoke insights into the people to whom you have to relate: classmates and professors, employers and coworkers, spouses and children, neighbors and fellow citizens, peoples of the whole world as it becomes more a Global Village.

However, the long-range goal could well be the assimilation within yourself of the healthiest aspects of all nine personality types: objectivity, caring, ambition, sensitivity, clarity, loyalty, spontaneity, courage, and empathy. Also, it should encourage us to be wary of each of their potential pitfalls: resentment, possessiveness, disillusionment, melancholy, isolation, distrust, arrogance, withdrawal, and frustration with life's limits.

The whole range of virtues and vices are what you need to grasp before you can lay hold of who you are and who you want to be, where you fit in at the moment and where you want to be as your life progresses.

The following tables may be helpful for clarification.

The key to Healthy is being anchored in things as-they-are, humble before the truth.

(+) ---------------SPECTRUM* ---------------(-)		
HEALTHY	**AVERAGE**	**UNHEALTHY**
1. Freedom; no pretense	4. Less open; more defensive	7. Anxiety; survival ploys
2. Some ego defenses	5. Ego dominates main asset	8. Neurotic; remaking reality
3. Healthy, but "touchy"	6. Self-centered; conflicts	9. Psychotic; denying reality

*Numbers in this table represent the decrease of mental health possible in all personality types.

TYPE	HEALTHY	AVERAGE	UNHEALTHY
1. REFORMER	Principled, objective	Impersonal, scolding	Inflexible, dogmatic
2. HELPER	Warm, welcoming	Manipulative	Guilt-mongering
3. ACHIEVER	Self-assured, honest	Image-conscious	Opportunist, sadistic
4. ARTIST	Intuitive, self-giving	Self-absorbed, moody	Alienated, morbid
5. THINKER	Visionary, innovative	Aloof, reductionist	Isolated, obsessed
6. TEAM PLAYER	Reliable, loyal	Partisan, blaming	Anxious, paranoid
7. SAMPLER	Lively, multi-talented	Sophisticated, greedy	Rude, impulsive
8. BOSS	Confident, assertive	Pushy, combative	Ruthless, vengeful

PERSONAL REFLECTION

Consider the checks you made next to the ninety statements about the Ennegram types, the more discursive descriptions of each type, and the schematic table above, and sketch out a first-draft description of who you are (admittedly, more or less) now. What are your personality habits—your attitude, your usual ways of perceiving, deciding, and living—that you've probably never examined before? Which of your habits should give you confidence for the future? Which do you suspect need some looking into, acceptance, and resolve to change for the good of your future life as a breadwinner, a spouse, a parent?

10.

NARCISSISM

> I don't care what you think unless it is about me.
>
> —*Kurt Cobain*

Consider the following statements. Do you agree or disagree?

1. In public, when you think everybody's looking at you, *they're* thinking everybody—including you—is occupied looking at *them*. Are you?
2. False humility is at least as debilitating to character as vanity.
3. The critical test of adulthood is taking responsibility for whatever you do or say.
4. It is rare for little kids to feel completely appreciated for who they are rather than for what they accomplish.
5. If you don't take care of yourself, who else will?
6. Self-preservation is the basic drive of animals, but human animals have higher inborn potentials than that.
7. The unexamined life is not worth living.
8. A faulty upbringing excuses no one.
9. No one should get too upset about trivial faults. They're negligible.
10. Your parents weren't compelled to let you be born.

TWO STORIES

Once upon a time, there was a Greek boy named Narcissus. This kid was so handsome that middle-aged matrons thought they were having cardiac arrest when he walked by. But it was worth it. Narcissus's mother, knowing the fierce cost of being gorgeous, broke every mirror in the house and forbade him *ever* to look at one. When he got to adolescence, he was constantly puzzled that damsels kept falling backward down wells staring back at him. Ah, but if Mama thought she could outwit the gods, she had another think coming! One day, Narcissus was out running in the woods and stopped to slake his thirst at a crystal pool. So slick and bright it was almost like a...mirror!

As he bent to drink, he saw this...gasp!...this *perfect* face! Talk about love at first sight! Narcissus sat and stared at that godlike image for hours. Finally, he couldn't resist! He had to reach down and embrace this splendor!

He fell in and kept swimming down, down, down, unable to grasp this treasure. He was swallowed up and never came back. So much for young Narcissus!

Narcissus wasn't in love with *himself*, but with an image of himself. If present day victims of narcissism really could *love themselves*, that is, respect and care for who they truly are, warts and all, they might become salvageable as human beings. In fact, the Greek root of the word *narcissism* is *narkoun*, "to benumb." It is the same root as *narcotic*, and the mirror is for the narcissist what the drug is to the junkie. Marijuana makes people giggle wildly, not because there's anything really funny. Pot stimulates a nerve. The fun's unreal, like being tickled. It blots out the insupportable really real. So does the self-deceptive image in the narcissist's mirror.

As it is, narcissists *detest* their shortcomings so badly they refuse to acknowledge their existence, and therefore hate and deny their real selves. Even their trivial flaws are monstrous because they are flaws in someone who really has *deserved*, by birth and by unequaled excellence, to be an archduke or a crown princess! Then, because they can't stand living inside a "host" they despise, they create an ideal self, a *persona*, which is the

Greek word for "mask." No one can talk to or know or love the real self, only the fabricated mask. They begin to live inside that "perfect, flawless" (completely self-deceptive) self. Nor will they tolerate criticism or ever admit they're wrong, not even to themselves. Anybody who finds them faulty is actually seething with jealousy of their superiority. (That's why siblings in folktales are always mean-spirited stepsisters and arrogant older brothers.)

Once upon a time—not nearly so far back as Narcissus—there was this best little boy in the world, who never did anything wrong—not because it was wrong, but because he convinced himself that if he did bad things, his parents wouldn't love him anymore. One day, Billy (for such was his name) and his less perfect eight-year-old chums were playing kick-the-can in the street and making a great deal of unseemly noise. An old grouch came out onto his porch and hollered at the boorish children to "haul their skinny asses out of there." So they went to play in a field. Ah, but once there, the boy in the group with the absolute least virtue found a dead rat! All those present agreed it would be a great idea to toss the said rat onto the old grouch's porch!

Guess who was deputed to carry out this quite reprehensible deed?

Trembling with the terror of unaccustomed guilt, little Billy crept from tree to tree, pinching the noxious rodent in his utmost fingertips, and hurled it blindly! He then ran like hell!

And Billy was me. (In fact, he still is.)

That evening, I was sitting doing something worthy (like reading a book, in summer!) The phone rang, and my dad answered it. I heard him say, "No. I don't think Bill would do something like that." My heart began to slam against my ribs like a pile driver. And my dad came over, the kindest, gentlest man I'd ever known, who loved me unconditionally. I was hoping. He asked, "Bill, did you throw a rat on Mr. So-and-So's porch today?"

I took a huge breath and said, "No."

And he believed me!

Well, I simply couldn't accept that. If I accepted it, I'd be admitting that I had, in fact, lied to my dad. That was simply intolerable. So I went out into the garage, and on the raw wood,

I scratched with a nail, "I get blamed." That was seventy-five years ago, and I can still see it, still feel it.

How many ways had I knotted the truth against itself? First, I wasn't blamed. Dad had believed me. So then it had to be his fault. It could not be mine. My image would be shattered.

There I was, just short of my eighth birthday, as yet incapable of spelling *prevarication*, still unaware boys were significantly different from girls, and I was already a full-fledged functioning narcissist—as self-deceived as the original Narcissus and in the same game with such world-class narcissists as Cleopatra and Vlad the Impaler.

Once again, Carl Jung says, the cause of all neuroses—trivial or tragic—is the inability to yield to the objective facts. And eventually, inevitably, the effort and anguish it takes to kid ourselves and everyone else becomes incredibly more agonizing than facing the unpleasant truth.

It would be years before I learned the difference between guilt and shame. Guilt is admitting the truth that "I *did* a bad thing." Shame is "I *am* a bad person." To be an honest, fair judge of yourself, you must learn and accept that crucial distinction between guilt and shame.

It would be slipshod and untrue to define narcissism inaccurately as self-love. Narcissism is no more love than Romeo and Juliet's passion was love. It was adolescent infatuation, just as Tristan and Iseult didn't love one another but were pixilated on love potion. Genuine love is not blind; being in love is blind. Infatuation is blind. Romance is a narcissism built for two.

THE CULTURE OF NARCISSISM

We live now in a culture of narcissism. Television, films, and nearly every other socializing, transforming medium makes the important (death, family, sex) trivial and the trivial (complexions, hair, pectorals) important. Nearly every advertisement you've seen since you first began to take in information and values has been a professionally executed attempt to make you discontent with yourself—your face, your smells, your urine retention, your clothing, your financial security, your insulation, your pest control, your swimming pool scum, your sexual potency. Where do all your imperfections end? So you desperately need lots of stuff for the narcissistic cover-up.

In 1979, Christopher Lasch published a book, *The Culture of Narcissism*, which has proven more and more prophetic every year since. He argues that western nations have succumbed to (and now more and more, all nations aspire to) smothering narcissism—not clinically self-indulgent hedonism, but a lack of self-esteem that requires constant validation. Less dramatic than operatic excess, *petty* narcissism will do just as well to ruin character and society as Roman orgies did. It may not be far from the truth to say that such a craving for center stage is at the root of the suicides of so many celebrities who had everything but despaired of life. Why do many otherwise intelligent people have to anesthetize themselves with drugs and alcohol from the really real? Why does every child now need a present when leaving someone else's birthday party so they don't feel left out? It's a gilded epidemic, proving that having too much is at least as ruinous as having too little. Nothing can be enough.

The Diagnostic and Statistical Manual of Mental Disorders (DSM-IV) of the American Psychiatric Association defines narcissism as a "pervasive pattern of grandiosity (in fantasy or behavior), need for admiration, and lack of empathy."

I once posed to my students the dilemma facing a new mother of choosing between leaving her place in the executive pecking order in a large corporation and risking her newborn child's need for a consistent caregiver for the first six months or so. A young woman said, "Sometimes you've got to think about *yourself*." That's what narcissism means, concretely.

The Industrial Revolution took parents and children from the home, broke the close family relationship with the parents in the shop or on the farm, ended the early conditioning of kids to working and to the intuitive assimilation of the parents' values and habits. However, with the success of monopoly capitalism, society offered a broadening sense of security and newly disposable income. Corporations found they had to pay workers a wage sufficient to make them also customers. World War II broadened young men's experience, introduced women to the broader work force, opened college education for veterans and triggered a dramatic move to suburban life.

In the process, it softened what was once the "hardy pioneer spirit." Advertising created "needs" that had never been needs before, like for Viagra and Dexatrim. Machines dominated life and threatened to reduce it to a soulless, materialist, consumerism that loomed in dystopian novels like *1984*, *Brave New World*, *Fahrenheit 451*, and *Clockwork Orange*. Mass production needed fewer skilled workers. It changed the interaction of managers and bureaucrats with workers from personal to distant and abstract, turned education into efficient schooling, which pointed young people not to become citizens of character but instead sifted the workforce for the economy. It siphoned off the brain surgeons from the entrepreneurs and the managers from line workers, and certified them for employment in the System. Everything became depersonalized. Consumerism addicted nearly everyone to distractions and recreation, the anesthesia of games and impersonal sex, and unrealistic sitcoms. Refusal to hold students to standards lest they become anxious or upset facilitated the emergence of a society of weak, ungrounded, defensive, insecure, and manipulative selves— like souls with rubbery spines or no spines at all. Commitment came only at the guarantee of loopholes and limits.

Lasch demonstrated that the culture has created generations now in constant need of *external* validation, incapable of "owning the self"—a kind of soul-bankruptcy. Too many, he argued, are not autonomous or self-motivated but driven by repressed rage and self-distaste, using others as objects for personal satisfaction but at the same time craving their sincere acceptance and approval. Lasch clearly saw it as an unrealistic world of pipe-dreams: "the fascination with fame and celebrity, the fear of competition, the inability to suspend disbelief, the shallowness and transitory quality of personal relations, the horror of death."*

He demonstrated how that infantile need has crept into every area of modern life: politics, sex, family, work, schooling, sports, and above all in a dread of the fact of aging and losing potency.

---

*Christopher Lasch, *The Culture of Narcissism* (New York: W.W. Norton, 1991), 176.

Watch TV shows that pan across the audience and see them claw toward the cameras like drowning victims, hoping to be somehow made real by the television. Notice how many shallow, beautiful people become "famous for being famous," like the Kardashians, the Baldwins, the Palins, the Osbournes, the Jacksons, Charlie Sheen, Paris Hilton, Tori Spelling, Snooki, and all the Neanderthals on *Jersey Shore*, who make $150K per show.

T. S. Eliot saw it as far back as 1925 when he wrote:

We are the hollow men
We are the stuffed men
Leaning together
Headpiece filled with straw. Alas!*

POP WARNER NARCISSISM

Not too many Kardashians are likely to pick up this book. But just as people who cheat on quizzes are in the same game as Bernie Madoff and people who use sexual tease are in the same game as prostitutes and pimps, but with less guts and smalltime opportunities, you don't have to be a star to be a certifiable narcissist. Petty bossy types and pity-rapists are in the same game as Hitler and Blanche du Bois—just not yet completely professional or big-time.

We live in a shared biological ecology—a web of relationships—in which, if any segment fails in its purpose, the whole system begins to falter, sputter, and then die. If big-time chemical companies spew pollutants, nobody will be able to swim in the rivers. However, it's just as destructive if somebody throws a single McDonald's box out of the car window and everybody else feels free to do the same. It results in a trash-filled world, which everybody has to share. But there is a perfectly parallel moral ecology made up of free human beings. One lie is trivial, like a single soda can out the window, *but* if everybody feels free to lie when it's convenient or drops commitments when they

*T. S. Eliot, "The Hollow Men," in *The Collected Poems, 1909–1962* (New York: Harcourt Brace, 1968), 77.

inconvenience them, then the moral system begins to falter, then sputter, and then die. And we all end up in a ruined web of relationships, where nobody can trust anybody else. Fifty years ago, Christopher Lasch had warned that it had been sputtering for a long time.

Check one more list of very petty actions. Do they seem so trivial that they almost excuse the perpetrators rather than embarrassing them for being childishly narcissistic?

–Parking in the handicapped space because I'm running late
–Spitting gum in the drinking fountain because the basket's down the hall
–Nudging into the head of a line getting onto a plane
–Leaving toast crumbs in the butter because it's trivial
–Snapping at customers because they're all faceless nothings in a line
–Splattering graffiti on a wall to let everybody know I was there
–Cheating for a few points because my dad will blow his stack
–Lying to my mom to avoid one more hassle
–Arguing with an instructor long after I realize she's right
–Leaving the toilet roll empty because I had more important things to do

None of the above actions merits a life sentence, but every single one mounts up, like the slow buildup of an avalanche. Far more importantly, they trivialize you. At one and the same time, each of those mounting selfish actions says,

My time and agenda are much more important than yours.

and

My faults are much more excusable than yours.

One would hope that any honest person would see in those two juxtaposed sentences

1. A blatantly laughable contradiction.
2. A pair of claims easily attributable to Hitler, Ayn Rand, Eddie Murphy, Friedrich Nietzsche, Nero, Oscar Wilde, F. Scott and Zelda Fitzgerald, Thomas Hobbes, Josef Stalin, Idi Amin, Gordon Gecko, Truman Capote, Howard Hughes, Charles Manson, Bette Davis, Oedipus, Madonna, Lady Gaga, Faust, Miley Cyrus, Hamlet, Marquis de Sade, Charlie Sheen, Simon Cowell. And the beat goes on.

How often we ease out from under by saying, "Who's not human, right?" Which is, to be honest, the same as saying, "Who's not stupid, right?"

PERSONAL REFLECTION

An integral part of Twelve-Step programs of self-reclamation is complete honesty about one's weaknesses—and strengths—and such a firm grasp of one's own reality that the individual feels strong enough to share them with one other trusted human being. Do you have someone in your life you trust so completely you could list what you truly believe are really healthy and unhealthy habits, which you should take meaningful steps to change? If not, can you say why not? If the reason is shyness or embarrassment, are those reasons worthier of protecting than ownership of your integral self? If not, do you really believe there should be?

11.

MOTIVATION

INNOCENCE OR INTEGRITY?
(BENTHAM, MILL, KANT, ARISTOTLE, AND AQUINAS)

> Where choice begins, Paradise ends, inno-
> cence ends, for what is Paradise but the
> absence of any need to choose this action?
> —*Arthur Miller*

As a child and adolescent, which was your habitual response
when any authority challenged your behavior, even if you didn't
vocalize the words?

–"I didn't do *anything!*"

or

–"Before you find out yourself, I want to tell you something I messed up."

The thrust of this course goes against what I believe has
been the dominant approach to teaching moral behavior once
academics took it away from storytellers. Those principled and
well-meaning learned folk who valued clarity over conviction
changed the process from an inductive journey of discovery into
a deductive classroom-ready plan starting from historically
recurrent, time-tested principles, ready for packing up before
any real journey even began.

The centuries-old method of spinning tales of heroines and heroes offered not a catechism of reasoned precepts, but focused a beginner's honest confusion into the character of a clearly inexperienced (therefore mistake-prone) protagonist, unexpectedly called out onto a perilous pilgrimage through personified forces of Good and Evil—a succession of human challenges. Oh, the heroes make mistakes aplenty, but there are always helpful dwarves, kindly witches, and sly foxes to steer— or at least nudge—them back onto the path of virtue. It seems that the motive was invariably to be a good human being, and not just avoid being a bad one. To admit guilt—"I did a wrong thing"—when it's appropriate, but never to submit to the Evil Force's contention that I'm shameful—"I am a bad person."

Therefore, this text has made a conscious choice to de-emphasize, almost entirely, experts considered the prime academic authorities on moral questions, even the Hebrew Scriptures and its "Thou-Shalt-Nots," which nearly every Westerner answers when asked about basic morality.

This course does *not* negate those authorities, nor does it in any way impugn the truths of their prohibitions. All the actions the religious and philosophical authorities reprehend are, in truth, reprehensible and should be shunned by any decent human. What this course tries to adjust is the sales pitch for a newcomer, who approaches the Human Questions for the first time as a thinking adult.

–"I don't want to be someone people can criticize."

versus

–"I want to be a person I can be rightfully proud of."

There's no way a text like this can give any profound or even serious insight into even the most influential of moral philosophers. Keep in mind that this text is sketching out a crude, primitive map, which can allow you to venture into more demanding waters if you choose.

The emphasis here is decidedly nontheoretical and more down-to-earth practical. Its aim is to point the way not to require a comprehensive academic command of the material, but to suggest reasons and insights that can help you—a unique individual—be a fulfilled human being.

It seems self-evident that valuing and desiring personal integrity is a more worthwhile goal than the ability to recall what even the greatest minds in history said about it.

MAJOR APPROACHES TO NORMATIVE MORALITY: AN OVERVIEW

Virtue: Natural Law / Human Rights— Aristotle (ca. 284–322 BCE) / Aquinas (1225–1274 CE)

There are, evidently, innate urges in all human beings that encourage them to push beyond their material/vegetative/ animal limits. Furthermore, these urges undergird the right and responsibility to use unique human intelligence to pursue certain natural goals, such as preserving and intensifying the sacredness of life, community, love, family, and truth. The inner nature of these natural goals enjoins on the human the duty to protect, enrich, and never to violate the means without which those goals are unattainable:

- –*Life*—no murder, savagery, war: nursing the future, enhancing growth and production
- –*Community*—no stealing, coveting, coercion, slavery: settling disputes, keeping peace
- –*Love, family*—no adultery, dishonoring parents: forgiveness, obedience, faithfulness
- –*Truth*—no lies, cheating, dishonesty: fostering learning, research, exploration

Those controls, known to most of us as embodied in the Ten Commandments of the Hebrew Scriptures, are found in nearly every other society known to historians, even though the divinities they worship are broken into many gods (Google "Ten Commandments in Other Religions").

However, some philosophers (Hobbes [1588–1679 CE]) hold that, by their nature, humans are not merely prone to evil but essentially savage, restrainable but never curable (see *Lord of the Flies*). In *Leviathan*, Hobbes asserts quite simply, "The life of man, solitary, poor, nasty, brutish, and short." Before him, Niccolo Machiavelli (1469–1527 CE) wrote, "It needs to be taken for granted that all men are wicked and that they will always give vent to the malignity that is in their minds."* John Calvin, the Reformer, (1509–64 CE), declared, "Original sin, therefore, appears to be a hereditary corruption and depravity of our nature, extending to all the parts of the soul, which first makes us obnoxious to the wrath of God, and then produces in us works which in Scripture are termed works of the flesh."† Of course, the emergence and the gradual dominance of empiricism/scientism would argue that no rules of proper usage can be written into the natures of things if there is no one like a Divinity to formulate and embed them. Things just...are.

Liberalism—John Locke (1632–1704 CE)

As its name suggests, philosophical liberalism is rooted in the freedom and dignity of the individual human person. It stands in staunch opposition to what preceded it: the authoritarianism evidenced in hereditary privilege, state religion, absolute monarchy, and the Divine Right of Kings. It was a result of the humanist Age of Enlightenment and itself gave birth to the American and French Revolutions.

Locke argued that there are certain unchallengeable rights rooted in the very nature of human, rational beings: the rights to life, liberty, and property. They are pre-government and were inherent in human beings from a state of nature, before there was a single law or a single authority. It was wicked for Cain to

---

*Machiavelli, *The Discourses*, bk. 1, chap. 3, pp. 111–12.

†John Calvin, *Institutes of the Christian Religion*, trans. by Henry Beveridge (Peabody, MA: Hendrickson Publishers, 2008), 152.

slay Abel, even though there were no laws and no authority other than the will of the Creator evident in his work. No human was objectively more worthy than another. All were born free and equal: two human qualities no one could legitimately take away or give away, any more than he or she could rightfully give away their souls, their selves.

However, Locke realized that humans aren't flawless. Rational beings had to insist on some *limit* on unchecked freedom. Open license led inevitably to chaos and suffering. Thus, human nature is restricted by the equally important element of *relationships*. Not merely, "What do I deserve?" but, "How do I fit in?"

Limits on human freedom are justified for both the believer and for the atheist. Theists acknowledge utter dependence on a Creator. Therefore, they are radically identified as God's property, God's workmanship, God's to dispose of. Atheists must submit to the truth that *rights* cannot *rightfully* negate other *rights*. Government by majority rule exists under tacit consent of the governed—that is, even though each one wasn't explicitly consulted about it, in committing themselves to live under this government, each has equivalently ratified its constitution and later legislation. Winston Churchill said it brilliantly: "Democracy is the worst form of government, except for all the others...."*

Utilitarian / Consequential— Jeremy Bentham (1748–1832 CE) / John Stuart Mill (1806–1873 CE)

The goodness or evil of any action arises from its total effects/consequences.

Bentham: The goal of society is "the greatest *pleasure* for the greatest number" (and fewest ill effects). Mill used the word *happiness* instead of *pleasure*.

---

*Winston Churchill, House of Commons, November 11, 1947, quoted in Richard Langworth, ed., *Churchill by Himself* (London: Ebury Publishing, 2008), 574.

The critical point, however, is discerning precisely what genuine pleasure/happiness *consists of* and who decides what actions conform to it. At the least, "pleasure/happiness" is the absence of pain. Bentham held all forms of pleasure equal, whereas Mill held for higher (intellectual) and lower (physical) pleasures and between enduring happiness and mere momentary contentment: "Better a human dissatisfied than a pig satisfied."

One might be tempted to suggest that it would be acceptable to torture one person if this would produce an amount of happiness in other people outweighing the unhappiness of the individual tortured. It was the argument used to defend the atom bombing of Hiroshima. However, this argument is well used to elicit support for measures on public assistance to the needy. Henry Ford used the notion to show that paying a generous wage, even at a temporary loss to company income, pays off in the long run when the workers can afford to buy Ford cars.

Unlike communism, which in its idealism, ignores human selfishness, utilitarianism assumes that enlightened self-interest is the best motive for acting decently. Those committed to that conviction have to find imaginative ways to show that unselfishness and altruism had to have seemed personally beneficial in order to be passed on through natural selection. Finding unselfish animal activity for those not of their species is difficult.

The Categorical Imperative— Immanuel Kant (1724–1804 CE)

Immanuel Kant taught that the moral (decent, rational, human) being is governed by what he called a "categorical imperative." It is "categorical" because it is unconditional, universal, and binding on all humans. It is "imperative" because it is a command rooted right into our humanity and our relationships. Our grasp of the categorical imperative is a priori, that is, it is self-evident without need of research or argument, such as I never met them, but I'm certain you had two parents, one male, one female. That inborn universal demand for human behavior can, indeed, be ignored, denied, and hushed up, but it remains real. Reality itself still says, "you ought."

Kant did not give an encyclopedic coverage of all possible specific violations of the categorical imperative. He offered no moral catechism. Rather, he posed a test:

> "Act as if the maxim of your action were to become by your will a universal law of nature."*

In other words, judge this possible action as if your choice would become a law binding on everybody on earth, all the time, as if *you yourself* were setting in stone a command that all other human beings must imitate or consider un-good.

For example, a will that decided to turn a blind eye and deaf ear to the suffering of fellow humans, according to Kant, "would contradict itself, inasmuch as cases might often arise in which one would have need of the love and sympathy of others and in which he would deprive himself, by such a law of nature springing from his own will, of all hope of the aid he wants for himself."† Consider the lesson learned by Ebenezer Scrooge.

Examples easily multiply. If you feel justified in cheating for a few points on a forgettable quiz, you're a fool to ask me to mind your wallet. If you routinely cheat your customers, you soon will have none. If you enjoy uncommitted sex with my son or daughter, don't be surprised if I feel equally free with either of your parents.

In 1961, the Nazi war criminal SS Lieutenant-Colonel Adolf Eichmann faced trial in Jerusalem for crimes against humanity. Eichmann declared with strong emphasis that he'd lived his whole life "according to a Kantian definition of duty."‡ He clearly had no idea whatsoever what he falsely claimed. He was simply a narcissistic little man camouflaging his mean-spiritedness in high-sounding verbiage. He flew in the

---

*Immanuel Kant, *Grounding for the Metaphysics of Morals*, 3rd ed., trans. James W. Ellington (Cambridge, MA: Hackett Publishing, 1993), 30.

†Ibid., 32.

‡Hannah Arendt, *Eichmann in Jerusalem: A Report on the Banality of Evil* (London: Penguin Classics, 2006), 135–36.

face of Kant's major demand that human beings never be treated with less than dignity. Had he discovered that he himself had even one Jewish ancestor, he would be obliged to kill not only himself but also all his children and grandchildren.

PERSONAL REFLECTION

Answer this hypothetical scenario. The police suspect someone you really love is dealing drugs to kids. They ask you if you will answer "certain questions" about his or her behavior. How would you respond? Much more important: Why?

Please consider seriously the PBS series that is available on the Internet, "Justice with Michael Sandel." Sandel is a Harvard professor of moral and political philosophy. The series offers twenty-four half-hour lectures covering a range of nonreligious approaches to behavior.

Part Three

VIRTUES

12.

HONESTY—
CONSCIENCE—
CHARACTER

> Integrity has no need of rules.
> —*Albert Camus*

Consider the following ten statements and whether you agree or disagree with them.

1. People dumb enough to leave their lockers open can't complain.
2. Lying to the insurance company isn't really cheating.
3. To say "I love you" while intimate with someone you don't care for is a lie.
4. If I work hard for the minimum wage, I can use the company photocopier to run off my resume.
5. A great deal of the research on the Internet is out there for anyone to use without fussing with footnotes nobody reads anyway.
6. If a friend got hold of a copy of a final, I wouldn't look at it.
7. Betrayals of truth inevitably snowball.
8. When even one student in a class cheats, all the others are the victims.
9. If you're not totally honest with yourself, the game's over, at least for you.

10. If I say I really want the goal but fail to take the concrete means to it, I'm lying.

A NAUGHTY STORY AND A SAD ONE

The first is the old joke about the man who asks a girl if she will sleep with him for a million dollars. Of course, she says yes. He then offers her two dollars and she slaps his face, saying, "*What* do you think I *am*?" He answers, "I know what you are. We are just haggling over the price."

Secondly, over the years, I've directed ninety-nine plays and musicals. On the sign-up sheet, after the usual contact details, I have a short paragraph saying, "If I'm chosen, I'll rearrange my schedule so I won't miss any rehearsals. I consider this a commitment," and the student then signs his or her name. Often, some would find the rehearsals too intrusive and would drop out without bothering to tell me. I'd call them up. It was always a shock to them! Why was it a shock? Because they didn't think they'd be missed! They thought that *little* of *themselves*? That bothered me more than dealing with the empty spaces when I was arranging chorus movements!

They offer a number of excuses, such as "I had a dentist appointment," "I forgot my SAT class," "My girlfriend had to be picked up," "I got chosen for another play." One actually said, "I wasn't having fun anymore." That was disheartening. I said, "But you gave me your word." They denied it. "But you signed your *name*. That's your *word*. When you put your *name* on the line, you put your *self* on the line." They didn't see things that way, even though human beings have been operating on that principle since there's been signature X's.

One girl started to cry, and her father grabbed the phone. "Listen, Father, you've got no business upsetting kids like that. She's going on the trip. They're only young once!" I asked him, "Is this ski trip more important than her word, her integrity?" He slammed down the phone.

When do these *kids* start growing up and honoring commitments? Who shows them how? When do they start *honoring themselves* if they can't grasp that their not showing up makes other people *rightfully* angry?

If someone offered you full college tuition and a job starting at $80,000 to tell one lie about a person you already dislike on national TV, would you do it? Don't answer too quickly.

When you tell yourself "I wish," "I'd like," or "I really want to," how often do you really, genuinely *mean* it? Don't answer too quickly.

When you say you need—and want—a good education, how many books did you read last summer beyond assignments? When you ride a bus, what's in your pocket, a book or an iPod? How often do you use CliffsNotes without the assigned book? How many hours a week do you spend on the phone with conversations not worth remembering? Don't answer too quickly.

Your parents pay you the equivalent of an annual salary of at least $55,000. According to the latest census figures, the median household income in the United States was $50,502 in 2011.* In honesty, where no one else can hear, can you say you give pretty much an honest day's work for an honest day's pay? Don't answer too quickly.

Those are distasteful questions, but they're an acid test of your honesty with yourself.

If I can buy your integrity for a few points on a quiz that tomorrow you'll forget you took, for an extra evening out in the pubs, or for a quick sexual hookup with someone to whom you're pretty indifferent, I can buy your soul for considerably less than a million dollars—probably five hundred dollars would do. We're not talking "sin" or "hell," just the right to feel honestly good about yourself.

Here, let me make you a solemn promise in exchange for another solemn promise. I can guarantee that you will be a valued employee, a treasured spouse, an honored parent. You will

---

*"How much do Americans earn? What is the average US income and other income figures. Fiscal cliff talks only useful in context of incomes," My Budget 360, http://www.mybudget360.com/how-much-do-americans-earn-what-is-the-average-us-income/.

be a contented human being if you make this pledge: "I promise that I will never lie to myself about myself."

TRUTH AND TRUST

Honesty negates narcissism. Truth is for narcissists what sunlight is for vampires.

The glue that holds together our web of moral relationships (human society) is trust. When I ride a bus, I need to have at least some trust that most of my fellow passengers are not packing guns and machetes or at least won't use them. A quarterback has to trust that his linemen won't flop down and let the opposition mangle him. We trust pilots, chefs, Amazon, credit card companies, and unseen people at the end of phone lines. Without trust, we become a nation of paranoids.

However, trust dovetails right into honesty. If I know someone gives in to cheating when it's easy *not* to (a quiz), I have no cause to believe them when the punishment is severe (losing a driver's license for a year). If, however, they consistently, forthrightly admit when they've done wrong, I'm tempted to believe them when everything points to their guilt but they claim they're innocent. ("I don't think Bill would do something like that.") A *habit* of honesty is always an investment in one's own *self*-interest. Nobody can find you out when you tell the truth—and the truth is always easier to remember.

Just as trust dovetails into honesty, honesty merges into truth. As we saw, truth is "out there." What I say is legitimate and trustworthy only if the objective evidence backs it up. The fabric of society depends on trust; trust depends on honesty; honesty depends on truth. The purpose of education (as opposed to mere schooling) is teaching people *to discover and grasp and speak and live the truth.*

It is not just to see the truth, but to yield to it, even when the Beast in me wants to blot out the truth, deny the truth, or change the truth to something false but more digestible. Truth is the only antidote to narcissism and neuroses: "Yes, my husband did leave, and he *won't* come back....Yes, I did fail, and I *deserved* to, and for these reasons....Yes, I did hurt her feelings, and I have to apologize." Facing the truth head-on is often painful, but the neurotic games we invent to avoid the unchangeable truth are always more bitter, more confusing, more self-destructive than yielding to the truth from the outset.

The first step toward wisdom and true freedom is calling a thing by its right name, to be honest about it to yourself. If a sexual act isn't the same kind of gift as a mother's unselfish act for her baby, don't call it "making love." Call it by the other harsher, truer word. It may be uncomfortable, but it's the truth. Fool everybody else, but don't fool yourself.

Aristotle says that we learn virtues by practicing them and making them habits. He could have said the same about vices. The first little lie is painful, but the next one is easier. Soon, lying has become as habitual as blinking your eyes. If you say you cheat only when you have need or you're kind but routinely destroy others' reputations, you've lost something precious. And if you only just noticed, it couldn't have been too important to you.

Some argue that, at times, telling the truth is too hurtful—and that's true. If she asks if you like her ghastly dress, say, "You look good in anything." If she presses: "If you like it, that's all that counts, right?" If she still persists, she asked for it!

Sometimes, the inquirer doesn't *deserve* the truth. For example, "Do you have a runaway slave in there?"; "Are you gay?"; or "Is your father a spy?" It will shock no one to hear that some people sometimes put their own self-interest above the truth for the most trivial reasons. But just as we saw earlier, in trivializing their mistakes, they trivialize themselves.

PERSONAL REFLECTION

In 1972, agents of the Committee for the Re-Election of the President broke into the Democratic National Watergate Headquarters and opened a tangle of dirty tricks using federal powers criminally. But President Nixon, the most powerful person in the world, chose to hang tough in denials for two full years, until he was forced to resign the presidency in August 1974.

In 1998, President Bill Clinton was overwhelmed by a seemingly endless investigation into alleged sexual misconduct in the Oval Office. When the evidence and scandal became inescapable, the most powerful man on earth defended himself against a grand jury by claiming, "It depends on how you define 'having sex.'" He was ultimately impeached by the House but acquitted of perjury by the Senate.

What would have happened, do you suspect, if—knowing the truth—each man had come clean, appeared on TV, and given the same remorseful speech each eventually had to give?

The more important question: Rather than being scandalized by the ignobility of such eminent men, has their example in any way had a positive effect on your own conscience? How?

13.

PERSPECTIVE

> Far out in the uncharted backwaters of the unfashionable end of the western spiral arm of the Galaxy lies a small unregarded yellow sun. Orbiting this at a distance of roughly ninety-two million miles is an utterly insignificant little blue green planet whose ape-descended life forms are so amazingly primitive that they still think digital watches are a pretty neat idea.
> —*Douglas Adams*

Consider the following ten statements. Do you agree or disagree?

1. Ignorance is curable. Dumb is forever.
2. The chance to grow is worth risking your comfort zone.
3. Without dissatisfaction, we'd still be howling back in the caves.
4. The unquestionably best weapon you can take into your future is the skills to think clearly and come to honest conclusions for unpredictable questions.
5. Reality is greater than any human mind has yet been able to encompass.
6. Better safe than sorry.
7. Truly educated people never stop broadening their horizons.

8. Curious people aren't just inquisitive, they're usually also weird.
9. There is a direct connection between IQ and wisdom.
10. The narrower your mind, the more your problems become out of proportion.

ANOTHER ONE OF THOSE GREEK GUYS

Long ago, in the Kingdom of Thebes, Queen Jocasta got this oracle that said her just-born son, as yet nameless, would grow up to kill his father and marry her. Well, Lady Jocasta was one very cunning woman and wasn't about to be snookered by a dysfunctional family of alleged gods. So she had a trusted shepherd leave the infant stranded on Mount Cithaeron. But, wouldn't you know, the shepherd went soft-hearted and gave the baby to a Corinthian shepherd who gave him to Polybus and Merope, King and Queen of Corinth, who named him Oedipus.

Oedipus was one sharp kid, baffling the bearded wise men with his cleverness and multiplying fifteen-place numbers in his head, while playing five chess games. However, when Oedipus was a teenager, the Oracle at Delphi told him the *same* prediction about patricide and incest, so, being a shrewd child of his astute birth mother, he, too, convinced himself he could outwit even those know-it-all gods, and fled Corinth to avoid harming Polybus and Merope. Of course, he headed straight for *Thebes*.

On the way, he encountered this old guy in a wagon with his retainers who somehow riled his adolescent feathers, so he slew the whole pack of them. After a while, he arrived in Thebes, where the citizens were reeling from the loss of their dear king, who just *happened* to have been overwhelmed by "a *band* of brigands" at the same crossroads where, according to the sole survivor, Oedipus had killed that old guy—really coincidental, right? At that time, a beast of mismatched parts called the Sphinx, who was ruining commerce by devouring visitors or passing merchants who couldn't answer a riddle, also bedeviled them. It goes without saying that clever Oedipus answered the riddle quickly, sent the Sphinx packing, slipped right onto the empty throne, and for good measure into the bed chamber of the Queen, Jocasta.

Jocasta and Oedipus were really smart. They were also really dumb.

Dumb has nothing to do with low IQ or National Merit smarts, nor with how many academic letters appear after your name. Dumb has to do with a lack of *perspective*.

Whatever name you give to the situation in which we humans have found ourselves since the beginning—God's creation, the State of Nature, the Realm of Fate, the Universe—humans did *not* make our environment nor its laws. Deny God, the gods, the Fates, or the laws of science as thoroughly as you choose, but we have to yield to The Rules of the Game, whatever ways we might maneuver the pieces to try and get away with it. No matter what name you give the Forces we contend against from birth to death, *we* don't control them and we can't evade them for long.

Even if Oedipus sneered at the gods, if he had even half a mind and was just a tiny bit less arrogant, he *never* would have killed *any* old man and surely wouldn't have been stupid enough to marry a woman at *least* fifteen years *older*! And *she* was just as know-it-all-stupid!

One of the prime goals of your sixteen-plus years of formal tutelage is to *humble* you before the facts of life without destroying your confidence, to prepare you for these predictable/unpredictable forces with confidence, imagination, and dignity.

You *can* play the game against He/She/Them with great wit and gusto, but don't get too arrogantly smarty-pants. The House *always* wins.

Never forget the name of Snoopy's theology book: *Has It Ever Occurred to You That You Might Be Wrong?* And remember the quote attributed to both Abraham Lincoln and Mark Twain: "Better to remain silent and be thought a fool than to speak out and remove all doubt." Barring those, remember O'Malley's Law: "The less you know, the more certain you can be."

Into the backpack you carry away from college, be sure to include words and phrases such as *maybe, perhaps, apparently, as far as I know..., the evidence seems to suggest..., I may be overstating more than I'd like to....* Almost surely, the majority of listeners will be ill prepared to admire your caution, but smart people *will* appreciate it—*and* you.

If you want to lessen the times you might be rightly judged as arrogantly dumb as Oedipus and Jocasta, make one more resolution: once a week (at least) take a half-hour walk alone and ponder the rock-bottom realities of who you are and where you fit in. You'll *never* regret it.

You're a human being, which, through no merit or achievement of your own, endows you with gifts no other creature we know of possesses. You have the capacity to learn, to love, to understand, and to empathize. *You* are capable of joy, peace, patience, kindness, generosity, fidelity, gentleness, and self-control, all of which elude the cleverest dolphin. Those strictly human qualities also elude inadequately evolved narcissists like Jocasta and Oedipus, Hamlet and Faust, Stalin and Hitler. Before your education was debased into mere job certification, it was intended to make sure those qualities don't escape you, too.

At the same time that your weekly soul check-up reminds you of your priceless value, however, make sure you (again) understand that the opposite is also true: everybody's important, nobody's essential.

See your unarguably empowered self located at the center of a web of real relationships radiating out and away from you: first, into the intense enrichment from a spouse, then a family, out further into your workplace, your neighborhood, and your city. In your imagination, project your soul energies out even further to your whole nation, to the huge hemisphere of this enormous planet, Earth. Then, let your awareness rocket outward, first, the mere four-and-a-half light years to our nearest earth-like neighbor, Alpha Centauri—actually 80,000 years' travel for our kind of lives—a briefer trip at the speed of light.

To get an even more realistic awareness of where you fit in, keep going across the expanse of the Milky Way Galaxy, 100,000 to 120,000 light-years in diameter. Then, travel further. Our galaxy is only one of what could be 500 billion galaxies. That's 1,000,000,000,000,000,000,000 x 500,000,000,000 km. And now experts even smarter than Oedipus, like Stephen Hawking, are postulating that our whole universe may be *one* of an *infinite series* of universes.*

Strain your eyes to see how much space—and importance—you have in that matrix. You're important, in a different kind of way from any rock or apple or bear *can* be. But the rock will last *much* longer than you will and a single meteoroid has more power than you'll ever have, *unless* you are in fact immortal. But that's a topic for an entirely different book!

Nevertheless, it's good to be aware of those undeniable objective facts when you evaluate your Grade Point Average, your popularity, and your bank balance. Against that unthinkably huge background, what you hold of desperate importance is actually quite dismissible, because our comeuppance is Death—and there are no U-Hauls hitched to hearses.

Awareness of your true matrix has a humbling effect, which is, of course, what the ancient Greeks insisted was the first baby step in the direction of human wisdom. It would be a heartbreaking shame if you spent so much time, money, and effort in college and missed that.

Some of the areas of instruction you find really valuable if your only interest is making a living may seem much less essential when you want to discover what human living is *for*.

Useless, that is to say, so-called unmarketable skills, like geography, cosmology, and astronomy put you in your place, which can be discomfiting. The courses often derided as air courses, like philosophy, theology, anthropology, history, art and music, and theater can be bewildering—almost always because the soul and mind of the recipient aren't large and sensitive enough to appreciate and encompass them. Honestly, I know of no one who has suggestions on how to animate a soul that's gotten as far as college age and never been ignited earlier. Confronting personal tragedy can do it, but that's hardly anything an educational institution could take upon itself to precipitate.

---

*See "The Known Universe," http://on.fb.me/1rX2TPi.

A narcissistic society that makes witnessing unreal death so commonplace and encountering genuine death so rare, as the King says in *The King and I*, "Is a puzzlement."

PERSONAL REFLECTION

Many beneficiaries of Twelve-Step Programs have difficulties admitting a deity or deny God completely, but they do yield to "a higher power." That could mean just "my gut instinct" or the example of others in the program. It could be what this chapter has described as the overall environment of any human's situation whose laws we must respect or pay the price.

No matter what your position about God, how do you personally react to the attitude toward human living manifest in the Reinhold Niebuhr prayer espoused by all such transformational programs?

> Grant me the *serenity* to accept the things that can't be changed,
> the *courage* to change the things that can be changed,
> and the *wisdom* to know the difference.

Do you find those three attitudes not only essential but also personally desirable?

14.

FREEDOM

If you want total security, go to prison. There you're fed, clothed, given medical care and so on. The only thing lacking...is freedom.
—*Dwight D. Eisenhower*

Consider the following ten statements and whether you agree or disagree.

1. Freedom exists only at the moment you give it up.
2. You can't make anyone love you more than he or she is able.
3. Those who form a personal ethical code are seriously limiting themselves.
4. Children who reject family conformity almost always embrace peer/media conformity.
5. Adolescents are eager to be free of parents' rules but not their savings.
6. To be genuinely free, you must first discover and honestly evaluate all the options.
7. You will never be completely free of your DNA, your parentage, or your past mistakes.
8. Nothing ventured, nothing gained.
9. There's a big difference between freedom *from* and freedom *to*.
10. Your freedom to swing your fist ends at the tip of my chin.

Freedom is a reality riddled with ironies and paradox. First, you can define *freedom*—which is very positive—only by negatives: not bound, not coerced, unrestricted. Second, freedom works only when you stop having it. When you stand in front of five doors and choose one, in that very act you deny your freedom to take the other four—at least for now. Third, freedom costs. It takes the effort to find what all your options actually *are*. You're not free to take a road you don't know about, and that takes time, patience, and effort. Then, to use the freedom, you have to commit yourself to that one to discover if it is, in fact, the right one.

Freedom's like money in your pocket. It's nice to know you have it, but it has no practical value until you give it up for something you want more than you want the freedom.

Most irritatingly, there's a big difference between freedom *from* and freedom *to*; between being unrestricted by outside pressure and actual freedom to act. It is like standing at the lip of a cold swimming pool. No one's pushing you, but you stand there: "One...two...here I come! Really? 59! 263! Here I come...!" Imagine yourself in your room studying for a chemistry test the next day. All your friends have a free morning, and you hear them jostling outside. Are you free, truly free to stay at the hateful desk? Or try this: The sexiest person you've ever beheld cozies up to you late in the evening and invites you to his/her room. Are you free to say, "I'm really flattered, but I'd only be using you as a sex object"? Are you free? Or are you a slave?

The media hype and the "Bachelorette" culture lead us to believe that we can be completely free. Not true at all! You'll never be free of the law of gravity, your DNA, the toxicity of cyanide, fire burns, rape degrades, the fact that dropped objects fall, and all of us will die. These are not opinions; they are facts. You'll never be free of the fact that the more intimate a relationship gets, the more human beings lay claims on one another, take risks, and get hurt. Not an opinion; a fact! You're free to divorce, but you'll never rid yourself of those shared years or responsibilities for your kids. You can never be free of the people you love. When they're suffering, you can't ignore them. Not an opinion; a fact!

Those actors on competitive reality shows seem to have limitless freedom. It's faked and a self-deception. They're actually abject *slaves* of their *own* hormones.

If you delude yourself that you can be totally free, you need no enemies. You're free to do *anything* you wish—within limits. You're free to jump off the Empire State Building, but only once. You're free to withdraw into lonely isolation, which negates all unpleasant (and pleasant) realities; free to blow the planet to smithereens; free to riddle a grade-school cafeteria with rifle fire. But you and anyone else involved are not free of the *consequences*.

Nor are you free of your own past. First, there are the cards you got dealt: family, economic bracket, DNA, neighbors, media values, as well as the way you've played those cards so far. Nor are you free of the society that helped socialize you—its relativism, subjectivism, materialism, and callousness. You'd have been a totally different you in ancient Rome or Nazi Germany.

Furthermore, unless you have the courage to be a hermit, your ideas and preferences are going to collide with other people's values and agendas. You're free to dress freaky if you don't mind being sneered at and ostracized. You're free to have wanton sex on your front lawn—for a time. You're free to demand your own way all the time—just get used to the silence and loneliness.

Finally, all the frustrating forces aren't outside you. There are other forces at least as vigorous inside: narcissism, inertia, and fear. Like reality show zombies, you can't even be free of your own moods and hormones—*unless* you make the considerable effort of will to master them, domesticate the inner Beast, the way the third little pig boiled the wolf and ate him, and co-opted its power.

Independence is something slightly different from freedom. Independence means you can stand on your own two feet. You don't need crutches like booze and dope. You don't even need the crutch of your peers' approval. And your parents have been working on you since you first breathed to become independent of them. You can stand alone confidently only if you have formed a personally validated character: an ego, a conscience, a soul.

PERSONAL REFLECTION

For you, personally, is the need to belong and to be accepted simply too strong to allow you to make choices with genuine freedom, and limited only by the objective truth about the *better* choice? What are the concrete, specific *external* influences on your true freedom—other people, other irresistible values and experiences? What are the *internal* forces that hamper your impartiality in choosing the best alternative—moods, undisciplined urges, biases, procrastination, inertia, and a narrow selfish focus? Be honest. You're talking to yourself.

15.

GRATITUDE

> Gratitude is not only the greatest of virtues,
> but the parent of all others.
> —*Marcus Tullius Cicero*

Consider the following ten statements and whether you agree or disagree.

1. No one is "self-made."
2. If anyone is honestly grateful, it should be visible in his or her life.
3. When you *make* good, something good inside you wants to *do* good.
4. The only good purpose in guilt is when it turns into responsibility.
5. What you do shouts so loudly no one can hear what you claim.
6. If your mother asks you to do something reasonable and you refuse, you've shown who you *really* are.
7. If teachers are constantly unprepared, they should be dismissed.
8. If students are constantly unprepared, they should be expelled.
9. Most of us take our giftedness for granted.
10. Don't complain about what you don't have till you've said thanks for what you do.

NOBLESSE OBLIGE

"Nobility Obligates"—being privileged imposes responsibilities. If you're lucky to have a car, even if you paid for it yourself, you have an obligation to treat it well and handle it responsibly. If you've been given life, and a life more privileged than most others on earth, honor should impose some owner's obligations. Those who by sheer luck are born into noble good fortune ought to act *nobly*. Those who have been *graced* should be grateful and *graceful*.

To understand what acting nobly means and what it takes to achieve it, you could consult a dictionary or an encyclopedia. Beyond the once-dominant (and subjective) restriction to those born of noble blood (as if there were such a thing), dictionaries offer such definitions as "Having or showing fine personal qualities or high moral principles and ideals, the promotion of human rights" and gives synonyms such as "worthy, decent, righteous, virtuous, honorable, upright, ethical, and reputable,"* which are as unhelpful as their definitions for *love*.

Alternatively, ponder the folks you've encountered in history or literature whom you immediately *feel* embody nobility, like Nelson Mandela and Jimmy Carter, where others clearly don't, like Nero and Darth Vader. Those who show us what nobility entails are those who seem to have worked their way up into those two highest-stage Kohlberg motivations.

The best definition might be "magnanimous"—*magna + anima*, "large soul." It means someone whose self is roomy, open, welcoming, non-judgmental, readily forgiving, and respectful of human dignity—*anywhere*.

What attitudes and actions come to mind when you think of Socrates, Jesus, Buddha, and Muhammed? What about Washington, Jefferson, Lincoln, Sojourner Truth, Oscar Schindler, Mother Teresa, and Martin Luther King Jr.? Warren Buffet and Bill Gates acquired multibillions with brains, hard work, and luck, but now they feel impelled to give back at least half of all their wealth to the society that enabled them to

---

*See Oxford Dictionaries Online, s. v. "noble," http://www.oxforddictionaries. com/us/definition/american_english/noble.

---

acquire it. Oprah Winfrey came from a dirt-poor pig farm in Mississippi to become arguably the most powerful woman on earth, and yet she seems to want to spend whatever life she has left helping the lives of those that life left out.

From literature, there is Antigone who defied the king to bury her brother and release his soul. Psyche, an adored, spoiled girl, rose to all challenges her peevish mother-in-law, Aphrodite, set her, using no more than her wits and her guts. Bishop Bienvenu in *Les Miserables* gave Jean Valjean not only the silverware he stole but two silver candlesticks to boot. Thomas More in *A Man for All Seasons* and John Proctor in *The Crucible* each went to his death rather than sign his name to a false confession—merely configurations of ink on a parchment. But it was their name, their word. Surely, Atticus Finch was noble: steady, wise, down to earth, willing to stand alone, a man of privilege among the downtrodden.

The very best source of intuition into what nobility means is to reflect awhile on the men and women you've known yourself—what human nobility meant to them, how it showed concretely in their everyday action and choices. But that can wait till the reflection.

A CONVICTION OF GIFTEDNESS

The trouble is that very few Americans consider themselves privileged. And yet, even those on third-generation welfare are, literally, materially better off than *most* other people on this planet. The reason is that the *dramatically* privileged in our society are so dazzlingly well off that it makes even those who are doing quite well look close to poor. Yet, if you have a stereo and TV, you have access to instant amusement no maharajah ever had. If you have spare change clinking in your pockets, you're the envy of most of the world.

You may be familiar with the following list that clarifies that giftedness by imagining the seven billion earthlings being reduced to one hundred:

–seven with a college degree
–twenty own 75 percent of all income
–forty live on two dollars a day
–sixteen are completely illiterate
–seventy are unable to read
–twenty-four have electricity
–twenty-three are without shelter
–thirteen are without clean water
–thirty are without waste disposal
–fifty are malnourished
–sixty are Asians
–seventy-five are non-white
–sixty-seven are non-Christian
–one is Jewish
–three are atheists

If you have a refrigerator with food in it, a closet with clothes in it, a bed, and a roof over your head, you're richer than 75 percent of the other people on earth. Daily, thirty-two thousand children die of hunger or curable diseases. Half a million children go blind each year for lack of vitamin A that costs two cents a tablet. A child dies of malaria every sixty seconds.

It's not your fault! You did nothing to be blamed for being lucky, nor anything to *deserve* it. Luck! Exactly like being born into the family of an archduke rather than, by chance, to a swineherd.

RESPONSIBILITY

You are not responsible for anyone else on earth having less than you do. However, now that your schooling has intruded on your comfort, you have *ipso facto* become responsible for what you *do* about that inequity—provided you want to be an adult with a right to feel good about yourself. But gratitude is impossible when you feel you *deserve* to be here, or that somehow the good luck of having these parents *entitled* you to more than the basics. Gratitude shows itself not in guilt but in responsibility.

The imbalance would not be rectified if all of us sold all that we have and gave it to the poor. Doing that would only increase the number of poor people in the global village. Nor will you personally—or all of us together—*ever* end the nearly bottomless sea of human suffering. God or not, coping with shortage now seems to be part of the cost of occupancy on Planet Earth that no one faced before. Trying to eliminate, or even significantly diminish, all human suffering is as futile and frustrating as trying to empty the Atlantic with a colander.

The best a person of honor can do to show gratitude for such staggering blessings is to choose *one* cause and do whatever you *reasonably* can, while still being responsible for the elements of the human web closest to you. In fourteen billion years, not even God has cured it all!

Year after year, social studies teachers offer at least a class or two on world hunger, infant mortality rates, life expectancy, and average income. Public service ads plea for donations by reminding us of bloat-bellied babies in Africa, bewildered refugee mothers, and flies drinking the tears of saucer-eyed infants. They're playing on your decency, your sense of guilt/responsibility. But if you don't have any significant money, you can't help much. However, if you deprive yourself of just one small purchase of an album on Amazon, it opens your perspective to realize that six months of pills against blindness cost the agency, Vitamin Angels, just twenty-five cents to rescue one child for one year. Hey! I'm *not* nobody!

No matter how little or how much you can give, your contribution will not significantly stem the tide of human suffering. However, it will almost certainly make a huge change in you— and yet these changes are just the result of the dramatic, vast, overwhelming evidences of human need.

Most of us look around at a group like a class and rarely focus on the people who are dressed more poorly than we are, have more blemished skin, are shy, overweight, and homely. They're not half-a-world away. You can light up their darkness at least for a moment with a gift as inexpensive as a smile and saying hi, which, at times, is harder to give up than money! It costs taking hold of your *self* and asserting your confidence in your *own* value.

Almost all the students I've had in a half-century seem to assume that their parents *had* to have them. No! They could have saved the quarter million and had a nice place at the lake instead. In the process, they could also have avoided learning diaper skills; walking you while you were teething; attending your plays, games, and recitals; enduring pointless arguments; and still loving you. And they do all that knowing—hoping—you'll come to them someday and say, "I've found someone I love more than I love you." Or, at least in a much different way, say, "Bye!"

How can you ever pay that back? You can't. And, amazingly, they don't even expect it!

What you can do—which is all that most parents really expect—is to make an honorable you.

As an integral part of forming that *you*, if either of those two people asks anything reasonable of you, you by God *do* it. There should be absolutely no question or hesitation about that. And you give them *better* than just a dutiful day's work for a more-than-adequate day's pay—not guilt, gratitude; not obligation, honor; and not duty, but love.

PERSONAL REFLECTION

Pick out four or five men and women you believe are fulfilled human beings, exemplary not for their bodily or mental skills or for their wealth, but for *showing* you what a praiseworthy human being looks and acts like. Sketch for yourself *concrete moments* you caught them being undramatically noble and self-forgetful. What do you suspect went into forming a character like that, someone who, more or less unconsciously, does the right thing simply as a matter of course? Don't rush your response. You're teaching yourself the self you want to be.

16.

RESPECT

> Without feelings of respect, what is there to distinguish men from beasts?
>
> —*Confucius*

Consider the following ten statements. Do you agree or disagree?

1. If you refuse to mind your own business, you have a more interesting life.
2. If you want to be useful, you have to be used.
3. Using racial or ethnic slurs is really a minor, careless bad habit.
4. In contrast to rocks, vegetables, and other animals, every human being is sacred.
5. It is not enough for a genuine human to say, "I take care of my own."
6. Concern for others completely unlike us seems to be a humans-only trait.
7. The Golden Rule isn't a matter of religion but of human survival.
8. Having at least one sibling is worth it in the long run.
9. Every other human I encounter is, inside, a "me."
10. I am human. Nothing human is foreign to me.

Some years ago, I read a news story about a fifteen-year-old boy arrested for the brutal murder of an old woman over thirty dollars. They asked if he felt any remorse. He was confused. "Why should I?" he said, "She's not me."

Brutal as it sounds, anyone who reads the papers knows that attitude isn't unique. How could any human have even the vaguest *sense of others* as equally human, and yet spray bullets randomly around a cafeteria or from the window of a car? How could anyone sharing the same invitation beyond other beasts strangle her own child and toss it into a dumpster? Could any civilized person drop megatons of explosives on a city knowing that most of the people below are surely noncombatants: children, nurses, nuns, judges, dancers, secretaries—not a single one personally responsible for any attack their leaders may have caused? All of those inhumanities seem to occur more than several times every day.

The primary task of parents and teachers—far more fundamental than making a living—is to civilize the self-absorbed Beast in their young, what Freudians call the id. They have not only to impose limits on kids' rambunctiousness, but also try to find ways to convince them to interiorize self-control on their own behavior, even when no authority will know or impose sanctions. Part of that instruction has always tried to stretch that awareness and concern *beyond* the self and the nuclear family to those nearby, in the neighborhood, work, and city. Less successfully and less often, some instructors try to expand awareness and concern to the whole human family and beyond that to a principled human life.

We find little basis for even minimal respect for others unlike us in the biological world from which we evolved. One life form preserves itself by destroying others. You may have seen the cartoon of the series of fish, each larger and with more impressive teeth than the one immediately ahead of it. It's become a cliche for the corporate jungle of monopoly capitalism: "Eat or be eaten." It's called "Social Darwinism." The jaguar stalks the gazelle and the wolf fells the lamb. Even the perky robin hauls the hapless worm up in its beak, as indifferent as that boy who murdered the old woman. The game of Monopoly begins as a perfect communism. Within a half hour, it's dog-eat-dog capitalism.

Two counterforces to successful humanization (morality) in more recent society should give us serious pause. One is what seems a general tolerance of inhumanity as insensitive (in a very genteel, well-mannered way) as the acceptance of blood violence in the Roman arena. By the time any normal child hits kindergarten, he or she has become accustomed to more gore than a barbarian rampaging across Europe fifteen hundred years ago. Granted, the blood is just corn syrup and red dye, and both the killers and the dead collect their pay and go home from the film studio at night, but there's nothing novel now for a child to see blood gush into the lens when someone's head has been transfixed by a broadsword. It's become commonplace, as negligible and undisturbing as sirens and graffiti.

The more disposable income you and your parents have, the more refined (if that word is appropriate) your experience of sadistic mayhem can be, branching out into video games at home (if you're well-to-do) or in game parlors (if you're not). Dehumanizing is an eighty billion dollar business, just in the games realm. That doesn't count gory action movies that, if they make less than a billion each, are limp losers. In many games, children routinely eliminate humans or humanoids and giggle as their tallies—"carnage factor"—mount up.

As those fathers told me when I called because their daughters had left the play cast after giving me their word, "Look, you gotta cut these kids some slack. They're only young once!" But how long does that last? Isn't it curable? Shouldn't it be challenged rather than approved?

The other counter-force emerging only very recently is the wrongful and devastating parental equating of "respect" for their children with "admiration" or "honor," no matter what the child does. It's the warped practice that demands everybody in the race gets a medal. That's quite justifiable in a Special Olympics race, where the participants are so impaired they deserve praise just for trying. But it ill serves children privileged with healthy bodies to be praised for doing what's legitimately expected of them, like being paid for merely passing a test or taking out the trash. The same is true for graduating simply on the basis of not having dropped out. That undeserved praise is an automatic affront to those who tried.

"Respect" is what anyone, who is human objectively, internally, worthier of deference than a dog or a daisy or dirt, deserves. As Kant pointed out, each other rational person is an autonomous self, an end-in-itself, and cannot rightly be used as a mere means. Basic respect is *owed* to other people not because of their pigmentation, their academic degrees, their purchasing power, or their armaments, but for something far more fundamental: their humanity.

Basic respect—independently of accomplishments— demands acceptance of the other's right to make choices, express opinions, and take justified actions; immunity from willful harm; and equitable treatment of the other as worthy of life, liberty, food, clothing, and shelter. *Honoring* means not praising but accepting them as unquestionably valid, as one honors a treaty.

That respect can *increase* in intensity because of the way individuals handle the invitation to improve on that basic endowment. Only then does the individual *deserve* greater admiration and praise. To accustom children to praise for attributes they did nothing whatever to merit habituates them to a wicked perversion of real life. Entitlement is a sure trigger for narcissism.

A sense of fairness and tolerance for others—respect— depends on a child's understanding and acceptance that the other person, child or adult, is a *fellow*, who fears the same things, longs for the same things, and is hurt by the same things. Kids can accept that they have to take turns, but they submit to that in the same uncomprehending way a puppy learns not to wet the rug or a child accepts that it's okay to bite the breadstick but not the cat's tail. But ever so gradually, obedience should evolve into genuine *felt* respect: "getting into the other's skin and walking around in it." The Latin root of the word *respect* is *respicere*, "to really *look* at."

Praise is reserved for the *exemplary*. An infant *deserves* a parent's enthusiastic "oohs" and "ahs" for taking those first few steps he or she has never accomplished before. But after a few years, they deserve no congratulations for getting up in the morning or for giving an honest day's work for an honest day's pay. If they expect admiration or even thanks just for being decent human beings, they'll live godawful thankless lives, and they'll take out their frustration on others in small ways or fatal ways!

Praise becomes valid when the recipient deserves it for acting "above and beyond" the call of ordinary human expectations. None of us needs to be taught to feel we deserve a bit of a thank-you for being more than usually thoughtful, for doing the job *before* being asked, for putting in more effort than usual, even when the effects were no better. Just don't *count* on it.

Think about those times. Well, just as *you* hope for praise for a job more than usually well done, so does your mom, as do even your intrusive and heartless siblings!

The very first requirement is *looking* at others with the same attentiveness as when you look in a mirror, especially the ones you're too used to: as they really are, worthy of attention and respect. Then, you need the skills mothers seem to have as a job requirement: hypersensitive antennae to read moods and needs when the other person can't yet verbalize them. Then, respect can bust open into empathy, and even kindness: "Hey, what's wrong? Let me help."

Herewith, I pose the acid test, which might burn a bit: When was the last time you said to your mother, "Mom, you look beat. Why don't you sit down and put your feet up, and let me finish that?" Ouch! How else will you learn the skills to notice your spouse, your kids—if you've yet to develop them for the person who loved you nine months before she saw your face?

PERSONAL REFLECTION

Hopefully, this course is helping you to elevate your awareness of the *sacredness* of human beings—not excluding yourself. Its hope is that respect and the concrete ways you express it will spread from self-respect to each of the members of your family, your habitual friends, your workmates, and fellow students. So far, that proposal is relatively threat-free, but reflect on how much further out into the web of human relationships you're *willing* to venture now. This isn't asking a commitment; just exploring possible areas of enrichment.

Is there some concrete way you could widen and enrich your *self* by reaching further? Of course there's a risk, but is it worth it? Has it been worth it in the past?

17.

EMPATHY

Pity may represent little more than the impersonal concern that prompts the mailing of a
check, but true sympathy is the personal concern which demands the giving of one's soul.
—*Rev. Martin Luther King Jr.*

Consider the following ten statements and whether or not you agree or disagree.

1. People who have suffered are the only ones with good stories to tell. They're interesting.
2. The only legitimate emotion allowed to real men is anger.
3. Locking oneself inside an iPod blocks out most of life.
4. Most often, when you trust others, they'll reward your trust.
5. Better a live slave than a dead hero or heroine.
6. People who beg on the street brought their situation on themselves.
7. As soon as you begin to compromise, you start to lose.
8. *Empathy, sympathy, compassion* are all "victim" words.
9. Experience without reflection is what happens to lab animals.
10. You can't crusade for all causes, but a person of character has to choose one.

KINSHIP

Every year when we discuss family, I show Robert Redford's film *Ordinary People*. Although I have now seen it many times, the ending after the son has finally been able to tell his father he loves him and the father has told him he loves him, too, brings tears to my eyes. One time, I mentioned that to a class of all boys, and a few of them went, "*Aww!*" Apparently, to feel deeply for strangers is very uncool.

I said, "You guys really *scare* me!" They sobered up very quickly. "Are your defenses *so* strong you can't allow yourself at least a bit of fellow-feeling for a man and boy, whose wife and mother just walked out on them, who just cling together in shared pain?"

One sneered, "Well, you can feel sorry for somebody without breaking down into *sobs!*"

He had to exaggerate my reaction into something absurd so *he* wouldn't seem so callous. Remember me as an eight-year-old, incapable of accepting that I'd lied to my dad. This guy was well on his way to being an accomplished narcissist.

I said, "How the hell are you ever going to share your wife's pregnancy or your children's confusions about being acceptable? When will you allow your human vulnerability to click on inside those macho Teenage Mutant Ninja Turtle shells?"

A larger question: Was the Teflon coating over those few boys' souls just part of a more *universal* modern psychological deadening, the general defensiveness that's almost essential today, at least in overcrowded, noisy, dangerous cities? People cocoon themselves inside cellphones to block out the chaos, walk corridors and sidewalks guarded by invisible blinders, focused on the elevator numbers to keep from intruders on my defenses? If you let in all the stimuli, you'll blow your mental circuits.

The general soul-numbing is understandable, for those who aren't weak enough to succumb to *real* drugs. Of course, if what makes humans different is the potential to know and love, it's humanly impoverishing. At the core of *Ordinary People* is the need of the mother, Beth, and the son, Conrad, to have control.

The elder brother, Buck, died in a boating accident and Beth and Conrad were the only ones who couldn't allow themselves to cry at his funeral. But Dr. Burger, the psychiatrist who finally chips away Conrad's defenses says, "If you can't feel pain...you won't feel anything else either."

That's why those macho boys scared me.

The survey statement is true: "*Empathy, sympathy, compassion* are all 'victim' words." Each one means "to *suffer with*." Typically, in my experience, those twentieth-century American boys were not *about* to take even the slightest risk of being victims. How will they ever learn to yield to the needs of those they love? Is that why half of all marriages now end in divorce? Does refusal of commitment to others begin *that* early?

Empathy is a reality inside a person that *resonates* with the anguish inside another human being, *identifies* with it. As the quotation from Martin Luther King Jr. at the opening of this chapter makes clear, compassion goes beyond pity, more than "feeling sorry for," which smacks of remoteness, only slightly warmer than indifference. Empathy presumes respect and goes further; it ups involvement beyond tolerance to engagement, even if limited. Respect is one step toward justice; empathy is one step toward love.

All of us like to believe we want to love and be loved. But so many people's defensive habits tempt me to believe they're lying to themselves, about themselves, and believing the lies. They just like saying it, but they're afraid of the cost of leaving themselves open to it. There is little chance that a person will love and be loved, at least to any extent, if they guard themselves from even *noticing* other people, distracted inside their phones, scuttling from class to class, eyes focused on the walkway, and going an entire semester not even knowing the names of the people on either side of them. That's Disney fairytale reality, where Prince Charming swoops out of nowhere on his white stallion and carries the misunderstood princess off to her wondrous castle. Good luck!

We can also be stingy with our limitless potential to love, restricting it in a very unloving way to a narrow, isolated group, which is also self-impoverishing. Nine times out of ten, when you offer someone your trust, that person will honor and reward your trust. The same happens when you offer empathy for someone's suffering. It enriches not only the receiver but the giver. Surely, one time out of ten you'll get scorched. We all have the scars to prove that. But to avoid that one loss, we willingly lose nine friends. That's even bad social Darwinism!

Novels, plays, and films can help evolve empathetic powers, if you're not too defensive against them. (Psst! That's why teachers have forced you to face those challenges all these years!) *The Elephant Man*, *The Color Purple*, *Death of a Salesman*, *Our Town*, *Forrest Gump*, *The Lion King*, *Shawshank Redemption*, *The Crucible*, *Billy Elliot*, *Schindler's List*, and *Paths of Glory*—the reason to rent and watch them is to feel your soul stir into life; to *feel* human.

Finally, empathy helps develop the very humanizing virtue of *forgiveness*. If anyone has had pesky, intrusive siblings, it's easy to fly off the handle at them. Try to remember what it was like at their age, confused, feeling left out of conversations, not quite able to understand—in fact, lacking precisely the virtue we're exploring here: empathy. One day, you'll likely be a parent yourself. Where do you find lessons to prepare a parent? Right here. Today.

Many sneer that empathy is a "sucker virtue"—and it surely is. However, all of us want our lives to be in some way useful, and yet, to be useful, we have to be used.

PERSONAL REFLECTION

This reflection is harder than you may at first realize. I've rarely had anyone answer it well.

Think of someone you can't stand, the very thought of whom makes you wince. That's the easy part.

Now, close your eyes and imagine it's full-moon time and, like Wolfman or somebody on *Twilight*, you're slowly, slowly transforming into that person. Like an actor preparing to inhabit a role, you're getting ready to get into that person's skin and walk around in it awhile.

Feel your facial structure ease around into his or her face, eyes, skin, and hair. Your body's elongating/shrinking/metamorphosing into that person's body. Feel what it's like inside there. Feel the heart quietly pumping, the muscle tensions.

Now, here it gets really difficult. Roam the innermost pathways of that person's feelings, attitudes to friends, family, you. What do you imagine would really hurt him/her most? What would give him/her an honest thrill? Don't oversimplify. How does it feel?

Now, here's the challenge. Picture that person in a communal situation you share—class, work, practice. Write down what it feels like, *inside*, being there with the others, guessing what they think of you.

This test is far more important than the SAT, the NMSQT, or the ACT.

18.

KINDNESS

"Hello babies. Welcome to Earth. It's hot in the summer and cold in the winter. It's round and wet and crowded. On the outside, babies, you've got a hundred years here. There's only one rule that I know of, babies—'God damn it, you've got to be kind.'"

—*Kurt Vonnegut Jr.*

Consider the following ten statements. Do you agree or disagree?

1. The fortunate and prosperous need people to whom to be kind.
2. By their very nature, boys are more aggressive and analytical, and girls are more intuitive and generous.
3. When a friend is hurting, sometimes touch is the only way to ease their pain.
4. Empathy makes your heart reach out. Kindness uses your hands.
5. Sexual stereotypes are cruel and impoverishing to both victim and perpetrator.
6. We have an enormous inner power to exhilarate others' spirits or stifle them.
7. Any male who can't say "I love him" about his best friend is emotionally crippled.
8. If you never let yourself be "taken in," you'll never see the inside of anything.

9. When you say, "Drop dead," aren't you glad you're not God?
10. Friendship means more than just being there. It means "being there alert."

During the first week of September 1997, everyone's life overflowed with pictures of two almost totally dissimilar women who had died that very same week: one, as beautiful as a young Greek goddess; the other, as wrinkled as a crone from a children's story book. Princess Diana of Wales was stunningly beautiful, regal, and radiant, even with her arms wrapped comfortably around a little Bosnian girl whose legs had been blown off by a land mine or cradling a dark baby gazing up at her flawless white face. The other was a tiny old nun, Mother Teresa of Calcutta, wrinkled as a walnut but exuding serenity, doing essentially the same things—cuddling infants, consoling lepers, and easing the final journey of the dying.

One was youthful and satin-skinned, schooled to privilege; the other was as leathery as a purse and vowed to poverty. Yet, each shared that same physical and psychological ease with broken bodies and spirits, and they couldn't restrain themselves from showing it. I found myself saying, "What a wonderful, almost tangible *aura* unaffected kindness ignites in a face."

Charity and courtesy can be faked; kindness can't be. Witness the contrast between idly (or grimly) dropping a coin in a beggar's cup and the ease of a mother's wiping the drool from her baby's chin. You experienced it (but almost surely have forgotten it) in the best grade-school teachers. It's second nature with the best nurses. That kindness is there in many males, too, but it seems almost that it has to be disguised in razzing and roughhouse. Kindness is sissy.

That confusion of sex (male/female, either/or, physical fact) with gender (masculine/feminine, more/less, psychological approximation) has caused more suffering than it ever had to. But you'll never go broke betting on dumb. Both Jennifer Anniston and Angelina Jolie have been paired with ultravirile Brad Pitt, but Angelina is more likely to play a kickass adventurer-Egyptologist and Jennifer to play kitten-cute prom queens.

Tom Hanks and Mark Wahlberg are both males and fathers, but Hanks plays persons of fragile sensitivity and Wahlberg (apparently contrary to the kind of man he really is), plays men who chew up crowbars and spit out nails.

The stereotypes are foolish. Some of the world's most successful rulers have been female (Elizabeth I, Indira Gandhi, Margaret Thatcher), while nearly all the world's best known artists, musicians, and cooks have been males. But stereotypes are also hard to uproot and are also impoverishing. With no formal teaching involved, they make too many girls hesitant to speak up and assert themselves, and too many boys say, "Aww!" at any expression of vulnerability. There are males who fear that if they show kindness to an outcast, their pals might call them "gay." Who in heaven's name would worry about the opinions of Neanderthals? Most of us.

I got a late lesson in human behavior in my senior year at high school. I share the story with every class I have, and they slurp it up, relishing every humiliating detail.

I returned home one day, and my mother informed me I was escorting (call her) Sylvie Smith to her senior prom. Sylvie lived only two blocks away; I'd gone to grade school with her. She was as pale as a peeled potato, had frizzy red hair, and wore granny glasses. There was not a bump on her I could discern. So of course I informed my mother in turn that I most certainly would *not* squire Sylvie to her prom.

Back Story: My mother was a woman of the assertive school that trained Medea, Lady Macbeth, and Ellen Ripley. One week, my piano teacher shifted my lesson from Wednesday to Saturday, when every kid in town went to the kids' matinee (two films, two serials, cartoons) and for only fourteen cents (seven coke bottles found along any road). It goes without saying where I betook myself. Suddenly, from the back of the darkened theater where I was with about five hundred other kids, I hear a voice remarkably like my mother's, yelling: "Where are you, Bill O'Malley? I know you're there!" Then, muttering about the cost of the lessons, she strode down the aisle and bumped her way across the row, grabbed me by the ear, and dragged me off to the lesson.

Thus, it goes without saying that I did, indeed, take Sylvie to her prom.

By now, my students are hooting!

It got worse, much worse. I didn't have my night license. So my dad had to drive us. We got there on *time*! So we were desolately alone! I tried every conversational ploy imaginable, including the causes of World War I. Nothing but muffled "Uhs." Then my pals started arriving with their drop-dead, witty, sharp-edged dates. Elbowing one another and jerking their heads at *us*. Besides that, I am, or was, one world-class dancer. Not so, alas, Sylvie. The shine was off my shoes in ten minutes. So, about 11:30, I said, "Well, it's getting late." So, I called my dad, and he picked us up, and we took her home.

The students, boys and girls, are now rolling in the aisles. Then I say, very, very quietly, "What a selfish son of a bitch I was."

Dead silence. Suddenly, they *feel* the meanness. They understand.

It was, almost surely, her first date, her first formal dress, her first night out from her very rigid family. And for three hours, I had thought of *nothing* but myself.

The class is really with me right then, because they've been there before—many of them at one time or other on *each* side of the insensitivity, the flint-heartedness and unkindness.

"What would happen," I ask, "if you went up to somebody unattractive at a dance and invited that person to dance? How much of your busy life would it take?"

After all these years, I can write the script before they even respond: "They'd think it was a trick...that it was condescending....They'd become a leech on the phone all the time." All of which misses the whole point, because the spotlight is still clamped firmly on themselves. For a few minutes, you'd have made somebody *happy*, and in the process, proven yourself valuable.

Are there no times in your life that you don't subject to a cost/benefit analysis? "There's only one rule that I know of, babies—'God damn it, you've got to be kind.'"

PERSONAL REFLECTION

Think of someone earlier in your life who unself-consciously gave you a gift of kindness—the person who taught you to read, whoever it was who cracked open algebra, the grade-school teacher who held your forehead while you threw up. Maybe the person who taught you to dance.

Write that person a note, trying to capture what that kindness—that kind person—meant to you. Make a good copy. Put it in an envelope and send it. It is only the cost of a stamp!

19.

RESPONSIBILITY

> Don't find fault, find a remedy.
>
> —*Henry Ford*

Consider the following ten statements. Do you agree or disagree?

1. Someone who makes the mistake of getting drunk is responsible only for that.
2. There's no such thing as an unjust profit. If they'll pay, it's okay.
3. The only ground for moral choices should be the well-being of one's self and family.
4. Writing a letter to a newspaper or a legislator is a waste of a stamp.
5. Commitment to principles sharply limits your freedom. (Think carefully on this one.)
6. Pleading victimization, for example, asking for an extension or make-up work, is almost always a declaration of flimsy character—a request from a child in an adult body.
7. The highest form of freedom comes with the greatest measure of discipline.
8. Many blame their faults on their personalities rather than blaming their personalities for their faults.
9. If not me, who? If not now, when?
10. Any growth as a human being is going to cost.

REFUSING TO BE A NOBODY

Consider some of the worthy figures who have been or are exemplary in embodying the qualities that specify our common human nature: knowing, loving, growing more profoundly understanding and caring. There were ancients like Moses, Socrates, Plato, Aristotle, Jesus, and Mohammed, and some fairly recent people like Abraham Lincoln, Florence Nightingale, Muhatma Gandhi, Helen Keller, Martin Luther King, Lech Walesa, and Nelson Mandela. There are some literary characters like Odysseus, Psyche, Theseus, Aeneas, plus newcomers like Dorothy, Frodo, Luke, Harry, and even a few personalities managing to rise above the general trivialization of humanity today like Oprah Winfrey, Bill and Melinda Gates, and Warren Buffet.

Besides having in common their exemplary humanity, each one is a former nobody. Each one was gifted in a way. But notice that a good many were gifted with disadvantage: Moses stammered; Jesus was a hillbilly carpenter; Lincoln was self-educated; and Helen Keller was deaf, dumb, *and* blind. Furthermore, every single one of them became *somebody* by rising to assert themselves over obstacles that they refused to consider unchangeable and yield to.

They took the first really big step in accepting that they were responsible for *more than just themselves*. Yet so many of us want, at one and the same time, to be standout individuals who are no different from everybody else, enviably common-place.

Conversely, that broader perspective of human concern displayed in those human heroes and heroines seems singularly lacking from the lives of heroes and heroines of the McWorld who had everything they'd been told would make them some-bodies—money, fame, sex, power: Elvis Presley, Marilyn Monroe, Janis Joplin, Jimi Hendrix, Jim Morrison, Kurt Cobain, River Phoenix, and Michael Jackson, to name a few. Sometime before he ended his life with an overdose, Philip Seymour Hoffman said, "I do understand what it is to not want to commit to someone, knowing that might bring pain or commit to a life that has to do with being responsible to people other than myself." Such a comment makes one suspect that an intensity of concern for those outside one's insulated cocoon is one of the *critical* components of human fulfillment and happiness.

What the humanly fulfilled heroes and heroines did share with the humanly impoverished heroes and heroines was *confidence*—in many cases, shaky confidence, indeed. Their courage wasn't the empty-headed bravado of those who cross Niagara Falls on tightropes. It was true courage, coward's courage—the courage that says, "I *can't*...but...I'll try." When the unhappy ones lost their confidence to cope, they fled life.

A well-to-do father of four once told me, "I made up my mind when I was a kid in high school that my kids would never have to wade through all the crap I had to as a kid. So, I did it, by God. I gave them everything I didn't have back then...*except* the one thing I *got* from having to wade through all that crap: spine."

As Aristotle said, you become brave by acting bravely, confidently, completely against your gut feelings, rising to the obstacles that challenge your confidence. Even though they had never known him, all those nobodies echoed the mad prophet Howard Beale in Paddy Chayevky's *Network*: "I'm mad as hell, and I'm not gonna *take* it anymore!"

Ah, but the radical question *then* becomes "Now you've got that out of the way, what do you do *next*?" Over fifty years, almost without exception, students I've taught have had great hearts, even though the McWorld was trying to get them to settle for distractions, the Yellow Brick Road to the suburbs, a pool, and crabgrass. Not that those things are bad, but is that all there is? By the time they're college sophomores, they've mostly settled for the nonpassing lane on the way to the MBA—afraid of anything risky that threatens their life's security (except booze and sex). They're so secure that they don't dare get upset or overwrought over anything much. Yet, to quote Gen. Colin Powell, "Being responsible sometimes means pissing people off."

If you can ignite that spark in yourself, then the question becomes one that many of us are *unprepared* for by our enforced schooling: problem solving. No one seems to have helped students bridge the gap between mathematical logic and philosophical logic. But then a further obstacle arises. Part of it is blamable on something apparently innocent and utterly trivial: the rise of the computer has given every student by first grade the skills to touch-type. Therefore, a major part of the population equates writing to typing. Turn on the machine and start tapping, as if thinking could be reduced to the same spewing one does on a random e-mail or texting.

It might seem unfair to blame the moral shallowness of today's society on kindly grade- and high school teachers, but if all teachers *had* assumed the task not of covering the matter but teaching kids to gather data, sift out the important, outline, draw a conclusion, and submit it to *ruthless* critique—if they taught kids to *think* carefully and honestly—we might be able to cut our police forces and prison populations in half, get our legislators in Congress to yield their vested interests to the needs of the general populace, and assure ourselves that the banking industry would never again bring us to the brink of another Depression.

Along with that tiny crack in the levee, my experience (in many schools and in several countries) says too many students have not been penalized enough—or at all—for blowing wind, what I've referred to elsewhere as "bushwah, piffle, blather, or worse." Nor have I ever found a student who wasn't honest, ready to admit, when confronted, what they wrote *was* truly "B.S."

What they needed to be taken to rigorous task for—what their bosses will expect from them no matter where they go—is *concrete specifics*. It's great to make students feel responsible for rectifying society's mistakes, for sharing the problems of their clients, defendants, patients, spouses, and children. But they're not going to help them simply by *feeling* genuine respect, empathy, kindness, and responsibility. Then, they have to face, "Now what are we going to *do*?" What *is* the problem? Where are its roots? What *concrete, specific* steps must we first recognize, then evaluate, then commit ourselves to—step-by-step? In your twelve years or more of schooling, has anyone ever taught you how to do that?

PERSONAL REFLECTION

Another problem when emergent adults confront the genuine obstacles to their personal fulfillment is that they feel *smothered.* They act with the blind emotions of someone still a child: "Oh, I'm such a helpless mess!" Not even a trained psychologist could help them if, when asked what's wrong, their only bewildered response is: *"Everything!"*

Focus, focus, focus! Right now, if you had to isolate just *one underlying* bad habit to which you can trace most of the bad habits that infect all your good intentions and hold you back from being the best self you can be, what would it be? Are you too narcissistic? Are you too unrealistic? Are you too unaware of any perspective beyond tomorrow and beyond your own skin and moods? Go back through the negatives in the Enneagram and analyze the basic need of the one person in your life who will determine everything else in your life: you.

If you don't do it now, when will you do it? Your boss, your spouse, and your kids are waiting.

20.

THE MORAL KEY

THE DIGNITY *IN* THINGS

> There are some things so dear, some things so precious, some things so eternally true, that they are worth dying for. And I submit to you that if a man has not discovered something that he will die for, he isn't fit to live.
> —*Rev. Martin Luther King Jr.*

Consider whether you agree or disagree with the following ten statements.

1. The schooling I've received has really stimulated my inner self, my soul.
2. Imagination is not as valuable in life as cold, hard reasoning.
3. Primitive people had a more life-enriching relationship with true natures than we do.
4. History is a record of gradual disenchantments.
5. There are real values that are not irrational, yet they are *non*rational. (What do those two words even *mean*?)
6. In our time, the sacred has been almost entirely overwhelmed by the secular.
7. We can't live meaningful lives without at least some symbols to capture our values.

164

8. "Rational animal" is about as good a definition of *humans* as we can get.
9. In a very real sense, the economy has become a religion.
10. In business, shrewdness is a greater value than morality.

THE "SACRED"

The words *sacred* and *holy*—like so many others—are too often restricted, even by scholarly dictionaries, to *religious* objects that are somehow ennobled beyond their everyday worth by an association with some divinity—God, or the gods, or the spirits. That's far too restrictively academic, probably because the subject itself eludes the particular skills and interests of most incisive academics. Many are only too happy to dump such impalpable realities into the bin of religion where they can ignore them more readily.

In the quotation from Martin Luther King Jr. above, however, the sacred has a richer, and more widely applicable, meaning than the exclusively God-related. It describes important elements in life *deserving* great respect, *entitled* to reverence and esteem, like "freedom is a *sacred* right." It's what the deist Jefferson meant when he used *inalienable* rather than venturing too deeply into religious territory from which he and his fellow revolutionists had wisely separated the state.

Every year, I ask college students what are the things, places, actions, and people that they and their peers would consider sacred, holy, and inviolable. While in the past there was a Niagara of "special stuff," now there's a long silence and bewilderment. The words *sacred* and *holy* have become foreign. In the world they grew up in, has the concept of the sacred been put aside and judged to be no longer meaningful? That's the feeling I get, though I could be wrong. Yet, when I express that, no one ever tells me I am.

It's hard not to believe that the media of all types have made what was once held as meaningfully sacred—love, sex, suffering, death—now trivial, commonplace, and insipid. Conversely, they have made what most thoughtful humans have always considered shallow, transitory, and scarcely worth notice—complexions, odors, constipation—worth the kind of concern and worry once reserved for objectively more substantial and meaningful realities.

One time when I asked a college class about what they held sacred, a young woman said, hesitantly, "Uh, babies...maybe?" But as we spun out the idea, it became clear that even if the words were unfamiliar, they really did hold friendship as sacred—and family, but not much more. Two-thirds of a class claimed that there were few-to-no heroes anymore. The investigative reporters of checkout tabloids make sure every celebrity's dirty laundry is available to the public, as well as their spouses' and their children's mistakes. Today, Achilles, Joan of Arc, and Florence Nightingale wouldn't stand a chance for very long.

In a *Daily Mail* survey in 2014, Britain's top ten ideal humans were David Beckham, Brad Pitt, Justin Timberlake, Michael Jackson, Jennifer Lopez, Robbie Williams, Orlando Bloom, Britney Spears, Keanu Reeves, Angelina Jolie. Jesus Christ was 123rd, tied with George W. Bush. With the notable exception of Ms. Jolie, are there many evident qualities of those chosen ten that penetrate below the surfaces?

PERSONAL INTEGRITY

This above all: to thine own self be true,
And it must follow, as the night the day,
Thou canst not then be false to any man.
—Shakespeare, *Hamlet*, Act I, Scene 3, 79–81

That advice of old Polonius to his son, Laertes, as he goes off on his own, has been mangled and fractured by a lot of lightweight minds who claim, "I gotta be ME!" when they haven't the slightest whisper of an idea who the hell they really *are*!

Inside themselves, they've got this really good and true, natural urge to be somebody, to go somewhere worthwhile. But they're so damn rambunctious to get moving that they won't take time to figure out where they want to go and what they have inside them to get them there. Vanessa Amorosi begins her song "True to Yourself" with a fatuous lyric that puts it perfectly. She sings of seeing in the distance a mirror of herself where she hopes to be someday.

Does it make any sense to use a *mirror* for a *map*? First, what you see in the mirror is where you already *are now*. Are you pointing yourself toward a future self who's no different? No better? Second, she doesn't even specify or concretize *what* she sees in the mirror, much less the potential as yet to be activated. Finally, hope, plus a few bucks, will get you on a bus, but it's sensible to find out where you're going before you do and how far your resources will go.

The purpose of this book is to make that a lot less haphazard than it is for most people. Furthermore, the lyrics of the song limit the considerations of her future only to what she sees in the mirror, like Narcissus. She limits the question to one, "Who am I?" and doesn't really begin to answer *that* one, except in clouds of empty platitudes. But she ignores the other equally pertinent question (unless she's already decided to be a hermitess): "Where do I fit in?"

Her decision to become a self in the society of other people puts a limit on what she can legitimately hope for. She really ought to accept and prepare herself for the one fact of life she's probably been shielded from too long: life is *not fair*. The other actors on "her stage" have their own agendas, their own priorities, many of which will directly confront hers, and not all of them will play fair. Count on that, too.

She also has to fit into a world in which the game rules were made up *long* before she was conceived of or conceived. Either she uses things for what they're designed or gets ready to take the consequences: their revenge. Leap off the Sears Tower, drink Lysol, tickle a tarantula, but don't be surprised if that choice destroys all your dreams.

Not only that, but there are no victimless crimes for two reasons: first, every single individual's violations of the moral web may seem trivial, but they slowly destroy the whole web; and secondly, if your trivial misdeeds hurt no one else, they harm you. They make you tough-souled and diminished as a person. You trivialize your actions—and thus yourself—till your soul is hard and pitted like the seed of a peach. This is fine as long as you're willing to live with that self, not to mention the way everyone else chooses to react to that kind of self.

A third delusion I've heard relentlessly over the last fifty years from sexually active males: "If she wants it as much as you do, who's getting hurt?" Well, both, in fact. They demean themselves to no more than two animals, humping (to be coarse, but accurate). If the other person *wanted* to be your slave or if they *wanted* you to help them commit suicide, would that make it acceptable? Furthermore, if he and she hold themselves so cheaply, their acceptance of their human triviality is hardly proof they're trivial, even though both of them are acting that way: cheap.

You can see the contradiction between "Well, *everybody* does it!" and "I gotta be ME!"

It's amazing how many really degrading things happen to people too lazy to think, too grabby to see beyond the present moment, and too childish despite their adult bodies.

There's something objectively disorienting—or it ought to be—in raising human babies on farms for human consumption, in setting live cats on fire, and in trashing all the uneaten bread from restaurant tables to keep up bakers' incomes. There's something humanly repugnant about treating a human fetus like a high school lab frog. There's something cheapening about treating human sex as if it were no more special, no more sacred, than mutual masturbation. Like it or not, even dishonesty on a quiz is different from cheating yourself at solitaire. Why? None of those actions are fitting because of the elements involved, their *inner dignity*.

DEHUMANIZATION: A WORLD WITHOUT SACRED OR SINFUL

"Now what I want is Facts [Mr. Gradgrind tells the teacher of his company school in 1854]. Teach these boys and girls nothing but Facts. Facts alone are wanted in life. Plant nothing else, and root out everything else. You can only form the minds of reasoning animals upon Facts: nothing else will ever be of service to them. This is the principle on which I bring up my own children, and this is the principle on which I bring up these children. Stick to Facts, sir!" (Charles Dickens, *Hard Times*)

As we noted earlier, there is no room in Mr. Gradgrind's school for fancy, imagination, intuition, the unquantifiable, or the sense of something *richer* than "Fact." In his school, a horse was not a noble beast, a snorting steed with flaring eyes, Bucephalus-Rocinante-Silver; it was "an equine quadruped." His students were not human spirits yearning for greatness, dreaming dreams, envisioning the unheard-of, exulting in the circus. They were "reasoning animals," to be sorted by his school into those capable of being managers and those destined to be no more than "the hands" in his mills. There is no sin in Mr. Gradgrind's school or world, except for sloth and lack of productivity, and nothing sacred except financial profit.

The progress of "civilization" has been, in a very real sense, a process of dehumanization. History is a story of disenchantments, not only in the sense of correcting naïveté, but of taking the magic out of everything. In primitive cultures—some few of which still exist today in the outback of Australia and the heartland of Brazil—the people's lives were surrounded and permeated by gods, magic, ritual, and enchantment. They found their meaning and purpose, as tribes and as individuals, by interacting with the powerful forces of nature. The yearly *rhythm* of natural change gave a rhythm to their own lives, a sense of rightness, wholeness, meaning, like an artfully composed piece of music into which they blended. It gave a center to their lives, a connectedness, a shared vision, and *coherence*. For them, that relationship with nature and life was "I-Thou" not "I-It."

Then as the Enlightenment and the Industrial Revolution began to spread over the civilized world, utilitarianism ("What works?") made far more rational sense than irrational altruism ("What's right?"). Mr. Gradgrind came into his kingdom.

In America, that hard-nosed, no-frills secular religion was first embodied in the practicality of Benjamin Franklin. To show how interchangeable Yankee shrewdness and religion have become in the American mind, many believe Franklin's dictum, "God helps those who help themselves," actually comes from the Bible! That, in turn, devolved into the cynical advertising ploys of Phineas T. Barnum: "There's a sucker born every minute," and H. L. Mencken's, "You'll never go broke underestimating the intelligence of the American public." And Barnum and Gradgrind are still riding high in the boardrooms of Madison Avenue, on the television, and the billboards. Buy, buy, buy! You *can't* have too much. Image outweighs substance; nothing succeeds like the appearance of success; it's not the gods that bestow success but consumption.

The economy is its own justification. If it's good for the economy, "it is of God."

The Law of the American Dream is subtler in its statements and more sophisticated in its methods than the Law of the Jungle, but it's no less savage. It's less meticulous in its strictures than the Law of Moses, but no less demanding.

The following analogy of the economy to idolatry might seem at first forced, but it will show how thoroughly the secular has replaced the sacred in every corner of our lives.

Just as the gods gave meaning, coherence, and purposefulness to more primitive societies, and Yahweh made sense out of life for Hebrews, and Christ validated even suffering and death for medieval and renaissance Christians, the economy now serves that purpose. In 1933, when Chicago invited people to celebrate "A Century of Progress," it stated, "Science discovers, genius invents, industry applies, and man adapts himself to, or is molded by, new things."*

Our lives are validated only insofar as we become grist for the Gradgrind mill: workers, consumers, managers, and investors who serve the "priests": scientists, inventors, financiers, and advertisers who answer our prayers for more new things, which our ancestors could not have dreamed of, much less coveted.

We are, most of us, willing devotees of the idol, Economy. Many accept uncritically the values of the modern world: blind faith in technology, gadgets, progress, and slavery to the electronic media. We're willing to accept that the soul of our society is not a shared spirit as it was for Washington, Lincoln, and Roosevelt, but a mass of electric circuits. Still, given the limits of the Monopoly game, we all do, unarguably, benefit: the harder we work, the more we have to spend; the more we have to spend, the more the Economy thrives; the more the Economy thrives, the more we have to spend. And on it goes.

Ironically, this fanatic religious campaign was able, in a kind of *1984* "Newspeak," to turn around completely the very *meaning* of the word *economy*. Before, it had always meant "thrift, conserving, buying carefully, frugality." Now it means precisely the *opposite*: "expansion, spending, the bullish market, the golden calf." As with all religions, the Economy through its advertisers is a work of *conversion*, a complete turnaround of values—even a complete inversion of what *value* now means.

Besides priests, there are highly valued "scriptures." For the elites, *The Wall Street Journal* and *Forbes*; for lower levels of the faithful, there are *People* and *Examiner*. They tell us what's important and *who*'s important; who are the "saints" who've "made it." And there are audiovisual "scriptures" as well, proclaiming the good news everywhere we turn:

---

*One of the 1933 Chicago World's Fair slogans cited in "The Chicago 1933 Exposition," in Steven L. Goldman, *Science, Technology, and Social Progress* (Bethlehem, PA: Lehigh University Press, 1989), 294.

"THE MORE THINGS YOU HAVE, THE HAPPIER YOU'LL BE!"

Like any religion, the Economy offers fulfillment: newer, improved, bigger, and livelier lives. It has successfully evangelized and secularized not only institutions but the very *consciousness* of the "congregation." We genuinely *want* what the "priests" and "scriptures" want us to want: more tangible proofs of our success; a culture of narcissism.

No drill sergeant, no voodoo hypnotist, no Siberian brainwasher—not even Hitler or Big Brother—ever had such coverage, such compliant subjects, or such sophisticated and successful methods as the huckster-priests of the unquestioned Economy. And we don't mind, really; after all, it's good for all of us. It's very thorough evangelization.

The moral code of the idolatry is strict: work and compete, that's how you'll find fulfillment, your real *value*—SATs, report cards, salaries, promotions, a new car, and designer jeans (which used to be poor peoples' pants). Efficiency and speed become demigods in their own right, to the point that one would rather have a tried-and-true fast-food burger than enjoy a meal. On the assembly line, one plugs in this part to a piece someone else assembled, hands it on to a faceless someone who paints it, who hands it on to someone else to ship, someone else to sell, and someone else to drive. It is soulless, but efficient. But we all really do "profit."

There are also secular rituals that celebrate competition and the Economy: Super Bowls, Olympics, World Series in which sport is no longer sportive; Academy Awards, Emmys, Tony Awards, Grammys, Country Music Awards in which the point at issue is hardly art; political conventions in which the point is rarely character but more often image; concerts, which are liturgies of the id; and shopping malls, which are cathedrals of consumption. Even taking a walk is no longer a chance to "stop and smell the flowers" or get a sense of the sacred in nature because that's short-circuited by the iPod keeping us plugged in to "the Energy."

With nothing but a calculatedly "soulless" background against which to measure themselves—unlike the sacred myth systems of the primitive, the ancient, the Hebrew, the Christian—the modern man or woman finds life segmented, One-Damn-Thing-After-Another, with no sense of meaningful coherence, no storyline. The surgeon can treat us merely as biological specimens in need of repair; the politician, as so many votes to open the door and then be forgotten; the general, as so many dogfaces to accomplish a task rather than sons and daughters and wives and husbands of somebody. The battle-weary teacher can deal with so many human beings as so many educands to get through the system, and the Economy's Gradgrinds can treat human beings as if they were merely "economic factors."

For all our speed and efficiency, for all our goods and services, for all our defenses against even inconvenience, and for all our better nutrition and medical care and life expectancy, are we demonstrably any *happier* than the primitive squatting among so many enchantments, the Hebrew clutching his prayer shawl and muttering prayers to Yahweh, the medieval peasant leaning her hoe on the furrow to say the Angelus? Do we have a more genuine sense of self, a more heartfelt sense of belonging to a community, a cause greater than the limits of our own skins, a truer sense of living purposeful lives than those simpler folk, benighted in naïveté, superstition, and magic? Are we missing something?

If what I have written is even sort-of true, then I hope that it is convincing you to probe for the objective truth beneath the surfaces, to wrench your mind and values out of the hands of manipulators.

INFORMATION VERSUS UNDERSTANDING

We have now eased into a new kind of education where electronic machines begin in great part to replace human teachers. It is, unarguably, more efficient. It's also easier to find talentless teachers more concerned with standardized tests than preparing human beings to think for themselves. Rather than comment on that situation, let me instead merely copy here the first questions from my ethics final and allow you to discover the dangers of that new adaptation for your own future children and their world.

1. In a situation of irreversible difference between two equally powerful nations, why would it be at least imprudent to program every possible variable into a super computer and let an electronic expert decide whether to declare war?

2. Why will empirical science never be able to resolve the question of when a fertilized ovum/zygote/fetus becomes a definitive human "person"?

PERSONAL REFLECTION

In no necessarily logical order, jot down the things you personally hold "so dear...so precious...so eternally true, that they are worth dying for." Then alongside each of these things give a few words explaining *why* you hold each sacred. If it's impossible to isolate and identify any such values, can you explain to yourself why?

Part Four

THE WEB

THE HUMAN ECOLOGY

INTRODUCTION

LAWS

So far, we've confronted the question, Who am I? Now we turn our attention to, Where do I fit in?

Truly smart young people tell me, "Society makes us...." That, they've been told, answers their legitimate "why" questions. Of course it doesn't answer anything at all. It's a dodge.

Who is Society with a capital "S"? Where is its office? Where do I go to lodge a contrary opinion or a complaint? The term is like Big Brother in *1984*, or like Professor Charles Xavier and Magneto in *The X-Men*, or whoever (really) controls *The Matrix*. Society is some mega powerful entity that's coldly analytical and spins out arbitrary obligations the way the simpler-minded pictured the Fates—the Greek *Moirai*, the Roman *Parcae*, the Teutonic *Norns*, Macbeth's Three Weird Sisters, or Medieval Christendom.

That delusion is okay for those who need their thinking done for them or someone to blame for never having learned to think. However, Society isn't any more an operative person than Santa Claus, although both are, indeed, real. They're both umbrella symbols.

Santa Claus brings together, in a jolly male, all the benevolent, watchful qualities folktales always attributed to Fairy Godmothers, Glindas, Gandalfs, Obiwans, and Dumbledores. Christians latch onto the same idea with the protective familial communion of saints, of whom Santa was reputedly one. They, in turn, were rooted in the protective spirits of the Roman household and in the quarrelsome Zeus family. Eastern societies and religions had the same congenial relationships with their ancestors. In your own personal life, Santa was *really* your parents who unselfishly gave credit for their own work and caring to a made-up old man who crept magically into your home on Christmas Eve, even if you lived in an apartment and had no chimney.

Society is probably also ultimately rooted in all those god-systems, but closer to home, the pronouncements of society were the products of tribal leaders at their wits' ends trying to keep the members from ripping off one another's property and wives and heads. They were men (and sometimes wise matriarchs) better able and more willing to think, to take the long perspective beyond their own animal selfishness. Think of the boys in *The Lord of the Flies*. We either have laws we all agree to respect, or we'll slip back into the primeval quicksand of animal savagery. Rules are in everybody's long-range *self*-interest.

Given that ever-present Beast in us, we also have to see not only that everyone keeps their selfishness in check but also that everybody—even the weak and less talented—has enough to survive (*distributive* justice: spreading around the common goods). And we have to make sure that labor and exchange of goods is fair (*commutative* justice: back-and-forth). And we need wise justices to mediate between parties when two legitimate rights conflict (*social* justice).

In a democracy, society is *us*. *You* have a right to have your opinion heard, but if you're too lazy or too shy or too hesitant to stand up, then you've automatically—*ipso facto*—chosen to *be led*—to let "them" take care of all that time-consuming, mind-bending stuff.

However, society is also a collective name for all the elements in a very real invisible reality, a web of objective relationships that arises from the simple fact that we share the same space and resources. We also (and this one is crucial) share the results of one another's choices!

LEGAL VERSUS MORAL

Laws are written for people who don't want the trouble of thinking for themselves. It should be pretty obvious by now that objective reality and therefore objective morality—the true determinant of rightness and wrongness—is not first in our heads but "out there" in the natures of things and that, even though it's not our subjective opinion, human beings *have* more objective value than cabbages, koalas, or curbstones. Therefore, whether there's a written law about it or not, it's immoral, less human, to treat anyone or anything in a less dignified way than its inner nature demands of any rational person.

There shouldn't have to be laws against spitting in a bus or leaving your dog's droppings for others to dance around or against treating humans like oxen or lab animals. But people do those things, and therefore there are laws and sanctions. If we live together, somebody has to ride herd on the ids of those who refuse to control their own.

That's the theory, but the lawmakers themselves are human, subject to narcissism. That's why we need a vigilant press and the courts and special prosecutors to make sure members of Congress don't become the paid employees of special interests to the detriment of the society. But just as the whole structure, the whole web of society, is glued together by trust and that trust depends on the honesty of at least most of the individual fibers (citizens), so, too, the whole web depends on the cooperation and *contribution* of each individual citizen. The whole web is only as strong as its slackest strands. The daily newspapers give evidence of how strong those are.

Furthermore, we contribute not just taxes to the communal reality but our souls—ourselves. It demands enlightened, self-possessed, committed members. That comes into constant conflict with the Beast in us, between the self-protective and the self-giving, between the utilitarian and the altruist struggle within every human being.

Utilitarian: I want to win.
Altruist: I want to do what's right.

Utilitarians are often engaged in games of hide-and-seek with the truth. Their vested interests get in the way of objective judgment: "How far can I go?...Is there a proctor or a cop close?...Is the punishment worth the payback?...It depends on how you define sex." Utilitarians rarely get beyond the very bottom of Kohlberg's stages. They have a great deal of common sense and enlightened self-interest. They usually think anybody on stages above them are naïve saps. In exactly the opposite direction, altruists want to have character, to invest the personal effort to achieve and maintain a personal human dignity.

What's stopping you from standing up and being counted, from making a difference, from being one of the people whom Dr. King said are "fit to live"?

Now this *is* a time to look into Vanessa Amorosi's mirror. What's holding you back from human fulfillment? Eldridge Cleaver said, "You're either part of the problem or part of the solution."* Is shyness robbing you of a far fuller life or belittling your importance? "Go along to get along"? If you resist putting up your hand in class, if you keep silent and gripe only to friends about an inadequate teacher or gouging cafeteria prices or lazy coaches, you are as guilty as anyone else that those injustices continue. And you're as guilty as anyone else when you moan that, "Nobody can do anything about anything!" And you're as guilty as anybody else that the web of human relationships— society—is so "weary, stale, flat, and unprofitable!"†

If you ever took hold of the reins of your own soul, refused to knuckle under to "Everybody says....Everybody knows.... Everybody does it!" *your* whole world would come alive!

---

*John Kifner, "Eldridge Cleaver, Black Panther Who Became G.O.P. Conservative, Is Dead at 62," *New York Times*, May 2, 1998.
†William Shakespeare, *Hamlet*, Act 1, Scene 2, line 133.

PERSONAL REFLECTION

Ponder this story: One Saturday afternoon, I was on my way to a high school football game, and I had on a pink shirt. A student came up and sneered, "I bet you've got pink *socks* on, too!" But I didn't. So I went out and bought a pair. Nobody tells me what I can wear.

21.

SEX AND GENDER

> What is most beautiful in virile men is something feminine; what is most beautiful in feminine women is something masculine.
>
> —*Susan Sontag*

Consider the following ten statements and whether you agree or disagree.

1. If your teenage son asked for ballet lessons, you'd have cardiac arrest.
2. Males may *feel* more sexual, but females *are* more sexual beings.
3. Female inequality in jobs is strictly a matter of male chauvinism.
4. Most women go to college just waiting till they get married.
5. Boys are, by their nature, more competitive and analytical than girls.
6. Industrial society is a "jungle" because it's nearly exclusively "masculine."
7. To advance in the professions, a woman has to be tougher than most males.
8. If there's a budget crunch in schools, what's immediately cut is the humanities, rarely the sciences and athletics.
9. There is something morally wrong about a woman flying a fighter plane in combat.

10. Men without sensitivity and women without confidence are severely deprived.

A great deal of pain and confusion could be avoided if people were more cautious in choosing words. But even learned commentators use *sex* and *gender* like synonyms. The sometimes tragic results are idiotic stereotypes in which females are treated as some kind of mutants or incomplete males. In old black-and-white films, they're merely silly: Me, Tarzan! You, Jane! In real life, they are dehumanizing, immoral.

The Reductionist Male	The Reductionist Female
muscular	delicate
analytical	bewildered
dominating	welcoming
decisive	submissive
cynical	gullible
lusty	proper
tireless	turns her ankle

In *My Fair Lady*, the fearsomely educated Henry Higgins stupidly–laughably–insists:

Why can't a woman be more like a man?
....
Men are so pleasant, so easy to please.
Whenever you're with them, you're always at ease....*

How about that for arrogant ignorance?

Contrary to the dualist, cartoonish simplification, there have been many quite successful female heads of state, surgeons, scientists, and nearly all the best known artists, musicians, and chefs in history have been males. Tom Hanks and Ernest Hemingway are both virile males and fathered children,

---

*"A Hymn to Him," in Alan Jay Lerner, *My Fair Lady*, music by Frederick Loewe, 1956.

but Hanks displays greater "feminine" sensitivity and Hemingway was more macho "masculine." On the contrary, it's hard to believe Ophelia and Lady Macbeth are the same species, much less the same sex.

Sex and *gender*, as anyone who has ever studied language knows, are not coterminous.

Sex: "male"/"female"—objective fact—physical—
either/or
Gender: "masculine"/"feminine"—subjective opinion—
psychological—more/less

Sex is a matter of either/or: fact. Lift the diaper, there's your definitive answer. Gender is more of *temperament*, which we encountered dealing with the Myers-Briggs Type Indicator and the Enneagram—*attitudes*: extravert/introvert; *perceiving*: sensing/intuitive; *deciding*: thinking/feeling; *lifestyle*: judging/perceptive. Those have *nothing* to do with determining your sexual orientation.

Masculine does not equal *Macho*; *Feminine* does not equal *Effeminate*. Nonetheless, people readily assert that it's not "normal" if a boy baby wears pink and a girl baby wears blue. This is another slovenly use of words. The word *normal* implies a *norm*. The meaning depends on whether the norm is based on the objective *nature* of a male or female, or merely on a subjective custom based merely on current tastes. Macho musketeers wore curly wigs with high-heeled shoes; Chinese women once had their feet cruelly bound to keep them tiny and utterly unlike cloddish male feet. Joan of Arc led an army, Madam Curie discovered radium, Scotsmen wear skirts, modern males wear earrings, and half the doctors in Russia are females.

Is a male ballet dancer or hair dresser immediately identifiable as gay and a female wrestler as lesbian? Only to Neanderthals—a quality formal schooling has been trying to exorcize since the very beginning; with uneven success.

The safer, more justified, assessment is "unusual to us."

The only objective difference between males and females are the genital differences—males with external genitals, females internal—and even they are the same for six weeks of gestation. Our hormones are the same, just varying levels. Those differences are real, and they do *matter.*

The philosopher Jean-Jacques Rousseau wrote, "The male is male only at certain moments, the female is female her whole life or at least during her whole youth."* The males' contribution to the procreative process is, to be honest, essential and consequential but laughably brief. Many young men simply don't realize that, though they may *feel* more breathlessly sexual in arousal, females *are* more sexual beings. Only they can menstruate, conceive, carry a fetus, deliver a baby, nurse—none of which the best-intentioned male is capable of doing—just as a rock can't reproduce, a carrot can't uproot itself, and an animal can't commit suicide. Facts!

Socialization—nurture as opposed to nature—however, has been manifestly unfair to females until only very recently. In the United States, the bastion of democracy, females were not considered legal "persons" (although corporations and ships were) and were not allowed the vote until August 18, 1920. An illiterate male had the franchise, not the president of Radcliffe College who had a doctoral degree. That is, manifestly, immoral.

As human beings, males and females, by their common human nature, are and should be treated as complete equals. Women are as (or more) intelligent, as (or more) resilient, as (or more) decisive. Advanced technology has eliminated even some of the usual physical male advantages. A woman can start a harvester, operate a crane, and press a rocket button as well as any man. It's unlikely, however, that science will devise a way a male can conceive a child.

Despite their human equality with males, in some situations, women's sex difference does intrude on her choices, or they can. If a woman chooses not to have children, by natural right, she should have all the opportunities of equally qualified males. But if she does choose to have a child, the *child's* natural rights to whatever gifts only his or her mother can give at least enter into the equation in ways they do not with a man.

---

*Jean-Jacques Rousseau, *Emile or On Education*, trans. Allan Bloom (New York, NY: Basic Books, 1979), 361.

When an infant is born, the first thing the caregivers must do is get the baby back as quickly as possible to the mother's heartbeat, which has meant assurance for as long as he or she has been alive. It's essential. It will be years before the child can think, connect cause and effect, and even differentiate self from the rest of the world. So infants became attached to mothers—physical contact with their mother's skin, stomach, heartbeat, body heat, smell, and movement. Secure attachments arise and stabilize from reliable, consistent, pleasurable patterns for comfort fixed in a baby's brain through the senses. Children who achieve attachment to *one* caregiver develop greater security, more emotional control, and greater confidence in facing new challenges. No matter how genuinely caring the staff of a child-care center, they are multiple and dissimilar. If that's the only recourse, if the mother simply *has* to return to work for both to survive, so it must be. But if her speedy return is motivated primarily by maintaining a level of lifestyle or her place in the corporate pecking order, the moral dilemma is at the very least complicated.

NATURE VERSUS NURTURE

The nature/nurture controversy has been sparking as long as the chicken/egg controversy. So don't expect it to be solved on this page. Whether you believe boys are aggressive and girls are adaptive because of the way they're made (nature) or the way they've been socialized (nurture) depends pretty much on which psychologist you read last. Whatever the complex of causes, we have to take each emergent adult as they find their selves. What appears here intends merely to help the reader be less uninformed.

Many psychologists maintain that, because a male child grows up with a person of the opposite sex, he develops his individuality by separation from her—putting up ego boundaries. On the contrary, a female child experiences herself like her mother and therefore doesn't feel that separation. Thus, they say, a female *usually/normally* begins to understand herself through vulnerability and connections. Females' internal worlds are more continuous with the outside world and have fewer ego boundaries. Therefore, some experts (surely not all) argue that masculinity (in either sex) is nurtured through separation and femininity through union; males become uneasy with intimacy, females with separation.

Again, that's surely not as universal or cut-and-dried as physical sexuality is. A little girl, just as a little boy, feels the same maternal abandonment at being weaned, potty trained, put outside to play, and abandoned at the kindergarten door. Nor can I accept that a boy, by his male *nature*, brushes aside paternal caressing because it's "sissy." That *does* happen, but abhorrence of sissiness, like all prejudice, has to be *taught*. Psychologists find that, up until about age three, both boys and girls try to get their way by hitting. At about three, boys continue to hit but girls stop. Instead, girls' ploys are subtler: "We won't play with *you!*"—instinctively (?) capitalizing on other girls' fear of exclusion. However, those discoveries fail to convince me that females would find solitary confinement more unbearable than a male.

Peer groups are a major factor in nurture, especially playtime. Janet Lever found that boys play outdoors more, in larger groups of broader age range, more competitively, and for longer periods—often because the game's prolonged by arguments over the rules, which the boys seem to enjoy almost as much as the game itself. In contrast, girls are more tolerant in attitudes to the rules, more willing to make exceptions to include the clumsy and unskilled (if they like her), and more open to innovations than boys. Girls would rather stop the game than argue, seeming to value friendships more than the game itself. Girls want to play, or so it seems; boys want to win.

Academic education always used to be a mechanism for curbing the competitive Beast, humanizing attitudes, perceptions, decisions, lifestyle—in a word: *values*. But the McWorld, which now subsidizes and governs the educational system, which now dutifully serves the McWorld, has changed diametrically in recent years, especially since the advent of Thomas Gradgrind: "You can only form the minds of reasoning animals upon Facts: nothing else will ever be of service to them."* Practical folks assert that education actually *means* science and math. Information is immeasurably more desirable than understanding it. The rest is "womanish." They argue that the more determining truth is "It's a jungle out there...a dog-eat-dog world...where nice guys finish last....Never give a sucker an even break....Your job is to find the other team's weak spots and *work* 'em!"

Those cynical lessons are *never* taught in any school—not explicitly. However, I've known college students who'd almost literally kill for a 3.6 GPA. And in every school I've ever served, the authorities spent more effort at exam time on training vigilant proctors than on training students who valued honor. (The *very* lowest Kohlberg motives.) Therefore, in both females and males, the "masculine" is held in higher esteem, the "feminine" is less worth consideration in a world where *value* now means "marketable."

What's more, at least in the first years when personal identities are *beginning* to coalesce, most of the authority figures are female, and it's a cliché that boys resist and girls accept. Then, in high school, when the individual is supposed to get a relatively firm grasp of personal identity, males and females are subjected to a regimen far more dominated by the left brain, "masculine" disciplines and where even the humanities are treated in an efficient, Gradgrind, multiple-choice way. Poems, plays, and novels are offered not to stir the soul but to serve as analysis-fodder: "How far was the protagonist's cabin from town?...Which character died clutching the conch?...What issues divided the family?" It's like hearing love analyzed by tax assessors.

PERSONAL REFLECTION

You're the board chairperson of an international manufacturing firm. Every branch factory is pumping out profit year after year—*except* the factory in Nowhereville. Despite changes

---

*Charles Dickens, *Hard Times* (New York, NY: Dover Publications, 2001), 1.

---

of management and work incentives, it's leaking red ink. The board meets and every member agrees: "Cut our losses! Close it down. Sell what we can and begone."

Except one member, who raises a truly foolish question: "What about the workers?" The others' jaws sag in disbelief. "What?"

"We're the backbone of the town's economy. What'll happen when their unemployment checks run out? There's nowhere to go for work. They trusted us."

Several respond. "Are we a charity?" And "Monopoly's the only game in town, friend."

"And what about the peripheral businesses like dry cleaners and gas stations and barber shops? And what about the tax base—the schools, water, trash collectors, first responders?"

Okay. You're the head of the board. What do you say?

22.

FROM ROMANCE
TO LOVE

> Love isn't blind. Being-in-love is blind.
> —*Victor Steele*

Consider the following ten statements. Do you agree or disagree?

1. Authentic love sets the other free genuinely to love others as well.
2. If Romeo and Juliet really loved one another, wouldn't they rather have had the other alive—even with someone else—rather than dead?
3. There are a number of similarities between being in love and chemical addiction.
4. Romance can usually last forever if guarded carefully.
5. Sex is too intoxicating for adolescents to handle it level-headedly.
6. Falling out of love is an opportunity for real love with the same person.
7. Many steady relationships are more inflexibly monogamous than most marriages.
8. Love without commitment is a misuse of the word.
9. The most profound way to show love is sexual intercourse.
10. People who share genuine love don't have to talk about it all the time and don't even think about it most of the time.

190

BLISSFUL BLINDNESS

Love is just one more recklessly applied label for countless realities unworthy of it: "I *love* your dress...pizza...June...Paris in the springtime." The verb is elastic but hardly enough to stretch from a mother's devotion to her newborn and to chocolate.

This word becomes especially endangered at the critical moment when a young person—having (supposedly) discovered and laid claim to a unique personal identity—feels a restlessness to leave the familial love of the birth nest and set out in search of a love nest of her or his own.

Two factors intensify that fragile encounter for a modern emergent adult, one as old as the caves, the other hardly a hundred years old: the rise of the omnipresent moral teacher, the television.

The first factor is that the urge to move on arises at the eruptive time of physical puberty. The two are Siamese twins. But during high school (a bit different for each person) comes the unlikely mix of, on the one hand, the potential for clear rational thought and, on the other, the swampy, earthy infusion of bodily hormones that turn the body into a stranger—stirring urges that the "victim" has little help comprehending. Fusing the two—body and mind—seems like a dualistic war between two hostile powers, and moralists for centuries (especially Puritans) found the two only barely compatible. Rather, the more realistic image of the call to merge body and mind is a marriage—the fluctuating halves of the Tao or the two opposite poles of a magnet fusing into a new power. The peaceful marriage of body and mind gives birth to the soul. However, no matter how helpful and sensitive the parents and teachers, the individual has to go it alone and accept reality as it's delivered.

So, you begin to *edge* out of the nest. And it's very precarious out there! Everybody you encounter, like every commercial, is a waiting mirror, reflecting your uncountable inadequacies. No matter how gifted you are, it often feels like being a rabbit in a forest infested with foxes. But then—almost exactly like Romeo and Juliet at the Capulet's masquerade ball and Maria and Tony at the gym dance in *West Side Story*—you encounter someone who (for whatever nonrational reasons) snags your attention, your vulnerability, your heart. Slowly, gradually, you inch closer, sharing meaningless chitchat that at least seems worth memorizing. Then, if you're lucky, it's like Dorothy in *The Wizard of Oz*: black-and-white flashes into Technicolor! You've rocketed out beyond the workaday, colorless routine into a fairytale. (In fact, the French word for fairytale is *roman*, the root word of *romance*). Just as in a drug high, you're now in a world where everything every day is merely Monopoly money by contrast. You're drunk—not on genuine love but on being *in* love. You now live in a different reality, about which those dull people Hogwarts students call "Muggles," haven't the slightest clue! They're incapable of seeing that she's a faultless princess and he's the gallant (for the moment, disinherited) prince.

There's nothing wrong with this bewildering elation. In fact, it's truly wonderful! And it's also essential. Who would be foolish enough to vow, in marriage, in the presence of others, to take responsibility for another (by definition, imperfect) human being, no matter what, till one of you dies, unless both were at least a little pixilated on l*o*v*e p*o*t*i*o*n?

The hardest thing to remember in that enchantment, when the unconditional love of infancy seems suddenly reborn, is that this situation is, in truth, not *real* long-lasting love, but *storybook* love. It's what more careful minds call *infatuation*. And as all love stories have manifested, it's almost impossible to communicate across the checkpoints on the borders between the two realities—romance and reality. It's a time when more than a few parents half-wish they'd gone into a monastery instead.

The second factor that makes this emergence into adult loving immeasurably more taxing today than for any other generation since the caves is the relatively recent development of the most persuasive agent ever known: commercial media. For the few hundred thousand years since *homo sapiens* first took their weight off their knuckles and stood erect, emergent young people didn't have to be formally instructed about the ways of pubertal attraction or even of the marital consummation of it after marriage. It took place in the common dwelling where everyone in the clan was aware of it.

However, in modern times, just as real death is at one and the same time hidden away from children but also endlessly unrealistically portrayed in films and TV, the same is true of sex. I say "unrealistically" advisedly because sex/love in the media is as phony and totally unreal as professional wrestling, to which it is also in many ways comparable.

I'm willing to bet you've never seen sex portrayed in media where the two operatives are ugly, or even unattractive. Even on the more permissive cable channels, rarely are the participants entirely unclothed, and *never* do they have to clean up afterward. Now that would be real, not storybook. But the real kicker is this: I'll bet you've never seen sex in the media when the two players are married. It's almost an iron rule. What's the effect of that on you?

Besides the media, science has also radically changed how humans deal with one another romantically by providing for the first time in history fairly dependable methods of artificial birth control. In so doing, though it hardly seems its intended result, for what seems like a majority of young people today, freedom to engage in sex without great fear of pregnancy has broken what has always been an objective, natural connection between the sex act and commitment of the two persons to one another. One young woman in a recent national survey put it perfectly, if somewhat unemotionally: "Sex used to be something you did only with your husband. Then it was only with someone you truly loved. Now it's for recreation."*

A few years ago, a male high school senior also put this quite new understanding of sex with equal clarity: "Look," he said in class, "if you *like* one another, it's just *natural*! If you're thirsty, you go to the sink and get a drink of water. If you're horny, you call your girlfriend." I said, "And you'd say you love her, right?" He said, "Of course." The two of us clearly had very different ideas of what qualifies as love.

Then, I said, "There are two words for having sex. What are they?" About five guys obliged me with the "F-ing word." I said,

---

*Cf. Christian Smith and Melina Lundquist Denton, *Soul Searching: The Religious and Spiritual Lives of American Teenagers* (New York: Oxford University Press, 2009).

"And what's the other?" The boy who first objected said, "Making love." And I said, "They don't call it 'making *like*.'" His face closed up like a fist, but it was the first time he finally grasped what I'd been talking about.

Just as an upraised middle finger speaks without words, so does the sexual act. You simply can't be more vulnerable than stark naked—which is why Nazi prison camps so often made the prisoners march naked, and why rape is a more heinous dishonor than murder, because the victim has to live with that degrading intrusion. Sex also is a sublime act of trust. If the he-man struts for his pals on Monday about how he scored with his girlfriend over the weekend, what guarantee has he that she's not telling her girlfriends, "Boy, there's a real deadbeat loser!"

When people justify their lack of control over their moods and feelings and act impulsively because of them, they tell, even themselves, "Who's not human, right?" which to an honest mind says the same as, "Who's not just an animal, right?"

Sex with a stranger, or even with someone you despise, would probably be gratifying. But in either case, it would manifest only one thing: me! Like graffiti. On the contrary, there are many people you love with whom having sex would be unsettling, just not right. In fact, it would spoil the friendship.

Then what makes the difference between being in love and the real thing?

LOVING

The way to establish a norm for the word *love* is to consider situations where there isn't the slightest doubt about its integrity, where there seems not the slightest whisper of selfishness: a good mother and her infant is one. The mother could probably sleep through an earthquake, but let that baby so much as breathe funny in her sleep, and that mom is out of bed like a pole vaulter. That's the real thing.

I got another fine example some years ago from a seventeen-year-old boy. He was very much in love with a girl but, as will happen, she developed an interest in one of his friends, who just happened to be better looking and wealthier. He told me later, crying, that he'd said to her, "If you honestly think he can make you happier than I can, that's what I want." That's the real thing.

More recently, a senior said to me one Monday, "Boy, I hated *you* Friday night!" I scowled, "Why?" He said, kind of sheepishly, "Well, her parents were out, and we were up in her room getting undressed. But I remembered what you said in class. So I stopped, and I said, 'I can't. I'd just be using you.' So I came downstairs and sat on the couch, and she came down and sat next to me, and said, 'I've never been prouder of you.'" That's the real thing.

If you have good parents, you've seen real love many times, when they call you up short on something unacceptable you did. At that moment, your face seems to be saying something like, "I *hate* you right now." And inside their heads, they're saying, "Right now, I'm not too keen on you either. But I love you enough that I'm willing to put up with you being angry at me for a while—just so you don't get hurt down the line." That's the real thing.

Genuine love isn't just a *feeling*. Love is an act of the *will*, a commitment that takes over when the feelings *fail*, when the beloved is no longer even *likable* for a while. Pose that definition to someone who's been married quite a long time, someone who's had kids and see if it stands up with experts in what loving *costs*.

When people say, "Sex is okay for us because we love one another," check it against that unarguable standard of what *love* means: I'd rather be unhappy with you than be happy with anybody else. If you truly believe you love one another, test it out. Give up the sex for a month and see which is more important: the other person or the sex. Just don't lie to yourself.

Here are three more factors to consider: need, kickback, and life-giving.

Need: No matter what your English teacher said, Romeo and Juliet didn't really live up to the test of real love. They *needed* one another because they'd lost the pampering of their parents and had yet to lay hold of a self. Each thought (wrongly) they couldn't be whole without the other. In his *Symposium*, the great Plato puts into the mouth of the playwright, Aristophanes, a creation myth (which he himself admits may seem absurd) that postulated that the early humans were of three sexes: the all-male; the all-female; and the androgynous, half male, half female. Zeus wanted to punish them for being arrogant, so he had them each cut in half. Ever since, people run around looking for their other half; some get jumbled, most end up with their opposites, and some end up with those of their same sex.

The same strain on the truth shows up in nearly every love song, most of which are really being-in-love songs: "You're nobody till somebody loves you." It also shows up in one of the most popular children's books, *The Velveteen Rabbit*, in which an allegedly experienced and therefore wise Skin Horse tells the newly arrived Rabbit, "When a child loves you for a long, long time, not just to play with, but REALLY loves you, then you become real."* The painful fallacy in that drivel is: How could anyone even *find* you—much less love you—if you're not real till they come along? Yet in the 1970s, a painful number of brides had that read at their weddings.

That explanation is as neat—and as dumb—as "I was a victim of the love potion." If all the other does is fulfill *your* needs, like the boy who said that his girlfriend is for him like a drink of water for *his* thirst, the only valid assessment is it's using a human being as a means.

Would you want to spend the rest of your life with someone who is meaningless without you around?

Kickback: Sex is such an instantaneous, thrilling return on a very ill-considered and impersonal investment, that it's difficult for someone with an honest, objective viewpoint to evaluate the relationship as much more than self-interested, with a thin camouflage of concern, no more genuine than a prostitute murmuring, "You're wonderful," in a customer's ear. Very often, boys feel they "have to score" or else doubt their manhood; girls feel they have to "give in" or go back to the embarrassing hunt for a new guy. Regardless, it seems a near-perfect example of Kohlberg's second stage of pre-adult moral motivation.

---

*Margery Williams, *The Velveteen Rabbit* (New York: Avon, 1999), 5.

Life-Giving: This is possibly the very best test of true love versus romance. Does it make each of the partners a better human being *outside* the relationship? Does it make them more sensitive to the unspoken needs of their parents and siblings, and more solicitous for their peers who are downcast, troubled, and withdrawn? That looks pretty genuine. Or, on the other hand, does it make them twitchier, oversensitive, quick to take offense, and secretive? Bad vibes.

No matter what your feelings about religion in general or Christianity in particular, the Apostle Paul has a description of real love even atheists find close to perfect.

> Love is patient; love is kind; love is not envious or boastful or arrogant or rude. It does not insist on its own way; it is not irritable or resentful; it does not rejoice in wrongdoing, but rejoices in the truth. It bears all things, believes all things, hopes all things, endures all things. Love never ends. (1 Cor 13:4–8)

Maybe if more people pondered those words, slowly, phrase by phrase, there might be a great deal less unhappiness around and fewer shattered expectations. But, of course, like freedom, like acting humanly, genuine love does *cost*.

Romance is very dramatic—operatic outpourings, thumping heartbeats, total domination of the mind. Real love is quite the opposite. The two people are so assured of themselves and of the other that there's no ground for jealousy. When there's a true cause for confrontation, they trust one another to have it out, forgive, and keep going. Real love is flipping-the-pancakes love. Real love is "No, go back to sleep, I'll get up and change her" love. Real love is cutting down on the drinking love. If it's dramatic most of the time, you're probably not in real life but in a soap opera.

PERSONAL REFLECTION

Almost surely, this chapter has taken a different viewpoint than you've been accustomed to on this crucial element in moral human life. From what I can gather, both grade and high school biology teachers treat human sex only concerning the mechanics, as if there weren't a quantum leap between animal sex and human sex. Understandably, parents are wary of intruding on your freedom to grow up, even though they're well aware from experience that sexuality in adolescence can be like alcohol to an alcoholic, "cunning, baffling, and powerful."* Most males I've taught get angry when I suggest that their mothers may know more about sex than they do. Not just the mechanics, not just how it *feels*, but what it *is*, what it *says*, and what it *costs*.

Just for yourself, write out what you honestly believe about the meaning of sex, romance, and unselfish love in a fulfilled human being's life. Share only what you choose to share.

---

*"How It Works," chap. 4 in *Alcoholics Anonymous*, 4th ed. (New York: A. A. World Services, Inc., 2001), 58–59.

23.

MARRIAGE

> Anyone who defines marriage by what goes on in the bedroom has never been married.
> —*Anna Quindlen*

Consider the following ten statements. Do you agree or disagree?

1. "Happily ever after" needs even more creative imagination than being in love.
2. A bridal couple doesn't know their marriage will work out; they're betting on it.
3. A wife's career should always yield to her husband's career.
4. The competition pervading schooling and society isn't good preparation for marriage.
5. Few people admire an adulterer or adulteress.
6. Divorces often happen because the couple hasn't kept working at their friendship.
7. Divorce has a more long-lasting effect on children than a parent's death.
8. If you have your honeymoon living together for a couple years before you marry, don't count on having a meaningful one after the wedding.
9. The wedding ceremony is only one event in the process of *becoming* married.
10. A couple is a lot *more* married on their first anniversary than they were at their wedding.

THE INNERMOST CORE OF MARRIAGE

In Thornton Wilder's play *The Skin of Our Teeth*, George Antrobus has come from a dalliance with a floozie and tells his wife, Maggie, he's leaving her and their two children because "a man has his own life to lead in the world."

Maggie says in response, "I didn't marry you because you were perfect. I didn't even marry you because I loved you. I married you because you gave me a promise. [She takes off her ring and looks at it.] That promise made up for your faults. And the promise I gave you made up for mine. Two imperfect people got married and it was the promise that made the marriage. [She puts her ring back on her finger.] And when our children were growing up, it wasn't a house that protected them; and it wasn't our love that protected them. It was that promise."*

That's the best statement of the essence of a marriage I've ever heard. In one word: a *promise*. That's the reason I called those girls who'd quit the musical. I wanted to take one small step to saving their marriages, even though they'd not even met the guy they'd marry yet. I wanted them to value a reputation for honoring commitments—that would let their bosses feel completely comfortable letting them close out the cash register, assure their children they never have to fear their mother would desert them. It's why I've tried all these years to encourage young people to honor their word as sacred, reliable, and inviolable; as precious as their own selves, their souls; and as indelible and beyond question as their love for their spouse and their children.

If adolescence is the greatest disequilibrium in a person's life, the commitment to marriage is a close second, despite all the happily-ever-after stories and songs. We're no longer considering an individual's relationship with his or her self. We're talking about two quite different selves finding not only peace, stability, and accommodation with one another, but also preparing a strong, nurturing environment for the next stage: parenthood.

---

*Thornton Wilder, *The Skin of Our Teeth*, Act II (New York: Harper Perennial, 2003), 81.

Most marital problems likely arise because neither of the two selves has, in fact, achieved a healthy, confident, positive self-ownership before they gave that self away. After the honeymoon, the couple has to avoid slipping back into the same old self-centered habits that preceded the self-forgetfulness of the romance. Because, once back into reality, the union reveals itself inescapably as not just physical but psychological: a blending of souls. Two inadequately owned selves are heading for a collision. Do they have the skills of confident self-transparency with the other, enough self-confidence *and* self-forgetfulness, enough love to compromise, empathize, forgive? When does a future marriage partner cultivate those sensitivities, if not now?

Romance is an absolute requisite for marriage. Without the breathless blindness that makes him a god and her a goddess, no one in their right mind would make a commitment so enormous with so few guarantees—and most often sworn to, in front of hundreds of witnesses: "I promise to be true to you, in good times and in bad, in sickness and in health. I will love you and honor you all the days of my life."

And that's not just sexual fidelity. It's the vigilance of the night sentry in battle, the attentiveness of the new mother, the watchfulness of a fine nurse. Perhaps it's unfair to suggest this, but one way to assess your *present* skills along those lines is to ask yourself about your usual sensitivity to your mother's moods, your creativity in restoring her usual serenity.

Marriage is a calculated risk—the more calculation beforehand, the better. But there's the dark underbelly of the rosy clouds of romance: Cinderella and Prince Charming are often so juiced up that they leap into love and forget to look first. Many, equivalently, join hands and jump off a cliff. Not smart. Blind faith is a contradiction and sheer idiocy.

Again, reality demands a hearing. If his great dream is to be a teacher and hers is to belong to a country club, it's time to ponder. If she sets her sights on being a surgeon and he's fast climbing in a corporation that often uproots executives, one or the other has to yield. Maybe it's really true that "love conquers all," but being in love doesn't have that toughness of spirit. If both dreams are, literally, incompatible, how would you suggest they solve it, right now?

Even when the two selves are as healthy as they can get at their stage of development and about as sure as anyone can be that "this is it," conflict is inevitable. Ask your parents. Do we sleep with the window open? Do we put the toilet roll overshot or undershot? Do we watch the Super Bowl and eat calf's liver? Ah, and the clincher: *Who controls the TV remote?*

If either *self* wins, then both lose. Marriage is perhaps *the* tightest moral relationship, and by that very fact, the one most susceptible to abrasions. And in flagrant contrast to romantic movies and sitcoms, a real marriage *demands* work, because once the two have made a permanent, public commitment, reality intrudes on the romance with conflicting job priorities, major expenses like houses and cars, and moods that are impossible to keep in sync.

For what follows, I'm indebted to a book called *The Good Marriage,** by psychiatrists Judith Wallerstein and Sandra Blakeslee, who interviewed couples who believed they had happy marriages as well as their friends who agreed to that. The book demonstrates understanding, sensitivity, and yet is remarkably down to earth. The authors suggest nine essential tasks married people have to acknowledge and deal with. I summarize them briefly here.

1. *Letting Go.* Marriage means a painful "leaving-behind" of unquestioned family customs, a room of your own, parents who usually had a handle on things, decades of a shared story. It's a real psychological disequilibrium, not rejecting the birth families but creating a whole different set of connections. If the true needs of the marriage conflict with the birth families, the marriage has to win. (Anybody who follows the example of *Everybody Loves Raymond* and moves across the street from their in-laws and leaves both front and back doors open so the mother-in-law

---

*Judith S. Wallerstein and Sandra Blakeslee, *The Good Marriage: How and Why Love Lasts* (New York: Warner Books, 1996).

can walk in anytime and sneer at the pasta sauce is feeble minded.)

2. *Partnership/Autonomy.* A truly tough one: become a "we" without losing either "I." If one partner dominates the other, it's not a marriage but a master/minion. There is a radical problem (especially for many males) in *self-disclosure*—fearlessly revealing the real individual beneath the fairytale princess and prince. This is a vulnerability even more profound than sex. He has to be able to say not only, "I'm mad as hell," but also "I'm so scared." She has to be free to say not just, "I'm hurt," but "No more, mister!" Like a mother's understanding of a child's needs before that child can speak, both partners have to be able to know when something is not being said.

3. *Accommodating Children.* A child forever changes what had been a two-person relationship. The child's schedule assumes control of all their plans. It's exhausting, and that can't help but affect the couple's patience with one another. Therefore, it makes eminent sense to resolve, no matter what the budget pinch, that they have at least one night a month to work on the marriage. It's not only important to them but to the children to sense that Mommy and Daddy have a secret love the kids can always depend on.

4. *Coping with Crises.* Some are foreseeable to anyone with perspective: the kids' stages of physical and psychological growth, paying for things, grandparents aging and dying, kids leaving home, and their own retirement. Others are unforeseeable: job loss, natural disasters, injury of a child, and sickness. But the crises offer them a chance to see what's truly important: "Well, at least we all got out alive."

5. *Space for Conflict.* Even constant, open communication can't eliminate abrasions, nor should it. Just as obstacles are the way an adolescent can rise to become a stronger self, confrontation helps them open up their souls wider, provided they agree long

beforehand that every time they conflict, it will end in a hug. In the Wallerstein-Blakeslee study, it was found that an amazing number of husbands said, "She takes no b.s."

6. *Maintaining Intimacy*. The security that comes with a vowed commitment often tranquilizes the passion of courtship; the other is less sexually intriguing, and years of bills, work, and dealing with kids can take the edge off. When you're just departing adolescence, it probably seems inconceivable there'd come a time when you have to make an act of will to have sex. Also, it's not unheard of that, just as Mommy and Daddy are getting romantic in bed, little Tiffany runs into the marital chamber with a report of a monster coming from her closet.

7. *Sharing Laughter*. Keeping the friendship alive and perking is essential. Couples have to keep teasing as friends do, defusing the bruised egos, and surprising each other: "What was the dumbest present I ever gave her? I wonder if they still make them." Again, it may be unfair to suggest you check your sensitivity to demonstrating love by how often you surprise either of your parents.

8. *Providing Soul Sustenance*. Souls aren't complete with a high school diploma. They need to be fed, prodded, and ignited. The absolute key is *noticing*: paying attention, hearing what's not being said. (How good are you at that now?) The researchers found that, although infidelity causes a lot of divorces, the need for psychological concern is equally important. If they don't find that at home, they might find it elsewhere.

9. *Remembering Romance*. Keeping a journal like the Personal Reflections in this text is a good way to keep oneself alive and to keep one's marriage alive and growing: "When was the very first time I laid eyes on this person who's shared so much with me? When

did I first suspect, 'I think this is the one'? How would
my life have been changed without him or her?"

Rising to these nine tasks should make divorce unthinkable.

DIVORCE

You have to prove more to get a driver's license than you
do to get a marriage license. You don't have to prove you're
level-headed, self-possessed, or a person of character. What's
more, the prevalence of divorce can't help but plant at least a
vague seed of "unless" in the marriage vows. One would think a
prenuptial agreement about disposition of property if this
"arrangement" *doesn't* work out would clearly invalidate the
promise, turn it into merely a legal contract, not a soul-to-soul
commitment.

Erikson's stages of human development outline the ideal
preparation for undertaking the commitment of marriage. It's
common to hear divorcees declare, "We just weren't ready."
Probably true enough, but equally probable are those who told
them that back then they didn't know what they were talking
about. For them, marriage is very little calculation and mostly risk.

Statistics suggest you have a greater chance of divorce if
your own parents were divorced, if you were married before age
twenty with only a high school education, if you came from a
very high or very low income bracket, and especially if there are
no children, which might be a reason many couples postpone
parenthood for quite some time.

However, the biggest problem is that two children in adult
bodies got married. They're still defensive, other-directed,
achievers versus strivers, oversensitive, and temperamental. The
qualities that make a good spouse and parent are the qualities
that make a mature adult.

Ask couples you believe have healthy, vibrant, life-giving
marriages what they find are the most needed qualities. These
are the ones I've gotten when I asked: openness to gripes, independence, flexibility, compromise without grudges, sense of

humor, *interested* and *interesting*, a good ear and a short memory, wholeness, and above all, forgiveness.

PERSONAL REFLECTION

If you're serious about preparing for your own future, think of three couples you know whom you believe have a happy, fulfilling marriage. (Don't pick anyone who's only been married for a brief time. Pick couples who have walked the walk.) Write concrete ways that *show* to an outsider the reasons you settle on these three unions. Avoid vague generalizations and focus on what they *do*. If you're preparing to be someone's spouse, it'll do you no good to feed yourself airy platitudes. Consider realistically how you can be a worthy partner?

24.

FAMILY

> My father used to play with my brother and me in the yard. Mother would come out and say, "You're tearing up the grass." "We're not raising grass," Dad would reply. "We're raising boys."
>
> —*Harmon Killebrew*

Consider the following ten statements and whether you agree or disagree.

1. No great harm is done to infants if their mother returns to work six weeks after their child's birth.
2. Better to be too lenient with children rather than risk being too strict.
3. Children need privacy but not *too* much privacy.
4. For their own sake, teenagers should begin to contribute financially to the family.
5. A teenage girl should not have to secure parental consent for an abortion.
6. Suicides of wealthy teenagers quite likely result from impossible expectations of life.
7. The hardest gift for parents to give is teaching their children the skills of fending for themselves.
8. "Helicopter parents" who hover over their children, shielding them even from the legitimate consequences of their poor choices, are poor parents.

9. It is far easier to be in charge of a business than in charge of a family.
10. Most people learn parenting recollecting how their parents acted, asking advice haphazardly, learning as they go, and not by studying as they do for other important jobs.

ATTICUS FINCH AND THE FAMILY

For the first couple of years, other than goo-goo eyes, there isn't very much return from the child for all the time, energy, money, toil, and availability parents are called upon to surrender. In fact, the parent-child relationship is strictly one way: unconditional, no matter what the infant does. In too many cases, that one-way situation lasts far longer than it should.

The fulcrum on which a family balances is the fusion of the parents. In many young marriages, two people offer their scarcely comprehended selves to one another. If there are unheeded, unhealed cracks in that parental balancing point, children may pay psychologically—for a lifetime—for shortcomings of which they're neither aware nor guilty.

Quite a few fathers, judging from written reflections and discussions, are warm but stern, their principal role being clarity and a flinty place against which to hone individuality. They are caring providers, arbitrators, and life managers. Their task is to give them the best they can and keep them from hurting others or themselves, or embarrassing the family. That seems what fathers offer and what kids expect. Mom's role is to be understanding, healers, and completely ignorant about sex.

Young people prudently anticipating eventual parenthood could do worse than read, reread, or rent the film of Harper Lee's *To Kill a Mockingbird* to find provocative clues to good parenting. In one scene, because a spiteful, sickly old woman has accused Atticus Finch of being "no better than trash" for defending a Negro in court, his son, Jem, with equal spite, uprooted the old woman's garden. Atticus doesn't impose an arbitrary sanction on the boy in reparation. Rather, he says,

"Son, I have no doubt you've been annoyed by your contemporaries about me lawing for [black folks], but to do something like this to a sick old lady is inexcusable. I strongly advise you to go over and have a talk with Mrs. Dubose."* Not "order"; "I strongly advise." The boy's free to take responsibility for his actions or not. He trusts the boy is ready to grow up.

As a result, Jem himself suggests he work on Mrs. Dubose's garden until it grows back. Wouldn't it be better if a parent said, "Could you help me understand why you did that?"—*first*, before imposing punishment? Atticus shows he understands, empathizes with, the instinctive reasons that impelled his son to such an impetuous act. But his *way* of handling the problem has more to do with helping the boy understand his relationships with other people than his relationship to a law, which was formed for people who didn't have parents like Atticus. Rehabilitation is more important than retribution.

A few times in my years of teaching, I think I may have gotten it right and used imagination in a crisis instead of the usual penal code. One time, I checked my grade book at the end of a quarter to see who needed reminding. Each weekly reflection was worth five, but I saw one line with a cluster of 5s in a different color red ink and different handwriting from mine. It was a boy who also had a small part in *Arsenic and Old Lace*, which I was directing. I told myself I wanted to handle this incident human-being-to-human-being, not turn him over—stimulus/response—to the cops.

"Dave, is there anything you want to tell me?"

There was an utterly innocent, uncomprehending look.

"Dave, did you tamper with my grade book?"

Instant connection!

"What...what are you gonna do? If you tell the office, they'll can me."

"I don't know." And I didn't. "Why not see me at rehearsal?"

---

*Harper Lee, *To Kill a Mocking Bird* (New York: HarperCollins, 1999), 119.

In the theater that afternoon, the cast was milling around the back. Dave met me at the lip of the stage, his lower lip quivering. "What...did you decide?"

"Dave, I'm just waiting for two words."

"You mean...you mean...I'm sorry?"

"Yep. If you really mean that."

"Oh, God, I'm *sorry!*"

"That's good enough for me. Welcome home."

For a second, he couldn't get a breath. Then he threw his arms around me and wept. I think he remembers that more profitably than being suspended or expelled. So many problems are easier if you develop a habit of *perspective*.

Another occasion, while grading senior AP English essays, I found two that were word-for-word identical. The students were each too smart to copy from one another, but on the Internet I found an essay they'd both spent ten bucks on. In the teachers' room, I told a couple of colleagues I was going to ask them separately for an essay, just three paragraphs: What does integrity mean? How does it feel when you lose integrity, and how do you get it back? One first-year teacher was quite irate. He said it was important—implying treasonous to evade—and that the boys be turned over to the discipline office so their misdeeds would go on their permanent records.

When the essays came in, one boy wrote that it was the first time in his life he understood what kindness meant. The other said he went to confession for the first time since eighth grade.

But the young teacher had gone to the school's president, who called me in and demanded that I give the boys' names to the office. I told him what I'd done and how they'd responded. He insisted, "All well and good, but...." I stayed firm, and it still feels very good.

Faced with his daughter's confession that she's unmarried and pregnant or a son's declaration that he's gay, a father has several options. First, to erupt, perhaps strike them in frustration after such a destroyed investment of concern. Second, collapse in shame and mutter, "What did we do wrong?" Third, take charge: "Now *this* is what we'll do." Fourth, wrap them in his arms and weep with them. At the moment, their pain is more important than his. Perspective!

Growing up, for parents as well as their children, means dying to the False Self, the remains of the narcissistic Beast in us: grabby, petulant, and thin-skinned.

MORALITY VERSUS COMPASSION

Morality means justice. The web of relationships in a family demand that, simply because they're all human. But family is far, far different from a village or a business or a country. The glue that cements this web is stronger than justice. It needs love. Not just a feeling but an act of *will*, a commitment that takes over when the feelings *fail*, when the beloved hasn't even been *likable* for quite some time.

In the best of families, love becomes contagious, spreading out into the whole web surrounding that tiny cell-society. How do you as a parent lead your children to take upon themselves a further burden of *compassion* even for those who don't "deserve" it: people that society finds problematic: homosexuals, chemical addicts, the deranged, third-generation welfare recipients. It is difficult to elicit in the young compassion for so many people "not like us." And that resistance is in the grain, from our simian ancestors.

My mentor, Atticus Finch, puts it as well as I've heard it when he tells his daughter, Scout: "You never really understand a person until...you climb into his skin and walk around in it."* Remember the personal reflection at the end of chapter 17 where you were asked to pick out the greatest outcast in the year and "get inside that person's skin and walk around in it for a while, and tell me what it's like to face a typical day *inside* that person." The descriptions that I receive—almost without exception—are totally from the *outside*: how others react to that person, not how the person feels *inside*. People feel sorry for the person, but they can't bring themselves to *become* that person, to have compassion for him or her—not *pity*, but fellow-feeling, which is

---

*Ibid., 33.

what, in fact, compassion means: "I suffer *with* you." But perhaps it's unfair to ask kids to understand what it's like inside someone else's skin when they can't understand the person walking around in their own skin.

Maybe when we open this up, you can share how to teach reciprocity, helping kids react to their bad behavior not from obedience or fear but from empathy, *realizing* that when I bop her, she feels exactly the way I feel when she bops me; to *feel* that she *is*, in fact, also a *me*.

VULNERABILITY

Too many parents place the children's need for security above the children's need to grow, despite the evident fact that insecurity—disequilibrium—is the requisite for growth as a human individual: birth, weaning, play years, schooling, adolescence. Robert Redford's film *Ordinary People*, mentioned earlier, is another casebook for parents, this time about the disintegration of a family. The mother copes by keeping everything "in control": the napkin rings, her son's frayed collars, the neighbors' opinions. When Conrad, the surviving son, goes to the psychiatrist, he says *he* wants "control." When, in the end, he and his dad finally speak as friends, sharing their separate weaknesses, he says, "I always used to think you had a handle on everything."

Too many parents try, for the best of motives, at least to give the *appearance* they have a handle on everything, in order to shield the children from suffering. But as Carl Jung points out, "Neurosis is always a substitute for *legitimate* suffering."* Life is difficult and uncertain; to shield at least adolescents from that truth isn't kindness. Parents' credibility isn't threatened but enhanced by an honest and vulnerable sharing of their own acknowledged shortcomings. It's the only way the child can get inside the *parents'* skin and walk around in it awhile. To shield children from the truth is to shield them not only from life but

---

*Carl Gustav Jung, *Psychology and Religion* (New Haven, CT: Yale University Press, 1960), 92.

from developing compassion. As we noted earlier, shielding them from harm shields them from developing character: spine. There are at least three basic elements to a happy family: communication, compassion, and forgiveness, all of which can be summed up as *vulnerability* to one another.

Communication is an easy word to bandy about, but we can often forget that genuine communication isn't just telling the other person all you know, even your most shameful secrets. That's only one side of a two-way street. You have also got to *listen*, really listen, looking the other person right in the eyes. You can't do that and erase the board or finish the ironing at the same time. Quite often you won't be spellbound by what the child (or adult) is saying. But that's where the love enters: the other person's more important than what he or she's saying.

Furthermore, you can't teach a child (or adult) until you hear his or her words with his or her mind, setting aside your own cherished convictions and sure-fire answers—climbing inside his or her skin. That's why every chapter opens with the initial statements and the concluding personal reflection—to help *you* see what you *really* think.

It's very difficult to *leave behind* your own preconceptions and get inside someone else's skin. How does a parent, for instance, put aside for a moment all the principles he or she has wrestled a lifetime for—to say nothing of the blind biases you can't even admit—in order to understand and *forgive* a child who breaks your heart? How do you get around the wound inflicted on *you* by your child's wounds? How does a youngster lay aside the confusion and hurt in order to understand and forgive *you*? Resentment is like taking poison and hoping the other guy dies.

At times, of course, the understanding and compassion *are* there, but the *words* aren't. At times, the shared truth is too enormous for words, as at a wake, and the only answer is arms around one another and mute tears. The family that has a barrier against touch and tears will find their mutual life far more difficult than families more comfortable with vulnerability.

Vulnerability is the one quality that ultimately separates humans from other animals. Animals always have their guard up, are always defensive, and always frightened by change. And we're partly animals, even though our human nature invites us further: to know more, to love more, and to grow more human. But that invitation to be more than merely high-level animals can be refused, as witness date rapists, Mob hitmen, and serial murderers. There's a whole spectrum to the meaning of *human*, stretching from Saddam Hussein to Mother Teresa.

Furthermore, even though we do accept the invitation to grow beyond our animal origins, we never leave our animal natures behind. It is rare to hear a biology teacher draw the radical distinction between humans and other animals. Whenever I give a questionnaire that says, "The law of *self-preservation* is the most basic law of specifically *human* life," almost all invariably check "True." So much for the invitation to vulnerability—and to transcendence.

Yet, without vulnerability, humanity is *impossible*. If we differ from our animal forbears in that we can learn and love, vulnerability is the *sine qua non*. How can you learn unless you're vulnerable to the truth, wherever the truth leads, no matter how much the truth threatens what we've long cherished? How can one love unless he or she is vulnerable to the beloved, no matter how inconvenient the beloved's requests, no matter how unlikable the beloved is at the moment? So many recent marriages break up because they're a union of two Teflon invulnerabilities. Once the honeymoon is over, once the love potion neuters down, it is time to dig out the prenuptial agreement.

And compassion is impossible without the self-esteem that *allows* one to be vulnerable. How can you get inside someone else's skin when your own skin's a fortress, beyond which everything becomes less and less real the further it gets? How can you genuinely understand another, yield *your* defenses to *their* pain?

That, of course, is what a liberal education is, or ought to be: to give people the ability to read books, climb inside other people's skins and walk around in them awhile. However, my experience is that the analytical left brain reigns supreme. Poems, plays, and novels are intended not to move the soul but to serve as analysis fodder. Beyond the empty rhetoric of the catalogues, the hard-nosed transcript, the GPA, and the SAT scores are what really count. Vulnerability seems harder and harder to come by.

One very real way to educe vulnerability in your children is through extracurricular involvement, and any parent who allows a child to leave school at the last bell ought to get a third of his or her tuition or taxes back. Being on a team forces a person to place trust in someone else, the beginning of vulnerability. Participating in plays can especially allow them to get inside another person's skin and walk around in it awhile, and explore the motivations of someone they may dislike—and what happens if whoever's supposed to come on stage *doesn't* appear? But at the curtain calls, you find in a way beyond words or question that being vulnerable pays off. As one teary football player told me after his first play, "I never realized. In a play, everybody wins."

Kids *want* to be vulnerable; they *want* to be an organic part of something bigger than themselves; they *want* to know and love. After all, that's their *human* nature inviting them. But they're afraid; afraid to be hurt again. What we have to do is be relentless in our efforts to build their trust, their self-esteem, and their willingness to *risk* losing something good, like their security, in order to get something better, like love.

My other mentor as a teacher is Annie Sullivan. For how many weeks did she draw incomprehensible signs in Helen Keller's stubbornly resistant hands? But she trusted; she trusted Helen, and more importantly, she trusted herself that she *would* find a way inside Helen's defenses.

There's a way into every kid's skin. I believe that any patient parent or teacher can find it. The only question left in this regard is, once again, When do you start to learn how? Like Harmon Killibrew's dad, one of the basic requisites of a parent is holding onto a long-view perspective.

PERSONAL REFLECTION

I once invited a physician friend to talk to high school seniors about careers in medicine. He was a neurologist and chair of the admissions committee of his hospital's medical school. I asked him, "Even to have the courage to apply to your medical school, a college senior would have to have almost a 4.0 GPA. What would be your first interview question? Without missing a beat, he said, "What was the last novel you read?"

Why would an expert think that question so critical? How could reading *fiction* make a better *physician*? Or for that matter a better parent? While we're at it, why have teachers been forcing you to read fiction all these years? Has it been just to keep your mind occupied?

25.

WORK

> Work is love made visible. And if you cannot work with love but only with distaste, it is better that you should leave your work and sit at the gate of the temple and take alms of those who work with joy.
>
> —*Khalil Gibran*

Consider whether you agree or disagree with the following ten statements.

1. Those in business simply have to resign themselves to keeping their moral principles very flexible.
2. One can't rightly have true self-esteem unless he or she works to capacity.
3. If you find a job you genuinely love, you'll never work a day in your life.
4. Work is not just a moral relationship to the task but to everybody else involved.
5. When you're employed, you owe an honest day's work for an honest day's pay.
6. In my education, I give my parents an honest day's work for an honest day's pay.
7. Overall, I'm genuinely proud of the way I work at my education.
8. Whenever I write something, I always work hard to make it worth reading and always make a thorough outline first.

9. Most of the time, I'm a self-starter. I'm not motivated by fear or hope of the reward.
10. I wish I were a better student but lack the motivation actually to do what that entails.

Jack and the Beanstalk never historically happened, but it carries a great deal of truth about taking possession of your own self and your own life. First, Jack was impelled by curiosity and confidence, and the willingness to put effort into both of those. However, even *after* he'd faced the tedious effort through a distance up that epic beanstalk *and* even knowing that in order to succeed, he was going to contend with unpleasantly ogreish and gigantic opposition, he still was willing to go up again, and again. Even after he and his Mum had more wealth than they could ever use in the bag of gold and the golden-egg goose, Jack went up for the singing harp—more precious than gold: his soul.

Why do you suspect that (a) stories of challenges and surmounting them is such a *consistent* theme going back as far as we have a history of storytelling and from every single culture all over the earth, and that (b) achieving those *same* qualities faced all of the heroes and heroines, without exception: Odysseus, Psyche, Abraham, the Buddha, Osiris, Aeneas, Jesus, Beowulf, Arthur, Robin Hood, Mulan, Boktu-Kirish, Siegfried, Geronimo, Sacajawea, Dorothy, Eliza Doolittle, Snow White, Frodo, Luke Skywalker, Harry Potter, Spider-Man? The same challenges, the same virtues—invariable. Why?

Is it possible that those earlier peoples—even without computers, iPods, and penicillin—just might have had more profound insight into what being human means than we do?

ACHIEVING VERSUS STRIVING

The suffix, *-escence*, is inchoative, that is, it designates not a single action but a *process* that's begun but not yet finished— as in *convalescence*, which describes a patient who's made a turn back to good health but isn't there yet; or *evanescence*, which describes a reality that's still there but starting to fade out.

You've surely met a few grown-ups who've reached middle age and are still less self-possessed than teenagers. Adolescence is inchoative adulthood. It's a process that demands attention every day, like luring a toddler to take just a few more steps. You should be more adult today than you were in ninth grade, even more than you were last week. All the healthy habits we've seen from the start: honesty, perspective, freedom, gratitude, respect, empathy, kindness, responsibility are the ingredients for self-ownership, none of which we share with other animals, and none of which move from potential to actual without effort.

Adult life isn't a sprint; it's a marathon. It takes a long time and work. And there are very few Gold Medalists. Winning isn't the only thing; it's the rare thing.

Every Olympic competitor trains at least eight years, gives total effort, yet all but three walk away empty handed. Does that mean the Silver medalist is just the first of the losers? Not a few people live their lives that way, in self-imposed frustration. Some students do a thoroughly committed job and get a C+, myself included. Others breeze along, without seeming even to crack a book, and pull down A's. That is definitely *not fair*; neither is life.

Teachers, coaches, and parents have probably told you that if you really put out the effort, you'll *surely* attain success, although they probably never told you in any meaningful way just what success *meant*, other than grades and a diploma and money. They really meant well, but they clearly forgot all the times *they* tried with all their hearts and lost. And I suspect the reason so many good-hearted young people give up on the educational enterprise isn't only that the "stuff" hasn't the slightest connection to what most people do with the rest of their lives, but because there's so little *felt* sense of *achievement*. Furthermore, the fault possibly lies as much with those in charge as with the dropouts themselves. The only motives the educators offered were grades, honor cards, and becoming a member of the National Honor Society. These are just short-term, sprint medals—nothing that gives value just in continuing to try, despite the lack of *concrete, immediate* reward.

The educators never tried to motivate with a sense of pride in the *striving* instead of the achieving. Many we've already noted—Elvis, Marilyn, and the others—achieved to the maximum but killed themselves.

Thousands prepare eight years for the Olympics but don't even make the team, plow through drama school and unskilled jobs like waiting on tables and taking walk-on roles without even an invitation to the Oscars, Emmys, or Tony Awards. Athletes ride the bench and serve as self-propelled blocking dummies for the first team, then retire with messed-up knees. The NFL is limited to 1,696 players, of whom only 10 percent in a given year can be quarterbacks, and only 7 percent of college seniors eligible get drafted. In just the first two tryout cities for *American Idol*, twenty-six thousand showed up, and there were eight more cities to go. There are 160,000 members of the Screen Actors Guild-American Federation of Television and Radio Artists (SAG-AFTRA). Figure the odds; calculate the heartbreak. You'd have a far better chance of being struck by lightning.

That doesn't mean everybody should aim low. Not at all! But everybody should be acutely honest with themselves, realistic. No matter *what* work you choose to support yourself and give shape to your life, the critical factor is your *motivation* and your *attitude*. No matter what ogres and wicked witches and giants and underhanded crooks you have to contend with, those two factors are in *your control*. That's perspective.

On the other hand, if you constantly assess your progress with countless measurements, you simply parcel the disappointment and frustration into daily masochistic doses. If you plant a carrot and keep pulling it up to examine if it's grown, guess what that does to the carrot?

If you lose heart, if you yield to depression or alcoholism or drugs, the reason is that you are most likely running the wrong race, which automatically wrenches your expectations out of whack. If you've got a sprint mentality, judging your self by factors of hundredths of a second, that's an extremely *shallow* accomplishment. Going to bed at night, proud of who you've been that day may be trivial in the McWorld, but in the Human World, that's what true success and fulfillment *means*.

Here, as elsewhere, there's an unstated and unquestioned *standard*. Which is more important: a country doctor who for generations has helped people through heart attacks and a heart-transplant surgeon whose picture is on the cover of *The New York Times Magazine*? A woman who doubles a national corporation's assets or one who's raised two children who are healthy, happy, and honorable? Annie Sullivan, who taught Helen Keller to communicate or the actress who (deservedly) won an Oscar for portraying her? Does anybody honestly know what *important* really means? Does it depend almost exclusively on publicity? Or does it depend on the breadth of your perspective?

Right now, at this stage in your life, what ways can you imagine to make your own kids know that they needn't be Number One as long as they're proud of trying their best? That you love them even when they don't bring home tokens to prove to *you* that *you're* a good parent?

MOTIVATION

In a lifetime, I've met almost no students who are really mean-spirited or ungrateful to their parents, once they're reminded about it. When asked why they don't work up to potential, they almost always say, "I guess I'm lazy." Nothing could be further from the truth. Look at those same people at a dance or at a close game, and they're clearly *not* lazy.

Here is another slovenly misuse of words: not *lazy* but *unmotivated*. Give them a reason, give them a cause, and they'll work—tirelessly, creatively, imaginatively—till they *drop*: Hockey, Art, Guitar, even mischief?

What might be *reasons* that the dilatory (Google the word) might have bypassed pride, not out of meanness but simply because the only motive for learning students have ever gotten from *anybody* is "You need a diploma for a decent job!"? You've heard that since first grade! And it's simply untrue—Bill Gates, Steve Jobs, Mark Zuckerburg, Ted Turner...and *nine* United States' presidents.

However, the big problem is that, right now you're more than fully subsidized like a pampered princess or prince, and the need actually to do real work for pay is far, far off—almost as unreal as death. I've had college seniors come into my dorm room in March all flustered, saying, "I don't know what I'm gonna *do* in three months!" I ask, "But what have you been doing for the last 16 years of your schooling?" They look at me as if I were speaking Mandarin.

"When I get out into the real world...." Where have you been since you were conceived?

Here are a few motives you may not have been offered that might ignite commitment:

1. *Habits.* Confucius said, "As grows the twig, so grows the tree." If you learned to beat the system in high school (and who didn't?), you were a tad short-sighted. It's unlikely that'll work with your bosses very long when they're paying you money to think.

2. *Honor.* In any given class, when I ask students exactly what their parents are paying for a year of college, there is only one or two who *know*. If you board, the common cost is about $55,000 for what amounts to about 36 weeks, times a usual adult 40-hour work week equals 1,440 hours. Unless my math is worse than I feared, that means most college students are being "paid" nearly $40 an hour. Enough said!

3. *The Shrinking Future.* Every year—in fact, every hour—that passes, the protected time withers away before you quite likely assume responsibility for another human being besides yourself, and perhaps another...and another. When does the responsibility thermostat click on?

4. *Honest Pride.* Recall the question in the Preface: "What gives you the *right* to feel good about yourself?" Is it your looks, your body, your car, your checkbook, your swimming pool, your GPA? How resilient is your measuring stick? What are the aspects of you that no one *can* take away?

5. *Control.* People who dodged the effort to learn how to think clearly and honestly are doomed to be life-long victims of people who have learned how. Such artful dodgers haven't the words or the logical structures to capture and express their honest convictions. They thought such skills had no purpose—when in fact they're the only means by which to find anything's purpose, including one's own. Words and logical structures help you handle more and more complex problems with far less *fear*.

PERSONAL REFLECTION

Be very honest with yourself. Has this chapter had any genuine effect on you personally? Not just your *thoughts* but your *intentions*?

26.

SOCIETY

> If everyone demanded peace instead of
> another television set, then there'd be peace.
> —*John Lennon*

Consider the following ten statements and whether you agree or disagree.

1. Slavery would be virtually impossible if citizens were willing to read, think, and stand up to be heard. Without those, at least mind-slavery is inevitable.
2. Corporations have stronger influence on public policy than any group of citizens.
3. Whoever buys illegal drugs or pornography, even in trivial amounts, is a contributor to the growth of organized crime.
4. If crime and the economy get out of hand, a president like Hitler could be elected.
5. Gay and lesbian teachers should be outlawed from teaching students of their own sex.
6. Heterosexual teachers should be outlawed from teaching students of the opposite sex.
7. Capital punishment has proven to be a deterrent to capital crimes.
8. Today, the U.S. Congress is governed, to all intents and purposes, by special interests.

9. The United States has a moral obligation to interfere with foreign governments when they can't govern their own citizens and jeopardize America's interests.
10. The media is in stronger control of moral values than any totalitarian government in history has ever been.

The root of *society* is in the Latin word *socius* (comrade, friend, ally), a gathering based on functional interdependence, common territory, and almost always an authority structure. As John Donne famously put it:

> No man is an island entire of itself; every man is a piece of the continent, a part of the main. If a clod be washed away by the sea, Europe is the less, as well as if a promontory were, as well as a manor of thy friend's or of thine own were: any man's death diminishes me, because I am involved in mankind, and therefore never send to know for whom the bell tolls; it tolls for thee.*

We're not just self-assertive individuals, but our animal descent retained our need for the warmth and safety of the herd. And our natural need since the rise of rationality is not merely for physical closeness. We need also to be psychologically meshed with other hearts, minds, and souls. The worst punishment, short of death, is solitary confinement.

Although becoming enmeshed in a society puts definite limits on freedom, most people find it worth the sacrifice. A society is collaborative, a pooling of diverse talents and skills that can enable its members to benefit in ways impossible for an individual. But any society is *not* what parents are to children. Just taking advantages of the common living demands that each member becomes *accountable*, which places further demands that individuals feel and act responsibly beyond themselves and their own. Each one owes the totality to develop the skills to make well-informed adult decisions about the common welfare,

---

*John Donne, "No Man Is an Island," from Meditation XVII, in *Devotions upon Emergent Occasions and Death's Duel* (New York: Vintage, 1999), 63.

safety, interlocked, and sometimes conflicting rights. At its most basic, civil society is about justice, not about love. However, if one purpose of society is to help humanize its components, then respect, empathy, kindness, and responsibility ought to be part of the package. All members profit with the strengthening of each element in the web.

Google can readily provide a history of societies, a subject relatively tangential to our interests here—hunter-gatherers, pastoral control of livestock, horticultural control of crops, feudal control of land, industrial control of production—separating into capitalist, communist, and socialist. Now the unifying factor is postindustrial control of information.

But the unitive motive (herding, farming, trades, mass production, and global markets) changes the manner and attitudes in which the people involved deal with one another morally. Up to as recently as fifty years ago, everybody in the camp, village, and neighborhood knew everybody else *and* everybody else's business. Bickering was probably more common, but so was lending a helping hand, which makes for far more genuine human involvement than when a huge segment of a society doesn't even know the people on the other side of their walls.

Unlike most of human history, most people today think of society as "them," not us—as in "Society *tells* us we have to..." and "When are '*they*' going to do something about...?" In a democracy, citizens with that attitude richly *deserve* anything they get: fascism, slavery, debtors' prisons, brainwashing, and worldwide financial collapse. Again, "If you are not a part of the solution, *you are* a part of the problem."

Here, we encounter again what we dealt with somewhat cursorily in considering the major opinions on roots of ethical behavior: character, prosperity, freedom, innocence, and integrity.

Originally, it seems, societies governed themselves by attempting to read "the will of the gods." Gradually, as humans developed greater competence and confidence and began to doubt the gods, they still couldn't avoid the evident need for control and laws if there were to be a peace beneficial to all. Therefore, they needed a compelling reason for voluntary conformity closer to home than heaven or Mount Olympus. Protagoras voiced the new touchstone of ethical behavior: "*Man is the measure of all things.*" Taking into consideration all the ways humans differ significantly from other animals, those in charge began to teach and govern guided by a conception of the ideal person: one who unearths and develops human faculties to the fullest. Aristotle asserted that the purpose of a good society is to promote the happiness of the *individuals* who compose it.* It should promote their pursuit of good lives. So a society is an atmosphere for promoting the virtues we've been considering all along.

Much later, during the Enlightenment, many of the most respected thinkers—even if they personally at least harbored the possibility of a Divine Power—wanted to distance themselves even further from divine motivation in order to purge their thoughts of slavish superstition, or at least as important, to preserve their purely intellectual, objectively unbiased academic purity. Because of their this-world limitations of moral obligation, they are called "materialist," and in many if not most areas of modern life, their theories are now predominant.

What follows is a brief summary of viewpoints to help you realize that understandings of the roots of morality are far more varied than most realize. There is absolutely no reason to remember the names and dates and particularities, unless you aspire to a career appearing on *Jeopardy!* It's far more important that you value and feel a need for personal integrity than that you know what even the greatest minds in history said about it.

> *Plato* (ca. 424–348 BCE) held that society is a hierarchic harmony in which everyone does his or her job. It has three functions: productive (workers), protective (warriors), and governing (philosopher-kings). A thinking aristocracy is the government advocated in Plato's *Republic*.
> *Aristotle* (384–322 BCE) maintained that "the political partnership must be regarded, therefore, as being

---

*Aristotle, *Politics*, trans. Carnes Lord (Chicago: University of Chicago Press, 2013).

for the sake of noble actions, not just for the sake of living together,"* and "the whole must of necessity be prior to [more weighty than] the part."† That held sway for the thousand years before Christ and even longer after, along with Aquinas (1225-1274). The purpose, *telos*, of each entity is revealed in the way it's made, its nature and evident purpose, and all human decisions should be based on that truth. It's the method and attitude used in this book.

Francis Bacon (1561-1626), on moral and political questions, advocated *empiricism*—inductive reasoning, "bottom-up" from concrete and specific to abstract and universal rather than deductive, "top-down" from time-tested principles applied to specific cases. He argued for the scientific method rather than authoritarianism. He opposed royalty and promoted a free parliament.

Thomas Hobbes (1588-1679) believed humans are savage at the core, and the only shield against savagery is a tacit [unwritten but accepted] social contract in which a (hopefully) wise and unbiased, absolute sovereign invokes particular limiting laws. Remember *Lord of the Flies*.

René Descartes (1596-1650) was a dualist, dividing reality sharply into opposing forces, antagonistic to one another—in contrast to the fluctuating opposites of the Eastern Tao we saw earlier. Though he never evolved a political philosophy, his need for certitude permeates all modern politics, even when the opinions are based on mere hearsay.

Baruch Spinoza (1632-1677) was almost completely opposite, seeing realities flowing into one another in a philosophy close to pantheism with a completely impersonal divinity. He strongly upheld a tolerant, secular, democratic society. Freedom of thought is absolute, freedom of speech is limited

---

*Ibid., 1280a, 31-32; 1280b, 40; and 1281a, 1-3.
†Ibid., 1253a, 5.

only in cases promoting treason, disobedience, or harm to others.

John Locke (1632–1704), the "Father of Liberalism," furthered the ideas of a social contract but disagreed with Hobbes about the absolute monarch, devolving that power to the consent of the governed. Humans have rights by their very rational nature, and the state exists to safeguard and promote those rights. He was the direct inspiration to those who wrote the U.S. Constitution.

David Hume (1711–1776) believed that society is best governed by a general and impartial system of laws, less concerned about the form of government, as long as it is impartial and fair.

Jean-Jacques Rousseau (1712–1778) believed in innate human goodness, opposite to Hobbes, influenced by the romantic idea of "The Noble Savage" supposed to populate the New World. He believed all our problems began with civil society, when "The first man who, having enclosed a piece of ground, said 'This is mine'....From how many crimes, wars, and murders...might not any one have saved mankind, by pulling up the stakes."* Remember *A Catcher in the Rye*.

Adam Smith (1723–1790), the father of free-market economics, saw that "the affluence of the few supposes the indigence of the many....It is only under the shelter of the civil magistrate that the owner of that valuable property...can sleep a single night in security. [Therefore] Men of inferior wealth combine to defend those of superior wealth in the possession of their property, in order that men of superior wealth may combine to defend *them* in the possession of theirs."†

---

*Jean-Jacques Rousseau, *The Social Contact & Discourses*, ed. Ernest Rhys, trans. G. D. H. Cole (New York: E.P. Dutton & Co., 1920), 207.

†Adam Smith, *The Wealth of Nations* (Hampshire, UK: Harriman House, 2007), 465.

Immanuel Kant (1724–1804) deemed that government is based on three basic principles: the liberty, equality, and independence of every citizen—not given but guaranteed by the state. The freedom exclusive to rational beings is the root of all other rights.

G. W. F. Hegel (1770–1831). His basic insight—far different from beliefs that the state is a separate "them"—is that the state should be an ideal *community*, not just a gathering of individuals with a common purpose (like strangers in an airport lounge), but a fellowship where the members are genuinely concerned for one another's welfare (like a team). Ideally, the individual is conditioned to universal concerns. As with communism, the theory seems to be unaware of what has always been called (for want of a better term) *original sin*: human selfishness.

John Stuart Mill (1806–1873), father of utilitarianism, held that government must seek to educate its citizens so that they pursue the *higher*, psychological pleasures—individual responsibility—recognizing that people are not merely hedonistic. Society encourages active participation by all citizens. A bad government forces its citizens to be passively obedient to the wishes and whims of a ruling elite, no matter how sensible those might be.

Karl Marx (1818–1883) held that, since the workers are, by far, the most numerous element of society, it is *their* happiness, not the pampered elite's that should be the goal of society. But since government has always been the elite's creation, it is their interests it has always catered to. The good citizen's task is to make things so bad that the elite will yield control.

Friedrich Nietzsche (1844–1900) believed that science and secularism had grown to a point where many people see God as no longer necessary. His radical questioning of objective truth had a profound influence on existentialism, nihilism (life has no

purpose), and postmodernism. As for the state's purposes: "Might makes Right." Power calls the shots.

Jean-Paul Sartre (1905–1980) maintained that humans
must create their *own* meaning and purpose in a
godless and objectively purposeless reality, and are
at their best rebelling against impersonal society,
and taking responsibility for their own actions
without coercion. His demand for self-reliance and
individualism seems strangely at odds with the
communism that he equally championed.

John Rawls (1921–2002). He felt that equality and freedom must yield to one another. The ideal market
promotes efficiency, and the ideal legislature leads
to fairness. If the majority's goals violate justice,
their desires "have no value." If we fail to see the
big picture and behave selfishly or unjustly, we
cheapen ourselves and feel shame. "Such actions
strike at self-respect, our sense of our own
worth....We have acted as though we belonged to a
lower order."*

This list was motivated solely in an attempt to demonstrate
how variegated the viewpoints and answers are. Similarly, the
following brief list of moral questions facing society (i.e.,
humans in a common, mutually beneficial web) is by no means
an attempt to solve the conundrums presented. It is merely an
attempt to deflate unfounded certitudes and bumper-sticker
solutions.

MORAL QUESTIONS

Abortion

1. The critical question about abortion is not whether
the means are professional or brutal but *what* is being

---

*John Rawls, A Theory of Justice (New York: Oxford University Press, 1971),
256.

killed. Should—can—such a decision of fact be settled by a majority of the nation's elected representatives or the Supreme Court, even if everyone were a trained thinker?

2. A human fetus is unarguably alive, and as a union of two human cells, it's unarguably a human entity. Can anyone offer sufficient evidence that killing it is *not* a homicide?

3. Given legal abortion, should a teenager require parental consent to obtain one?

College Situations

1. A freshman receives notice of his assigned roommate, and they begin to correspond by e-mail. The roommate declares that he's openly gay but neither flamboyant nor promiscuous. Can the other roommate demand to be reassigned? What if the person were of a different race?

2. You and your roommate share a class and, for a final paper, shared notes. Because you're quite well-versed on the subject, he/she asks if you'd proofread and offer suggestions. Is that okay, using you as just another learned source? What if, however, you realize that he/she has frequently copied word-for-word from sources you yourself consulted without attribution? If you raise the issue and he/she refuses to change, should you simply back off?

3. Your roommate says that the next day he/she might need the room to be alone with his or her current love interest. If there's a handkerchief on the doorknob, stay away. You pay half the rent. Do you have the grounds—and the guts—to deny the request, especially knowing the roommate will spread the news that you're a prude?

4. One of your best female friends is, in all honesty, not homely but certainly plain. But lately she's constantly bubbly. Suddenly, she has taken up with a guy whom

you don't particularly trust. She tells you in confidence that he's saying to her that, if she really loved him, she'd have sex with him. How do you respond?

Immigration

1. Just as no one has the right to set up a squatter's camp on my property, does a government have the right to disperse illegal immigrants, even if it means depositing them in some uninhabited place to fend for themselves?
2. Given the Declaration of Independence's core assertions about the right to life, and thus to food, clothing, and shelter, rooted not in citizenship but in humanity, should the government feel responsible for sustaining illegal immigrants until they can be returned to their home countries?
3. If your next-door neighbor hired workers who spoke little English but a language you understand, and you gathered from their speech together that they were undocumented, should you report the situation, especially presuming they would lose their livelihood and be deported, after all the difficulties they went through just to get here? The problem isn't cut-and-dried.

Utilitarianism

1. "The greatest good (or least harm) for the greatest number" is the argument used to justify the atomic bombing of Hiroshima and Nagasaki in 1945, killing about 260,000 civilians and permanently damaging far more, which did, effectively, avert an invasion estimated beforehand at two to four million American casualties, including four to eight hundred thousand dead and five to ten million Japanese

deaths. Is such a mathematical equation with human lives warranted?

2. Is it even possible to foresee all the critical consequences of a moral choice? For example, Prohibition enhanced organized crime exponentially, as does the war on drugs; safety measures lead people to feel safer than they are; requiring taller smokestacks merely spread pollution farther and produced acid rain.

3. If the government is sure beyond reasonable doubt that a terrorist has planted a bomb to explode in two more days in some heavily populated area that he refuses to reveal, and if he has resisted hours of physical torture, is it justified at least to threaten to torture his only child?

Majority Rule

1. Should majority rule determine which behavior is allowed and which is punishable when it is clear the overwhelming majority are illiterate and ill-informed?

2. Is the invocation that the majority opinion carries the question merely a restatement of Nietzsche's doctrine of might makes right?

3. Can/should a chief of state gear his or her choices to fairly reliable opinion polls? He or she does, after all, claim to represent the will of the electorate.

4. Does the government have the obligation to think *for* those citizens who clearly refuse to think for themselves? What is the right/obligation of the wise to control the foolish?

War

1. The law requires that, for major departures from the status quo, like allowing the vote or restricting the

rights to sell and use alcohol, the Congress must pass an amendment that, in turn, must be approved by three-fourths of the state legislators. Should that same broad consent be required for declaring a war that will, inevitably, cost many citizens their only lives?

2. Should a citizen who can establish a genuine opposition to *any* war or to the reasons for a particular war be required to perform some other kind of civilian service for the duration?

3. In a battle, when your officer gives the command to attack a hill bristling with mortars and machine guns, you realize that complying with the order is, equivalently, suicide. Do you have any alternative? Refusing an order in combat allows the officer to shoot you.

Education

1. Given the value of separation of Church and State, is it a false dualism to constrain public schools from explicitly teaching morality, since that is an intrusion on freedom of conscience and the establishment of religion?

2. Can a school system legitimately dispense free condoms or free Bibles?

3. Avoiding any particulars restricted to any religious denomination, should public school biology classes be required to explore the dramatic psychological difference between human and animal sex?

4. What concrete specific actions by a student— cheating, bullying, drugs—should guarantee expulsion? Does the school have an obligation to help rehabilitate the culprit rather than merely pass on the problem?

5. Can a high school senior justly be forbidden to bring a same-sex date to the prom?

Premeditated Homicide

1. If most philosophers agree that each human (not just each American) has an inalienable right to life, does a human have a right to give up that life and commit suicide? Can society legitimately forbid a competent health provider from assisting the suicide of someone whose illness has made every day of life a torture?
2. A survey of professional criminologists shows that 88 percent are against the death penalty. Many states without it have a lower incidence of capital crime. Is there a reason to retain it? The majority might likely agree to keep it, even though many others evaluate it not as a deterrent or even a punishment, but simple savage vengeance.
3. If a government can empower citizens to kill enemy citizens in battle, if urban crime got out of hand in a city, could it also empower citizens to hunt and kill *fellow* citizens in vigilante groups? It would be an efficient solution to a lack of trained police.

Personal Freedoms

1. Congressional Research Service in 2009 estimated there were 310 million firearms in the United States with a population of 307 million, not including weapons owned by the military. In 2010, there were 19,392 firearm-related suicides and 11,078 firearm-related homicides in the United States. It could be argued that anyone who killed themselves or others must be mentally unbalanced. Can a government limit the rights of competent citizens in order to curtail the erratic behavior of a minority?
2. Except for moderating situations of citizens' conflicting rights (joint property, inheritance taxes, etc.), is a government competent to legislate who may marry whom?

3. Few could argue that commercial advertising is a very effective method of training citizens, especially children, to value greed as a virtue instead of a vice. To be honest, greed is *the* motive that keeps our economy perking. Also, research on violent television and films, video games, and music reveals unequivocal evidence that media violence increases the likelihood of aggressive and violent behavior in both immediate and long-term contexts.* However, almost the sole source for such information about the media for most citizens is the media. What recourse does a concerned parent have?

Collective Responsibility

1. Should the citizens of Germany today feel some kind of personal responsibility for what their ancestors did to Jews and Slavs in the Nazi camps?
2. Present-day Americans were in no way responsible for the inhuman treatment earlier Americans inflicted on Native Americans, on African slaves, and on Japanese-Americans in World War II. But are we in some way responsible for encouraging our representatives to try to rectify the inequities that resulted from those mistakes?
3. Is there some national situation you find totally inequitable or some injustice closer to home that you believe can and should be corrected? You're quite likely not responsible for it having occurred, but could you offer a letter to a newspaper or legislator that may not assure a change but would serve at least as one more irritant that could push someone with more power than you to take action?

---

*Craig A. Anderson, et al., "The Influence of Media Violence on Youth," *Psychological Science in the Public Interest* 4, no. 3 (December 2003): 81, http://public.psych.iastate.edu/caa/abstracts/2000-2004/03abdhjlmw.pdf.

PERSONAL REFLECTION

Choose any single issue from the previous lists. Write why you found it more intriguing than the rest. Is there one issue that you feel personally responsible for and would like to do something concrete and specific about that situation? When? "If you're not part of the solution...."

Appendix

Dilemmas for Discussion

You're a student, drinking with a friend in her dorm. After a couple of hours of drinking, your friend starts to feel nauseous and passes out. Worried, you want to go to the RA for help, but you're also afraid you'll get yourself and your friend in trouble. Your friend has already been caught drinking and is facing expulsion if caught again. Do you protect your friend from being expelled by looking after her yourself, or do you call the RA and get in trouble?

———◆———

Mrs. Esposito sits in the emergency waiting room, scrubbing the tears from her tired face, mumbling, "Why?" You're the intern who just informed her that her ten-year-old son, Cisco, probably suffered a blood clot as a result of his fall from the jungle gym, and in the ambulance, the clot traveled to his brain and ended his life. But she keeps asking in that weary voice, "Why?" You've already *told* her why, several times. What are you doing wrong?

———◆———

Your friend, Pat Heffernan, is married to Tom, a successful, much publicized lawyer running for district attorney. He says that she's essential to his confidence on the campaign. They have two daughters, Megan and Monica, both pretty and popular, but lately sullen and unwilling to talk more than a few mumbles to their parents. Pat invites you to lunch.

"Even though the campaign keeps us away most evenings and weekends, we have a live-in cook who's been with us since the girls were babies and who loves them as much as we do. We've tried to give them everything, to show interest in everything they care about. I brought these two girls into the world. And now they're like strangers. What can we do?"

———◉———

Corlene Stewart is a very gifted African American senior on scholarship in an elite high school and is determined to become an attorney to pay back her hard-working parents for all their sacrifices. She's a candidate for an endowed college scholarship for the senior with the highest SAT scores. All the other possible candidates are very well-off and have taken a prep course that was way out of her family's reach. Her boyfriend, Jamal, at times gets angry about the unfairness of that, and it's difficult to deny it. On the afternoon before the exam, the principal's secretary asked Jamal and two others to help carry the cartons of exams from the shipping dock to the office. As the secretary put the cartons into the safe, Jamal memorized the combination, came back that night, stole one exam, resealed the carton, and left unseen. At midnight, he calls Carlene and offers her a free ride into her future. Do you support Jamal's actions?

———◉———

All through grade school, the kids called Amelia "Miss Piggy." By the first year of high school, she'd had enough. Without advice from a doctor and to the consternation of her mother, she drank nothing but a diet shake at breakfast and lunch and ate two grapefruits at dinner. Within a few months, she became quite slim, although with shadows under her eyes and often feeling listless and drowsy, unable to concentrate for long. Her mother pleaded with her to start eating again, but she refused. She was acceptable now—or at least not rejected. Boys were starting to talk to her.

Her mother tried to force her to a doctor, but she kept quoting the long-dead Duchess of Windsor: "You can't be too rich or too slim."

You're her best friend or a boy who suddenly has noticed her. What do you say to her?

———◈———

Gordy Byrne had a first date with Anita Bonneville, Miss Just-About-Everything, whose father was a brain surgeon. There was no way he could show up in his dad's ten-year-old Chevy. So he pleaded (on his knees) with his best friend, Joey, for just one night, to borrow the keys to his parent's new Audi, since they were in Florida for another week. Reluctantly, Joey agreed. The evening was perfect, until Gordy had too much to drink and Anita took a cab home.

Gordy zoomed along the freeway, so nauseous and dizzy he almost missed the exit to Joey's house. As he backed up to make the turn, he slammed into a guard rail. Shocked into sobriety, he opened the car door and threw up. The right rear fender was scraped. Gordy drove to the nearest open gas station. The mechanic, just a young guy, guessed it would cost about five or six hundred to repair. The only person Gordy knew with that kind of disposable cash was a guy he'd known in grade school named Stu Masterson, who dealt dope. What would you advise?

———◈———

Keith Pulaski is sitting in his dorm room looking at a tower of texts and notes for a paper on "Shakespeare's Attitudes toward Women," which is due tomorrow. He's gotten a good start when Art Frawley sticks his head in the door and says, "Keith, come on. We're goin' down to Saki's for a beer." Keith feels everything in him straining toward the door. "Sorry, Art. I've got a paper." Art says, "Get an extension over the weekend." Keith tries to hang tough. "Don't want it hangin' over my head. Have a good time." Art makes to go but pulls back into the door-way and says, "You know that Fran Whatsername you were staring at today? She's gonna be there. Her roommate told me she'd like to meet you." Keith gave him a scowl. "You're puttin' me on." Art raised his hand. "Swear to God! Just an hour. We'll be back real early." What would you do if you were Keith?

⸺◉⸺

Your friend, Sarah, is unexpectedly pregnant. She thinks she has no other alternative than an abortion, which you yourself (reluctantly) believe is premeditated homicide. You're the only one she trusts and asks if you'll go with her anyway. Will you make her face it alone?

⸺◉⸺

Matt Grimes and Missy Elkins have been going together for four years. Both have good jobs and both eventually want children. They believe they truly love one another enough to have a good life together. Again and again, Matt's asked Missy to marry him, and she really wants to. However, her mother's death two years ago was enough to shock her father from his alcoholism, and he's kept a tight hold on his sobriety since then. Missy's the only one of her siblings still in the city, and she's lived with her father since her mother's death. She's afraid that, if she leaves, he'll fall back. Matt's been patient a long time. What should he do?

⸺◉⸺

Kenny Lindner sat with his hockey coach, "Packy" McGuire, on the office couch. He'd just told the coach that, through his own stupid fault, his GPA had slipped just below 2.0. He was so cocky about being a superstar that he'd slacked off and would be ineligible to play until he pulled it up. He was desolate—having let down Packy and the team. Suddenly, Kenny just started to sob. Then he sobbed even harder for being so unmanly, crying like a girl in front of his coach.

Suddenly, the coach's weight shifted, and Kenny felt Packy's arms around his shoulders, saying, "It's okay, son. It'll pass."

Kenny jackknifed to his feet, scrubbing at his eyes. "Thanks a lot, coach," he muttered and shoved out into the hall, dragging for breath. Who could he tell about the old queer?

⸺◉⸺

Connie Cepeda has never been more than almost average in anything, but when her family came to the States, she had high hopes. That lasted only awhile. Her high school teachers seemed interested only in the smart ones and the troublemakers, and the "stuff" was meaningless to her. *Pride and Prejudice* might as well be about Martians, and did she need geometry to be a waitress and a mother, which seemed her inevitable future? The science teachers might as well be talking Chinese.

Connie's mother cleans the house for your mother and has asked her to ask you to talk to Connie. You're in college and understand, yes? Connie needs someone her own age to give her a reason she can appreciate to stay with it, when her only response is, "What's the use?" What do you do?

———◈———

Pat Ganley is a teacher of eleventh-grade English who just welcomed Mrs. Bloodworth, a parent who's taken her (severely) to task for subjecting her daughter to a novel called *Catcher in the Rye*. "Judith brought the book to me, and I was simply *appalled* at the language. These are *children*!" Miss Ganley pointed out that all the students were well past puberty, capable of having children themselves. She asked if Mrs. Bloodworth had read the whole book. "Surely you're joking. One needn't sit through an entire pornographic film to know it's obscene."

Can you help Mrs. Bloodworth cope with this situation?

———◈———

Kathy Beglan is a college sophomore. Both her parents are attorneys, and since she was small, they both hoped their only child would choose to be a lawyer, too. But after a service project in the inner city, she's told her parents, "I've been so lucky that I want to give something back. I want to give two years to the Peace Corps before law school." Her parents are flustered. What will that do to her career? Kathy says, "I'm thinking about what it'll do to *me*." Her dad says, "This Joan of Arc business is very noble, but you've got to be practical, honey." She's going home again for Christmas and asks if you've got any ideas.

———◈———

As soon as Beth and Roger got engaged, Beth had the wedding planned down to the ring pillow. You're Roger's cousin, delighted for them both. Beth's a take-charge girl and will be good for Roger who could use structure. In ten years since college, Roger's bounced around: accountant, grade school teacher, store manager. Now he sells office equipment, involving a lot of east-coast travel, and he's doing well.

One Saturday evening as you came through a restaurant bar to meet a friend for dinner, you stop short. At a table in a dark far corner was a man who looks exactly like Roger, and just as you're about to call his name, Roger kisses the man he's with. What do you do with this information?

━━◈━━

Chris, a lifetime family friend, is the personnel manager for a firm you apply to in your senior year of college. Even though there are others more experienced, he puts you at the top of the list, you're hired, and you do splendidly. So splendidly, in fact, that after a few years, you're made area manager for your section of the country. Chris is up for promotion. He's not the best candidate, but he's serviceable. Which prevails: personal loyalty or company loyalty? Your employment depended on him. What does friendship mean?

━━◈━━

You are part of the select committee appointed to ratify applications for permission to torture terrorist suspects. Mr. Ahmed Kujur, a naturalized American-Saudi citizen, has been arrested by the FBI on suspicion of planning to bomb Grand Central Station in New York City. He is a member of two groups with affiliations to the Taliban and Al-Qaida. They have been tied with money donations that appeared in banks in Yemen immediately following Mr. Kujur's business visits there for his import-export carpet business.

Three different informants claim they have overheard him speaking to the same three employees of his firm about a Day of Reckoning. Mention was heard by two on the day before the start of Ramadan, Tuesday, July 9, 2013.

Today is Thursday, July 4. The FBI has had Mr. Kujur in custody since Monday, using all conventional means of interrogation. He denies any guilt and refuses to speak, although his experienced interrogators are close to certain he is involved and that the attack will take place as scheduled. The government now petitions the committee for permission to send Mr. Kujur to an undisclosed "black site" in North Africa where he can be subjected to less conventional means of obtaining information. How do you vote?

He has not been sent (yet), but Mr. Kujur's involvement is now confirmed because of a telephone call received an hour ago that the terrorist cell has kidnapped the mayor's daughter from a school for special education students. If the government doesn't release Mr. Kujur, they will begin sending body parts of the girl, beginning with her ears, then her fingers.

In a new development, the FBI has discovered that Mr. Kujur's son is a prisoner detained on Riker's Island in New York on a charge of carrying a concealed weapon in an attempt to rob a convenience store. Do you have any suggestions as to what should be done?

—=◉=—

Indentured servitude was debt bondage in the early American colonies. Farmers, planters, and shopkeepers in the colonies needed free workers before potential workers set up their own farms. A solution was to transport a young worker from England or Germany, who would work for several years to pay off the debt of travel costs. During the indenture, servants were not paid wages, but received food, accommodation, clothing, and training. After a previously agreed number of years, they would be free.

Most white immigrants arrived in colonial America as indentured servants, men and women under the age of twenty-one. Typically, the father of a teenager would sign the legal papers and work out an arrangement with a ship captain, who would not charge the father any money. The captain would transport the servants to the colonies, and sell their legal papers to whoever needed workers. In the seventeenth century, nearly two-thirds of settlers to the New World from the British Isles came as indentured servants. With this information, respond to the following questions:

Should Mexicans accept lower than minimum wage?

If she wants it as much as you do, who's getting hurt?

—=◦◉◦=—

Few people need more than one kidney. However, most countries ban offering kidneys for sale, even though there is always a need. If each person enjoys radical ownership of his/herself, suppose a farmer in India wants more than anything to send his bright son to university, why can't he offer his kidney to someone who can easily afford to underwrite the entire cost?

If so, then two years later, should he be willing to offer his second kidney for his second son's boost in life, even if it means his own death?

—=◦◉◦=—

You're the supervisor of a border control unit along the Rio Grande River, separating Mexico and Texas. Very heavy rains from a hurricane have swollen the river so that it has made crossing very dangerous. But, still, the illegal immigrants are seeking to enter the United States, despite the grave risk. Five aliens trying to cross the river were swept away and will surely drown. You only have two boats. You dispatch one boat, manned by one Border Patrol officer, who is a single, Caucasian male, in an attempt to rescue the five illegal aliens.

Later, you observe that the boat has capsized before reaching the aliens, and now the officer is in danger of drowning. You know that you do not have the time or resources to rescue both the officer and the aliens. Do you send your remaining boat out to rescue your officer or do you order it to pick up the five aliens and allow your officer to drown?

—=◦◉◦=—

Under Elizabeth I of England, to attend a Roman Catholic Mass was treason, as was harboring a Catholic priest in your home, subject to impoverishing fines, imprisonment, torture, and death. Some, usually priests, had to decide how, in conscience, they should answer the judge's "bloody question": "If England were attacked, would you support the Queen or an army blessed by the Pope?" As the historian, William Haugaard, says, "To Elizabeth this was a political question; to the priests, a complicated problem of conscience with no simple answer."* The conscientious Catholic was plagued with many questions: Should I outwardly attend Anglican services while refusing inwardly or secretly hearing Mass? Should I, as a judge, swear the Oath of Supremacy, withholding true allegiance in my heart? Should I, as a Jesuit, deny my name, my true reason for traveling hither, my religious profession, and my faith? What should I, as a Catholic gentleman, say to the pursuivants at my door when they inquire about the priest hidden in a secret closet of my house?

---

*William Haugaard, *Elizabeth and the English Reformation* (Cambridge: Cambridge University Press, 1968), 327. On the "Bloody Question," see Philip Hughes, *The Reformation in England*, vol. 3 (London: Hollis & Carter, 1954), 352–56.